Controversies in Economics and Finance

To Nisreen, Danny, Ryan and Ivy

Controversies in Economics and Finance

Puzzles and Myths

Imad A. Moosa

Professor of Finance, Royal Melbourne Institute of Technology (RMIT), Australia

Edward Elgar
PUBLISHING

Cheltenham, UK • Northampton, MA, USA

Published by
Edward Elgar Publishing Limited
The Lypiatts
15 Lansdown Road
Cheltenham
Glos GL50 2JA
UK

Edward Elgar Publishing, Inc.
William Pratt House
9 Dewey Court
Northampton
Massachusetts 01060
USA

Paperback edition 2021

A catalogue record for this book
is available from the British Library

Library of Congress Control Number: 2020940496

This book is available electronically in the **Elgar**online
Economics subject collection
http://dx.doi.org/10.4337/9781839105623

ISBN 978 1 83910 561 6 (cased)
ISBN 978 1 83910 562 3 (eBook)
ISBN 978 1 80220 328 8 (paperback)

Printed and bound by CPI Group (UK) Ltd, Croydon, CR0 4YY

Contents

Figures

Tables

Preface

Controversies in economics and finance take the form of puzzles, paradoxes and myths. Puzzles and paradoxes, which are equivalent, arise because of firm belief in a theory that is not supported by casual empiricism or formal empirical evidence. They can also arise from an observation that allegedly cannot be explained. Myths, on the other hand, arise in normative economics out of differences in opinion or value judgement. It follows that what is a myth for one economist is not a myth for another.

I got interested in the study of puzzles, having done a significant amount of work on the Meese–Rogoff puzzle that macroeconomic models of exchange rate forecasting cannot outperform the random walk in out-of-sample forecasting. Following extensive research, I reached the conclusion that this is not really a puzzle, even though some eminent economists have, for some reason, taken it too seriously and considered it a challenge to the prestige of international economics and finance. For me, the real puzzle is to regard the Meese–Rogoff results as representing a puzzle. Since I embarked on a study of puzzles in the fields of international finance, international economics, macroeconomics and finance, I have found out that all of these puzzles can be explained intuitively, without the need for complex models or the extravaganza of econometrics. I have also reached the conclusion that some of the alleged puzzles are silly and some are dumb.

I like to write in the normative tradition of what ought to be, which (unlike the positive tradition) requires the expression of opinion. I have learned, however, that opinion can be expressed only if it can be supported with logical arguments and evidence. I hold the view that it is a myth that the puzzles of economics and finance are puzzles, but I do believe that myths are abundant. In March 2020, central banks resorted to interest rate cuts to counter the adverse effects of the coronavirus outbreak on the economy and financial markets. This response is ridiculous, but it is based on the widespread myth that interest rate cuts can be used to revive the economy and inject life into financial markets. When the Fed realized that cutting interest rates down to 0.5 per cent could not do the job, those in charge went all the way to zero, even though they perhaps knew that this would not work either. This book is about demonstrating that puzzles in economics and finance are not puzzling at all, and that what some economists see as undisputed facts of life are actually myths.

Writing this book would not have been possible without the help and encouragement I received from family, friends and colleagues. My utmost gratitude must go to my wife, Afaf, who bore most of the opportunity cost of writing this book and helped with the drawing of diagrams. I would also like to thank my colleagues and friends, including John Vaz, Kelly Burns, Vikash Ramiah, Mike Dempsey, Larry Li, Liam Lenten, Brien McDonald and Nirav Parikh.

In preparing the manuscript, I benefited from the exchange of ideas with members of the Table 14 Discussion Group, and for this reason I would like to thank Bob Parsons, Greg O'Brien, Greg Bailey, Bill Breen, Paul Rule, Peter Murphy, Bob Brownlee, Jim Reiss and Tony Pagliaro. My thanks also go to friends and former colleagues who live far away but provide help via means of telecommunication, including Kevin Dowd (to whom I owe intellectual debt), Razzaque Bhatti, Ron Ripple, Bob Sedgwick, Sean Holly, Dan Hemmings, Ian Baxter, Basil Al-Nakeeb and Sulaiman Al-Jassar. Last, but not least, I would like to thank Alex Pettifer, the Editorial Director of Edward Elgar Publishing, who encouraged me to write this book.

Naturally, I am the only one responsible for any errors and omissions that may be found in this book. It is dedicated to my daughter Nisreen, my son Danny, my grandson Ryan and my granddaughter Ivy.

Imad A. Moosa
2020

Abbreviations and acronyms

ABC	Australian Broadcasting Corporation
AIDS	Almost Ideal Demand System
AIG	American International Group
ARCH	autoregressive conditional heteroscedasticity
ARDL	autoregressive distributed lag
BACE	Bayesian averaging of classical estimates
BKK	Backus–Kehoe–Kydland
BLS	Bureau of Labor Statistics
CAPM	capital asset pricing model
CBO	Congressional Budget Office
CDO	collateralized debt obligation
CEO	chief executive officer
CEPR	Centre for Economic Policy Research
CFO	chief financial officer
CIA	Central Intelligence Agency
CIP	covered interest parity
CNBC	Consumer News and Business Channel
CPI	consumer price index
CRA	credit rating agency
DMP	Diamond–Mortensen–Pissarides
DSSSD	downside semi-standard deviation
DW	Deutsche Welle
DW	Durbin–Watson
EFTA	European Free Trade Association
EMH	efficient market hypothesis
EPSU	European Federation of Public Service Unions
EU	European Union
FCIC	Financial Crisis Inquiry Commission
FDR	Franklin Delano Roosevelt
FH	Feldstein–Horioka
G7	Group of Seven
GARCH	generalized autoregressive conditional heteroscedasticity
GDP	gross domestic product
GFC	global financial crisis

GMM	generalized method of moments
IMF	International Monetary Fund
IQ	intelligence quotient
LTCM	Long-Term Capital Management
MAE	mean absolute error
MP	Mortensen–Pissarides
MPC	marginal propensity to consume
MSE	mean square error
NAFTA	North American Free Trade Area
NASA	National Aeronautics and Space Administration
NBER	National Bureau of Economic Research
OECD	Organisation for Economic Co-operation and Development
OLS	ordinary least squares
PPP	purchasing power parity
PSIRU	Public Services International Research Unit
PWC	PricewaterhouseCoopers
R&D	research and development
RBA	Reserve Bank of Australia
RIP	real interest parity
RMSE	root mean square error
SD	standard deviation
SEC	Securities and Exchange Commission
TBTF	too big to fail
UAE	United Arab Emirates
UEH	unbiased efficiency hypothesis
UIP	uncovered interest parity
UK	United Kingdom
UN	United Nations
UNDP	United Nations Development Programme
UNESCO	United Nations Educational, Scientific and Cultural Organization
US	United States
USSR	Union of Soviet Socialist Republics
VAR	value at risk
WTO	World Trade Organization

1.　Puzzles and myths: a general overview

1.1　THE CONCEPT OF PUZZLE

This book is about puzzles and myths in economics and finance. It seems appropriate, therefore, to start by defining and describing the concepts of 'puzzle' and 'myth' before embarking on a discussion of specific puzzles and myths that arise in various research areas such as international finance and macroeconomics. This section is about puzzles as understood in general terms, whereas the concept of myth will be dealt with later on in this chapter.

A puzzle is an enigma, an observation that baffles or confuses observers. It could be a question that is yet to be answered or an unresolved problem that is intricate enough to be perplexing to the mind. The word 'puzzle' is a synonym of 'paradox', albeit with a subtle difference: a puzzle is anything that is difficult to understand or make sense of, whereas a paradox is a self-contradictory statement that can be true only if it is false, and vice versa. We will find out, however, that paradoxes in economics are puzzles, or allegedly so, which (for some reason) are called paradoxes rather than puzzles. For example, the Gibson paradox (that interest rate and the general price level are positively correlated) can readily be called a puzzle because the underlying empirical observation is not consistent with some theory. It will be argued later that the Gibson paradox is neither a paradox nor a puzzle.

According to Danesi (2018), 'the English word *puzzle* covers a broad range of meanings, referring to everything from riddles and crosswords to Sudoku and conundrums in advanced mathematics'. The word appeared for the first time in *The Voyage of Robert Dudley Afterwards Styled Earl of Warwick & Leicester and Duke of Northumberland*, a book that was published around 1595, in which the word 'puzzle' was used to describe a game. According to Danesi, it is most likely that the word 'puzzle' is derived from the Middle English word *poselen* (to bewilder or confuse), which is associated with endeavours to solve puzzles.

Danesi (2018) also refers to a definition put forward by a brilliant puzzle-maker, Scott Kim, who defines a puzzle as 'something that is fun and has a right answer' (Kim, 2006). Scott Kim's definition, therefore, encompasses two characterizations: (1) a puzzle is a source of fun; and (2) it has a right answer. These two characterizations imply that puzzles represent a form of play that is distinguishable from other forms of play, such as games and toys. The *Random House Dictionary* defines a puzzle as a 'toy or other contrivance designed to amuse by presenting difficulties to be solved by ingenuity or patient effort'. This definition implies that the two main skills required for solving puzzles are ingenuity and patience.

1.2   THE PUZZLES OF SCIENCE

In science, puzzles are typically unsolved mysteries that have defied scientific and technological progress. For example, we still do not know why we need to sleep, why we do not feel the earth spinning, and where Earth's water came from. We do not know what the universe is made of, how life began, whether or not we are alone in the universe, why we dream, and whether or not time travel is feasible. These are puzzles because of the unavailability of a universally acceptable answer for any of them.

In mathematics, a large number of puzzles or problems have not been solved yet. Distinction is typically made between mathematical problems and mathematical puzzles, based on the recreational characteristic of puzzles (the latter are supposed to be recreational). However, this distinction is only valid for non-mathematicians. In this sense a mathematical puzzle is what follows in the sequence 2, 5, 11, 23, 47, . . . (the answer is 95) whereas a mathematical problem is working out the integral of x^x. For mathematicians, however, mathematical problems that baffle or confuse are, by definition, puzzles. If a puzzle must have a right answer, according to Kim (2006), then finding what follows in the sequence 27, 46, 29, 49, 34, . . . is not a puzzle, although it looks very much like a puzzle. This is because the sequence is a collection of random numbers between 1 and 50 (generated from a uniform distribution), in which case the following number could be anything between 1 and 50; hence no right answer. Alternatively, it makes sense to suggest that this is a puzzle but that Kim's definition is wrong.

In 2000 the Clay Mathematics Institute suggested seven Millennium Prize Problems and offered a \$1 million prize for solving each puzzle. Out of the seven puzzles, only one has since been solved, the Poincaré conjecture, not that it was an easy task. The conjecture can be traced back to the beginning of the 20th century when Henri Poincaré, a French mathematician, was working on the foundations of topology (a branch of mathematics that deals with the geometrical properties and spatial relations unaffected by the continuous change of shape or size of figures).

Over time, the conjecture proved to be extremely difficult to solve, but after nearly a century of failed attempts, a brilliant Russian mathematician, Grigori Perelman, presented a proof of the conjecture in three papers made available in 2002 and 2003 on arXiv. As a result, he was awarded the Millennium Prize of $1 million, which he declined.

Does the Poincaré conjecture sound like a puzzle in general terms? It was an unanswered question and unsolved problem that baffled and confused mathematicians for more than 100 years. Further properties of the Poincaré conjecture that are shared with generic puzzles are that it has a right answer and that its solution requires (enormous) ingenuity and patience. Puzzles are written, and this particular puzzle was written by Henri Poincaré. However, it would be a stretch of imagination to suggest that it is a source of fun and amusement, even less so as a form of play, except perhaps for a genius such as Grigori Perelman.

1.3   THE PUZZLES OF ECONOMICS AND FINANCE

The puzzles of economics and finance predominantly take the form of empirical or conceptual anomalies that allegedly remain unresolved and present a challenge to economists. Empirical anomalies, hence puzzles, arise when the implication of a theory is inconsistent with observed economic data; that is, when empirical testing does not support the theory. Alternatively, a puzzle arises when an observed phenomenon cannot be explained. In the second case, however, once a puzzle has been established, various plausible explanations are rejected by the originators, no matter how plausible they are. This is why, once perceived, the puzzles of economics and finance tend to persist and thrive.

The problem with the description of a puzzle in economics – that theory is inconsistent with data – is that it is based on the assumptions that the observed economic data are measured correctly, that the techniques of econometric testing are valid and produce consistent results, that economists conduct research because they are on a quest for the truth without any biases, and that economics is as rigorous as physics because economic phenomena are governed by laws, the laws of economics. A puzzle arises because of firm belief in theory, so that when empirical testing rejects it, a puzzle arises. This makes one wonder: why bother about testing the theory in the first place?

Testing economic theories is based predominantly on faulty data. In the natural sciences, investigators make their own measurements through experiments (as in testing Boyle's law) and other scientific procedures; for example, by measuring the distance from Earth to a certain galaxy or the height of a mountain. In economics, however, the economy itself generates data in vast quantities. In essence, economists use accounting data representing recorded transactions and activities. The problem with accounting data is that they are not collected for the purposes of a specific project that an economist is working on. This causes all sorts of problems, as the economist does not have any control over non-experimental data. Econometrics is used to deal with or solve problems such as measurement errors, but whether or not the treatment is adequate is a different matter. It certainly is not.

Baltagi (2002) argues that the data collected for applied econometric research are not ideal for the economic question at hand because they were posed to answer legal requirements or to comply with the rules set by regulatory agencies. Griliches (1986) describes the situation as follows:

> Econometricians have an ambivalent attitude towards economic data. At one level, the 'data' are the world that we want to explain, the basic facts that economists purport to elucidate. At the other level, they are the source of all our trouble. Their imperfections make our job difficult and often impossible . . . We tend to forget that these imperfections are what gives us our legitimacy in the first place . . . Given that it is the 'badness' of the data that provides us with our living, perhaps it is not all that surprising that we have shown little interest in improving it, in getting involved in the grubby task of designing and collecting original data sets of our own. Most of our work is on 'found' data, data that have been collected by somebody else, often for quite different purposes.

To do what scientists do, Griliches (1986) goes on to say the following:

> The encounters between econometricians and data are frustrating and ultimately unsatisfactory both because econometricians want too much from the data and hence tend to be disappointed by the answers, and because the data are incomplete and imperfect. In part it is our fault, the appetite grows with eating. As we get larger samples, we keep adding variables and expanding our models, until on the margin, we come back to the same insignificance levels.

The conventional wisdom that the techniques of econometric testing are valid and produce consistent results is questionable because econometrics is a con art that can be used to prove anything. Any negative evidence can be turned to be supportive by using different techniques, different data sets, different functional forms, and so on. Empirical evidence on an issue is always a mixed bag and never consistent. This is why every economic theory has supportive, unsupportive and neutral empirical evidence, depending on what the researcher feels like. And what the researcher feels like depends on ideology, the urge to prove a prior belief, or the desire to please a journal editor or a potential referee. This issue will be revisited in Chapter 5 where we examine the myths of econometrics, and referred to repeatedly when we consider individual puzzles in Chapters 2–4.

1.4 THE CONCEPT OF MYTH

Myths, which have been an integral part of humankind's entire history, are traditional or legendary stories, usually of unknown origin, and typically involving a hero or an event. They are symbolic tales of the distant past, ancient stories that are believed to be true. They can be found in every culture, where collective myths make up the culture's mythology. The word 'myth' can be traced back to the word *mythos*, which means a story, while the term 'mythology' denotes both the study of myth and the body of myths belonging to a particular religious tradition. The terms 'myth' and 'mythology', as we understand them today, arose in the English language in the 18th century. Myths are neither wholly true nor wholly untrue, and although some modern usages of the word have connotations suggesting that myths are irrelevant or wrong, this is not necessarily true.

Myths are characterized by certain features. McDowell (1998) describes myths as 'counter-factual in featuring actors and actions that confound the conventions of routine experience'. He argues that myths often involve extraordinary characters or episodes that seem impossible in our world, but 'the extraordinary feats and traits of mythic protagonists are possible only because they attach to a primary and formative period in the growth and development of civilization'. Myths may appear to be in opposition to science because they are not testable. Magoulick (2015) identifies 12 characteristics of myths, including the following: (1) a story that is or was considered a true explanation of the natural world; (2) characters are often non-human, such as gods, goddesses and supernatural beings; (3) the setting is a previous proto-world (somewhat like this one but also different); (4) they depict events that bend or break natural laws; and (5) they evoke the presence of mystery, the unknown. For some scholars, myths are inaccurate accounts of real historical events.

The themes of several noteworthy myths have been retold in various ways across many cultures, predominantly the 'creation myth' and the 'flood myth', which are popularly retold within the context of religion. The creation myth involves humans, the universe, or some other element of life. The flood myth depicts a great flood sent by God to destroy humankind, often as a form of punishment for forgetting the power and importance of divine rule. For example, the biblical story of Noah's ark is a representation of the flood myth in Christianity (and Islam). Furthermore, most religions have a form of creation myth that explains the existence of the universe and humankind.

1.5   THE MYTHS OF ECONOMICS AND SCIENCE

Peet (1992) attributes the rise of myths in economics to the 'lack of validity of much of standard economic theory', which 'comes mainly from within the economics profession itself'. Effectively, this means that myths are associated with neoclassical economics. He goes on to say the following:

> Much of theoretical economics has ceased to be related to real human societies. This is part of the reason why mainstream market liberal economics on the one hand and anthropology, sociology, and psychology on the other have drifted so far apart. The latter are based largely on empirical observation; the former, largely on a nineteenth-century logical-mathematical approach.

He quotes Peter Wiles as saying that 'the main thing that is wrong with economics is its disrespect for fact', and that 'it is perfectly possible for a science to be sick, and ours [economics] is now'. Myths in economics may not be myths for all. What is a myth for one school of thought is an undisputed fact of life for another. This is so much the case because, as Peet puts it, 'the scope of positive economics is smaller, and that of normative economics larger, than is frequently claimed by economists'. Normative economics involves value judgement on what ought to be, but what ought to be for Economist A is not so for Economist B. For A, private ownership of production facilities is conducive to efficiency and wealth creation, which is a myth for B.

For Peet (1992), myths arise in mainstream neoclassical economics, which follows the methodology of physical science. For example, he attributes the 'myth of rational behaviour' to the observed behaviour of particles in classical physics, which is assumed to be present in human behaviour. While rational behaviour is at the core of neoclassical economics, it is rejected by those studying behavioural economics, which has elements of psychology. Therefore, rationality is a myth as far as behavioural economists are concerned, but it is an undisputed fact of life for those believing in the principles of neoclassical economics.

Peet goes on to examine a number of myths arising from neoclassical economics, including the myth of bounded rationality, whereby people make decisions without perfect knowledge. In some respects, however, this approach is an alternative view to that of neoclassical economics, reflecting the fact that human behaviour consistently violates the principle of rationality. Unlike straight rationality, the proponents of the bounded rationality approach agree with the proposition that people have limited cognitive capabilities, implying limitations in attention, perception, memory, and abilities to process information and communicate.

Other myths arising from the nature of neoclassical economics include the myth of utility, as Peet argues that 'the presumed existence of utility is rooted in political-economic beliefs and ideologies rather than empirical science'. Discounting is a myth when it is applied to human life because (at the appropriate discount rate) it leads to the conclusion that one life today is worth 150 lives ten years from now. Then there is the myth of the invisible hand, that each individual who acts in their self-interest promotes the interests of the society, and the myth of stability, that the world is an unchanging, static system, or else it changes slowly. These may be myths for Peet but not so for neoclassical economists.

Science has its own share of myths, even though myths and science may be viewed as being diametrically opposed to each other. In the 1960s, Popper (1963) put forward the view that 'science must begin with myths, and with the criticism of myths'. It seems that myths are present in science because, as Peet puts it, 'there is a long history of gullibility, ignorance, and stupidity among scientists'. Scientific objectivity is a myth as scientists may take on responsibility for pronouncements in areas beyond their expertise, which is a consequence of having an inflated opinion of their ability to determine the truth of a situation from what is often nothing more than a cursory study.

1.6   ECONOMIC PARADOXES

Skousen and Taylor (1997) refer to three types of paradox in economics: (1) everyday observations that appear to defy common sense; (2) paradoxes that have perplexed economists in the past but have since been resolved to a certain extent; and (3) empirical or conceptual anomalies that remain unresolved and present a challenge to today's economists. Most of these paradoxes, however, sound like puzzles, in the sense that they are yet-to-be-answered questions. For example, the diamond–water paradox can be stated as an unanswered question (why is diamond more expensive than water, when the latter is by far more useful?) or it can be viewed as a self-contradictory statement that water is by far more useful, yet cheaper than diamond.

An example of the first type of paradox is the observation that some supermarket items sell for more per ounce in larger sizes. This observation is not difficult to explain, in which case it is hardly a puzzle or a paradox: it is one reason for the need to protect consumers from corporate greed.

In the absence of legislation requiring them to display unit prices on the products, supermarkets can generate more profit from large items (such as a 20 kg sack of rice) than small items by: (1) selling a big product for more than the number of units multiplied by the unit price; and/or (2) reducing the product size (the number of units) at the same price. In both cases, these are easier to hide in a big product than a small one. In fact, reducing the product size at the same price has been a common practice. Greenwood (2018) expresses this situation eloquently by saying that 'all around you, all the time, many consumer products are growing lighter, thinner, less substantial – all while maintaining the same price'. She also has the following to say:

> It's probably happened to you in a supermarket aisle, or maybe at home while making a favourite family recipe. You'll notice something odd – a can of tomato soup seems to hold less than it did, or the tuna used to be enough for three sandwiches, not two. It might dawn on you in the bathroom, where last month the household went through twelve rolls of toilet paper, up from the usual 9 or 10.

This is not a new phenomenon, but rather an old practice. In the early 1960s, the Committee on the Judiciary (1961) published a report in which the following question was raised: 'How badly have consumers been fooled?' The report makes it quite clear that 'if per-ounce cost as well as the unit cost were stamped on the package, the consumer would have no difficulty in making comparisons'. This observation is easy to explain in terms of corporate greed; it is not a puzzle, a mystery or a paradox.

An example of the second type of paradox is the diamond–water paradox of why diamond is more expensive than water. There seems to be a contradiction that although water is more useful than diamond in terms of survival, the latter commands a higher market price. It is strange that economics students are still told that this is a paradox, when the first thing these students learn is scarcity: that excess demand for a commodity brings about a high price. More than 200 years ago, Adam Smith presented a simple but plausible explanation for this paradox. In his celebrated work, *The Wealth of Nations*, he wrote the following (Smith, 1776):

> What are the rules which men naturally observe in exchanging them [goods] for money or for one another, I shall now proceed to examine. These rules determine what may be called the relative or exchangeable value of goods. The word VALUE, it is to be observed, has two different meanings, and sometimes expresses the utility of some particular object, and sometimes the power of purchasing other goods which the possession of that object conveys. The one may be called 'value in use;' the other, 'value in exchange.' The things which have the greatest value in use have frequently little or no value in exchange; on the contrary, those which have the greatest value in exchange have frequently

little or no value in use. Nothing is more useful than water: but it will purchase scarcely anything; scarcely anything can be had in exchange for it. A diamond, on the contrary, has scarcely any use-value; but a very great quantity of other goods may frequently be had in exchange for it.

Smith's explanation is based on the labour theory of value. An alternative explanation is based on the theory of marginal utility: diamond is more expensive than water because it is consumed to a level at which the marginal utility is still high, whereas water is consumed to a level at which the marginal utility is low. There is indeed no contradiction between the two explanations. It takes hard work to produce a given quantity of a scarce product, which means that it will be consumed to a level at which the marginal utility is still high. The same reasoning is valid for numerous commodities that are in short supply, including truffles, saffron and caviar. In general, a commodity commands a high price if it is scarce while the demand for it is rather strong, the magical term being 'excess demand'. As I was writing these lines I decided to conduct an experiment by asking my wife, who has never studied economics, to come up with a reason why diamond is more expensive than water. Without hesitation, she said 'scarcity'. There is no paradox here, but I can see a puzzle, which is why economists still talk about the water–diamond paradox when it is intuitively easy to explain.

Most (if not all) of the paradoxes in economics can be explained easily. Most, if not all, of the paradoxes arise because of the elevation of economics to the status of physical science. In the latter, studying the effect of x on y is conducted in a laboratory where any other variable that affects y is controlled. Economists try to do the same by running a regression of y on x and including the control variables $z_1, z_2, \ldots, z_n$ in the regression. The problem is that in economics we cannot control for anything, in which case we employ the *ceteris paribus* assumption, even implicitly. Economists come up with a theory stating that x should affect y in a certain direction, but when that is not observed it becomes a paradox. The problem here is that in theory we can assume that nothing else changes, but in reality everything changes, and some of these changes are not quantifiable or even observable. The elevation of economics to the status of physical science gives rise to paradoxes through another channel. An economist comes up with a theory that is rather elegant mathematically, but when this theory is tested the results are not supportive. This becomes a paradox, arising from belief in the power of econometric testing in revealing the truth.

Paradoxes arise in various fields of economics, including public economics, methodology, macroeconomics, microeconomics, environmental economics and international economics. In public economics we have the

Downs–Thomson paradox that improvements in the road network will not reduce traffic congestion. This is not a paradox, even by the principles of economics, the very basic theory of supply and demand. Improvements in the road network involve the provision of new roads and the upgrading of existing ones. Congestion will be reduced only if improvements do not bring about an increase in the number of road users. Traffic grows for natural reasons, such as population growth and rising standard of living, but this is not all. Bad roads entice people to use public transport, but good roads make it more convenient to use private vehicles. In general, more and better roads attract more traffic. Traffic density does not depend on one factor only, the quality of roads: we may find traffic jams where roads are really bad and where roads are good, and vice versa. Traffic density depends on other factors such as the quality of public transport and, most importantly, taxes. Traffic jams may be caused by households having more than one car. Doubling vehicle registration fees is more effective in reducing traffic jams than building new roads. This paradox is not a paradox: road improvements invite more traffic, in which case traffic jams are likely to worsen.

Another paradox in public economics is the Tullock paradox that rent-seekers wanting political favours can bribe politicians at a much lower cost than the value of the favour rendered to the rent-seeker. A simple explanation for this paradox is that rent-seekers are greedy and politicians who render services to rent-seekers are cheap and corrupt. Corrupt politicians may be content with small bribes because they do not want to make it obvious that they are receiving bribes by exhibiting lavish lifestyles. Moreover, corrupt politicians compete to offer favours to rent-seekers, thus bidding down the cost of rent-seeking. Guided by marginal analysis, rent-seekers offer bribes only if they think that they will get more in return.

In methodology we have the Easterlin paradox, which arises from the observation that happiness is an increasing function of income on a cross-sectional basis, but it is not so on a time series basis. This is a paradox only if happiness as a function of income is a universal law that holds anytime, anywhere. It is not a law, and happiness depends on more than income with cross-country variations; after all, money cannot buy love. From an econometric perspective, there is no reason whatsoever to expect cross-sectional evidence to be consistent with time series evidence. Typically, economists do not produce both time series and cross-sectional evidence on the same issue, but rather they mix data and run a panel regression, where the results turn out to be all over the place. Panel regression is no more than a ploy invented initially to boost sample sizes; it is a con job. The Easterlin paradox is not a paradox.

In macroeconomics we have the Gibson paradox: the observation that interest rate and the general price level are positively correlated when they should be negatively correlated. Interest rate cannot be positively or negatively correlated with the general price level for the simple reason that the two variables behave differently. The general price level moves predominantly in trends, while interest rates move predominantly in cycles. The general price level hardly declines, whereas the interest rate exhibits swings in either direction. The movement of the general price level over time is smooth, whereas the interest rate is volatile. If anything, the interest rate is more likely to be positively correlated with the inflation rate, as envisaged by Irving Fisher, than with the general price level. But even positive correlation between interest rate and inflation may or may not be observed.

The expectation that the general price level and interest rate are negatively correlated is based on a combination of the quantity theory of money and the loanable funds theory. More money leads to a higher price level and also to more loanable funds, which should bring down the interest rate. Hence prices and interest rates should be negatively correlated. However, interest rates do not only depend on the money supply, or the supply of loanable funds, because other factors come into play as the interest rate assumes different roles: the cost of borrowing, the return on investment and a monetary policy tool. Furthermore, a monetary expansion may lead to a higher or lower interest rate as it exerts a negative liquidity effect, a positive price level effect and a positive inflationary expectations effect. The resultant of these effects may be positive, negative or zero, depending on their relative sizes.

Even correlation between the interest rate and inflation may be positive or negative. It is positive according to the Fisher hypothesis where the interest rate represents the rate of return on investment. In this case, when inflation or expected inflation rises, investors demand a higher level of interest rate to preserve their real return. The Fisher hypothesis is definitely valid in times of hyperinflation, and this is why interest rates in countries experiencing hyperinflation may be in three, four or even five digits. On the other hand, if the interest rate is looked upon as a monetary policy tool, a higher expected inflation rate leads to a policy decision to raise the interest rate, which presumably brings inflation down. This means that interest rate and inflation are negatively correlated, albeit with a time lag.

Another paradox in macroeconomics is the Norwegian paradox that Norway's economic performance is strong despite low research and development (R&D) investment. This is not a paradox, at least if growth is what is meant by 'performance'. The underlying assumption is that growth depends on one factor only, which is R&D investment, but this is not the case. Studies of economic growth identify some 60 or so factors that explain cross-country differences in growth. For example, Norway's economic growth has been propelled by North Sea oil and perhaps by pro-people socioeconomic policies that enhance human capital.

In microeconomics we have the Giffen paradox, which is a paradox because it violates the 'law' of demand, when in fact there are no laws in economics and because, as usual, the effects of other factors on demand are ignored. Basic microeconomics tells us that demand depends negatively on the price of the commodity, positively on income, positively or negatively on the prices of other goods, positively or negatively on taste, positively or negatively on regulation, positively or negatively on technology, and so on. A rise in the price, therefore, will not necessarily reduce demand. Also at play is the elasticity of demand: when demand is inelastic a price rise brings about no change in demand, perhaps even an increase, as consumers reallocate expenditure from one good or a class of goods to others.

In microeconomics we also have the Jevons paradox and the Khazzoom–Brookes postulate. The Jevons paradox is the observation that consumers tend to travel more when their cars are more fuel-efficient. The Khazzoom–Brookes postulate is that improvement in energy efficiency boosts energy consumption. Improvement in fuel efficiency brings down the cost (price) of travel, leading to an increase in demand. The same applies to increasing energy consumption. It seems that if consumers demand less travel and less energy as the price declines, that would be more like a paradox.

Yet another paradox in microeconomics is the Icarus paradox, the observation of businesses failing abruptly after a period of apparent success, where this failure is brought about by the very elements that led to their initial success. According to Miller (1992), success seduces companies into failure by fostering overconfidence, complacency, specialization, exaggeration, dogma and ritual. Overconfidence is a well-known behavioural bias, which may take one of three forms: (1) overestimation of one's actual performance; (2) overplacement of one's performance relative to others; or (3) excessive confidence in own beliefs. The third form is quite common, and it can be hazardous by leading to unpleasant outcomes, particularly if the beliefs are unfounded, defy common sense, or when they cannot be substantiated. Overconfidence on its own can explain why a business may fail if success induces overconfidence. This is not a paradox.

In environmental economics we have the green paradox, which is not a paradox. It is the observation that an environmental policy aimed at slowing down global warming ends up accelerating it. This is not a paradox, because the producers of fossil fuel determine the aggregate rate of extraction that maximizes their net worth in the long run. If environmental policy becomes progressively greener, this will motivate those producers to extract resources at a higher rate, thus aggravating global warming. The profit maximization postulate is at play here.

Last, but not least, paradoxes arise in international economics. The first is the impossible trinity of fixed exchange rates, independent monetary policy and free capital movement. This is not a paradox, but rather a typical situation of choice and trade-off; these situations often arise in economics and finance. As a matter of fact, even two of the three may not be compatible. A fixed exchange rate is not compatible with free capital movement unless the central bank has adequate financial resources to defend the fixed rate by intervening in the foreign exchange market. A fixed exchange rate is not compatible with an independent monetary policy. For example, the central bank cannot set the interest rate at a level that is different from that on the currency to which the domestic currency is pegged, otherwise opportunities will be created for riskless arbitrage profit. Then we have the Lucas paradox that capital does not flow from developed countries to developing countries despite the fact that developing countries have lower levels of capital per worker. This paradox can be explained easily in terms of the phenomenon of home bias, which will be examined in Chapter 3.

1.7   WHAT IS NEXT?

In this chapter the preliminaries have been presented: the concepts of puzzle, myth and paradox, both in general terms and what they mean in economics and finance, where paradoxes are essentially puzzles. We considered some paradoxes, such as the Downs–Thomson paradox, the Tullock paradox, the Easterlin paradox, the Gibson paradox, the Giffen paradox, and others for which some simple explanations were suggested. We also considered the meaning of myth in general and more specifically in economics. We will later see some interaction between myths and puzzles, in the sense that some puzzles are based on myths, and that myths can arise from firm belief in puzzles, no matter what plausible explanations are presented to solve these puzzles.

In the next eight chapters we will consider in detail some puzzles and myths. In Chapters 2–4 we examine puzzles in international finance, international economics and macroeconomics, and finance, and argue that none of them is a puzzle. In Chapters 5–8, some myths (which, for some reason, are considered by some economists to be facts of life) are analysed in the fields of econometrics, laissez-faire, financial economics and macroeconomics. In Chapter 9, the mother of all myths, that the British royals attract tourists and pay for themselves, is debunked. In Chapter 10 we consider puzzles based on myths as well as a hypothetical puzzle, a silly puzzle and a dumb puzzle.

2. Puzzles in international finance

2.1 INTRODUCTION

In the macroeconomic approach to exchange rate determination, the exchange rate is envisaged to be a function of some macroeconomic variables such as inflation, growth, the money supply and interest rates. The earlier form of the macroeconomic approach is the goods market approach, whereby the demand for and supply of currencies came from the cross-border buying and selling of goods and services (that is, current account transactions). Hence, a country with a current account surplus would have an appreciating currency, and vice versa. This approach is typically represented by the flow model of exchange rates in which the exchange rate between two currencies depends on relative output (growth), relative prices (inflation) and the interest rate differential. It is also represented by purchasing power parity (PPP) whereby the exchange rate depends on relative prices only. The failure of this approach is indicated by the dismal performance (in terms of explanatory and predictive power) of both PPP and the monetary model. The failure can be attributed to the fact that international trade accounts for a tiny fraction of currency trading, meaning that only a small portion of foreign exchange turnover is used to finance the buying and selling of goods and services.

In the 1970s the asset market approach emerged in recognition of the observation that currencies are bought and sold to finance the cross-border buying and selling of assets (capital account transactions). This approach is represented by various forms of the monetary model of exchange rates as well as the portfolio balance model and the currency substitution model. These models have also failed as predictive and explanatory tools. The problem with this approach is that it is based on the assumption of homogenous beliefs and expectations, which is inconsistent with the huge trading volume in the foreign exchange market, let alone that it is counterintuitive.

The microstructure approach has been developed as an alternative to the macroeconomic approach to exchange rates. Lyons (2001) defines the microstructure approach in terms of 'the process and outcomes of exchanging currencies under explicit trading rules'. At the outset of Chapter 1 of his book, *The Microstructure Approach to Exchange Rates*, Lyons tells the following interesting story:

Ten years ago, a friend of mine who trades spot foreign exchange for a large bank invited me to spend a few days at his side. At the time, I considered myself an expert, having written my thesis on exchange rates. I thought that I had a handle on how it worked. I thought wrong.

As in the asset market approach, the demand for and supply of currencies in the microstructure approach are attributed to cross-border trading of assets. The distinguishing feature of this approach is that it relaxes three unrealistic assumptions of the asset approach by recognizing that: (1) some information relevant to exchange rates is not publicly available; (2) market participants differ in ways that affect exchange rates; and (3) trading mechanisms differ in ways that affect exchange rates. Lyons argues strongly for the ability of the microstructure approach to explain three puzzles: (1) the exchange rate determination puzzle, that exchange rate movements are virtually unrelated to macroeconomic fundamentals; (2) the excess volatility puzzle, that exchange rates are excessively volatile relative to fundamentals; and (3) the forward bias puzzle, that excess returns in the foreign exchange market are unpredictable and inexplicable. Even though the microstructure approach is more consistent with reality than the other two approaches, it does not have a monopoly over the ability to explain these puzzles, simply because they are not puzzles.

In this chapter, these puzzles are examined. The exchange rate determination (or disconnect) puzzle and the excess volatility puzzle are related, if not identical. Exchange rates are not related to macroeconomic fundamentals and they are too volatile relative to fundamentals. These puzzles are discussed primarily with respect to the monetary model of exchange rates. The purchasing power parity puzzle is a special case of the exchange rate determination puzzle. While the determination puzzle, excess volatility puzzle and PPP puzzle are about the explanatory power of exchange rate determination models, the Meese–Rogoff puzzle is about the predictive power of these models. These puzzles are about the behaviour of the spot exchange rates between two currencies and how the behaviour is related to macroeconomic fundamentals. The fifth puzzle discussed in this chapter pertains to the relation between the spot and forward exchange rates.

2.2 THE EXCHANGE RATE DETERMINATION PUZZLE

The exchange rate determination puzzle is the observation that exchange rate movements are virtually unrelated to macroeconomic fundamentals, such as interest rates, inflation and growth. It is indicated by the weak explanatory power of macroeconomic exchange rate determination models, and some observations about exchange rates not responding, or responding in the wrong direction, to changes in macroeconomic fundamentals.

I will start by telling a real-life story from the first half of the 1980s when the dollar was going through a period of consolidated strength to reach the highest level ever, in effective terms, early in 1985. At that time I was an economist in an investment banking firm. One week in 1984 the United States (US) prime lending rate declined by some 50 basis points while the growth rate of the US economy was revised downwards, which should have led to depreciation of the dollar. Yet, the US currency appreciated by about 2.5 per cent in that same week. My boss called me to ask for an explanation, wondering what had happened to economic theory (and implying that economists like me could not explain real-world phenomena). Obviously, he saw a puzzle, something happening in reality that defied economic theory. I decided to run a regression of the dollar's effective exchange rate on the US growth and interest rates. I found that these two variables explained 27 per cent of the variation in the exchange rate. So I told my boss that other factors, some of which we did not know and some which could not be measured, must have been changing in a manner that supported the dollar. I suppose that I convinced him, because he did not fire me.

The super-strong dollar phenomenon of the 1980s is perceived to be a puzzle because economists (or at least some of them) think that exchange rates are related to macroeconomic fundamentals by a law of physics, just like the relation between the volume of gas and the pressure exerted on it (Boyle's law). However, this is not the case, as technical factors may not only affect exchange rates but also they could dominate and overwhelm macroeconomic fundamentals. Even the effect of fundamentals could be anything: positive, negative or zero. The currency of a country that is growing faster than its trading partners may appreciate or depreciate. A rise in the domestic interest rate may lead to appreciation or depreciation of the domestic currency. As we are going to see, different models of exchange rate determination produce different predictions and provide different explanations as to what happens to the exchange rate when a macroeconomic variable moves one way or another.

Let us consider further examples on the peculiar behaviour of exchange rates that makes the lives of financial journalists and foreign exchange dealers rather difficult. It is quite common for a financial journalist to write a story attributing the appreciation of the dollar to a rise in oil prices, and a few months later the same journalist would write a story telling us why the dollar depreciated because of higher oil prices. Economic theory can be used to show that a change in a certain macroeconomic variable can have a positive or negative effect on a particular currency. A rise in the growth rate can be interpreted to be a bullish signal, since growth boosts corporate profitability and leads to a thriving stock market; but it can be interpreted to be a bearish signal, since it leads to the growth of imports and hence deterioration in the current account. A rise in interest rate may be taken to be a bullish signal, since it implies that domestic assets have become more attractive; or a bearish signal, since a higher interest rate depresses the economy. Monetary expansion leads to inflation, which is bad for the domestic currency; but it also forces the central bank to react by raising interest rates, which is good for the domestic currency. A smaller budget deficit, in the absence of a change in saving–investment balance, leads to improvement in the current account, which is good for the domestic currency; but lower borrowing requirements by the government ease pressure on interest rates, which is bad for the domestic currency.

The reason why financial journalists and foreign exchange dealers have difficult jobs is that exchange rates are difficult to judge. The following are some pitfalls that they often fall into:

- They tend to look at one variable in isolation, whichever happens to be fashionable at that time. Exchange rates do not behave in response to one factor or a small number of factors, except in one case: hyperinflation. Explaining the behaviour of exchange rates or forecasting them on the basis of inflation, interest rates, commodity prices, current accounts or oil prices in isolation of other factors is hazardous. This is actually the reason why a large number of foreign exchange dealers lost their jobs in the 1980s when they kept on predicting the depreciation of the dollar, which did not materialize until March 1985.
- Failure to distinguish between the short-term and long-term effects of fundamental variables on the exchange rate. A single factor may have a positive effect in the short run and a negative effect in the long run.
- Failure to identify reverse causation. For example, is it that improvement in the current account leads to currency appreciation, or that currency depreciation leads to current account improvement? Both of these propositions are valid, but the effects occur over the short and long run.
- Failure to identify the effect of news; that is, unanticipated changes in the variables affecting the exchange rate. What matters is not what is announced, but what is announced relative to what had been anticipated. Announcements are not news in an economic sense. An announcement has a news component if the announced value is

different from the expectation prevailing prior to the announcement. An announcement of a 5 per cent inflation rate or a \$5 billion deficit in the trade balance may be good or bad for the underlying currency, depending on whether the anticipated figure prior to the announcement was higher or lower than the announced figure.

A conclusion that always follows when exchange rates defy conventional wisdom, and move in a way that is contrary to what had been anticipated, is that fundamentals do not matter. Fundamentals do matter, but not to the extent that makes the relation between them and exchange rates something like a law of physics that is obeyed by all market participants. Another pitfall is that the foreign exchange market is often viewed as a mechanical system that is expected to work as designed. Thus, pushing the inflation 'button' should move the market in a particular direction and in a predictable manner. When this does not happen, a conclusion is reached that inflation does not matter. The same applies to all other fundamentals, but this is not the way to judge the importance and relevance of fundamentals.

Let us now examine the explanatory power of the basic flexible-price monetary model, which is derived by combining two demand for money equations (relating demand to output and interest rates) with PPP. In a testable form, the model is written as:

$$s_t = \alpha_0 + \alpha_1(m_t - m_t^*) + \alpha_2(y_t - y_t^*) + \alpha_3(i_t - i_t^*) + \varepsilon_t \qquad (2.1)$$

where s is the log of the exchange rate, m is the log of the money supply, y is the log of output, i is the interest rate, and an asterisk denotes the 'foreign' variable, such that the exchange rate is measured as the price of one unit of the foreign currency. This model is based on the proposition that excess demand for money denominated in a particular currency leads to the appreciation of that currency, and vice versa. It follows that a country experiencing rapid monetary growth, slow output growth and a high interest rate (relative to its trading partners) will have a depreciating currency, and vice versa. In terms of equation (2.1), this means that $\alpha_1 > 0$, $\alpha_2 < 0$ and $\alpha_3 > 0$. The model can also be written in a general testable form by relaxing the assumptions of symmetry (the equality of income and interest elasticities of the demand for money) and proportionality (a one-to-one relation between the exchange rate and the money supply) to obtain:

$$s_t = \beta_0 + \beta_1 m_t + \beta_2 m_t^* + \beta_3 y_t + \beta_4 y_t^* + \beta_5 i_t + \beta_6 i_t^* + \xi_t \qquad (2.2)$$

where $\beta_1 > 0$, $\beta_2 < 0$, $\beta_3 < 0$, $\beta_4 > 0$, $\beta_5 > 0$ and $\beta_6 < 0$. Other models of exchange rate determination tell us different stories. In the flow model, for example, rapid output growth leads to deterioration in the current account and hence domestic currency depreciation. In the same model, a rise in the domestic interest rate leads to domestic currency appreciation. In the sticky price monetary model, a rise in the domestic interest rate leads to currency appreciation. Even if we believe in the power of these models, we should not expect the exchange rate to move in a particular direction when interest rates and output growth change, because we do not know which of these models is the true representation of the facts on the ground. I suppose that none of them is, because exchange rates are determined by more than macroeconomic fundamentals. As a matter of fact, none of these models can explain a typical phenomenon in the foreign exchange market, which is bubbles followed by crashes.

In the following exercise we examine the explanatory power of the monetary model for the exchange rate between the pound and dollar using quarterly data over the period 1983:1 to 2016:3 (obtained from *International Financial Statistics*). The money supply is taken to be the broad money aggregate (M3 for the US and M4 for the United Kingdom). Output is proxied by industrial production, and interest rates are medium–long government bond yields. The exchange rate is measured as the price of one dollar, which means that a rise in the exchange rate implies dollar appreciation. When the model is estimated by ordinary least squares (OLS) over the whole sample period, it gives the following results (t statistics in parentheses):

$$s_t = -0.305 - 0.185(m_t - m_t^*) + 0.316(y_t - y_t^*) - 4.579(i_t - i_t^*)$$
$$(-4.88)\ \ (-8.24)\ \ \ (7.02)\ \ \ (-4.57)$$

$$R^2 = 0.46 \quad SC = 86.77 \quad HS = 1.77$$

All of the estimated coefficients are statistically significant but the signs are exactly the opposite of what is implied by the model. While the estimated equation passes the diagnostic for heteroscedasticity $(HS \sim \chi^2(1))$ it fails the diagnostic for serial correlation $(SC \sim \chi^2(4))$, perhaps implying misspecification. When the model is estimated as an autoregressive distributed lag (ARDL) model, we get the following:

$$s_t = -0.618 + 0.931s_{t-1} - 0.184s_{t-2} - 0.289(m_t - m_t^*) + 0.244(m_{t-1} - m_{t-1}^*)$$
$$(-2.93)(11.07)(-2.23)\phantom{s_{t-2}}\ (-4.13)\ \ \ \ (3.47)$$
$$+ 0.103(y_t - y_t^*) - 0.011(i_t - i_t^*)$$
$$(3.09)\ \ \ (-3.35)$$

$$R^2 = 0.82 \quad SC = 2.15 \quad HS = 0.01$$

*Figure 2.1   Actual exchange rate relative to monetary model prediction
              (GBP/USD)*

The ARDL equation passes the diagnostic for serial correlation but the
signs of the coefficients on the contemporaneous variables are still opposite to what is implied by the model.

In Figure 2.1 we observe the actual values of the exchange rates and
those predicted by the model over the sample period. We can see that the
model gets it wrong by up to 25 per cent on the upside and 19 per cent on
the downside. More importantly perhaps is that the estimated coefficients
could be positive or negative, depending on which part of the sample is
used. Figure 2.2 exhibits the rolling coefficients using a window size of 24
quarters; that is, the first rolling regression is estimated from the first 24
observations, then the sample is updated by dropping the first observation
and adding a new one. We can clearly see how unstable the model is.

Lane (1991) lists six reasons for the apparent failure of the monetary
model, bearing in mind that it is derived by combining two demand for
money functions and purchasing power parity. The first reason is the unre-
liability of the demand for money estimates. The second is the assumption
that the parameters in the demand for money functions are equal in both
countries (the assumption of symmetry). Third is the violation of purchasing power parity and the implied stationarity of the real exchange rate.
Fourth is the empirical failure of uncovered interest parity (UIP), implying
either risk neutrality or that exchange rate risk is entirely diversifiable, let

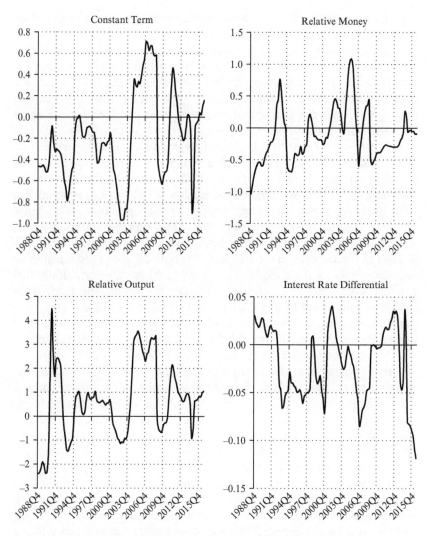

Figure 2.2   Rolling coefficients (window = 24)

alone that it is misspecified as we are going to see later. Reason five is the assumption that the money supply is exogenous, which rules out the possibility of policies initiated by feedback. Last, but not least, is the possibility of bubbles which, if present, would contribute to the empirical failure of the monetary model, since it is difficult to distinguish bubbles from omitted variables and specification errors. Lane defends his arguments with numerous related empirical studies to reach the dismal conclusion that 'it is perhaps less surprising that the (monetary) model has failed empirically than that it ever appeared to succeed at all'.

A question that arises here is whether or not macroeconomic fundamentals do matter. Some economists wonder whether exchange rates are determined by fundamentals or by speculation, implying that the two are mutually exclusive (for example, Dixon, 1999). Hence, what these economists have in mind is that speculation cannot be based on fundamentals but rather on some sort of extrapolation of past values of the exchange rate. These observations have been wrongly interpreted to imply irrelevance of the macroeconomic fundamentals envisaged by asset market models of exchange rate determination (Moosa, 2002b). It can be demonstrated that the empirical failure of fundamental models is not inconsistent with the relevance of fundamentals. The proposition of disconnect between exchange rates and macroeconomic fundamentals is based on the empirical observation of disparity between the actual behaviour of exchange rates and what is implied by fundamental models. Hence, the argument goes, fundamentals do not matter because these models do not work. While there is no doubt that macroeconomic models of exchange rates are inadequate, this inadequacy cannot be interpreted to imply the irrelevance of fundamentals. This interpretation is far-fetched because it implies that the foreign exchange market is governed by an iron law embedded in the underlying fundamental model, and that this iron law is observed and obeyed by all market participants.

These arguments overlook the fact that the foreign exchange market is not a mechanical system that moves according to a predetermined, yet-to-be-discovered formula given the empirical failure of the exchange rate models that have been developed so far. This flawed line of reasoning results from the wrong perception, which Harvey (1993) describes by saying that 'markets are perceived as quasi-physical phenomena composed of a system of deterministic laws leading to predictable outcomes'. The problem with this line of reasoning is that when these predictable outcomes do not materialize, the conclusion that jumps to the forefront is that fundamentals do not drive the foreign exchange market: rather, the driving force is yet to be discovered; this is a very convenient excuse if one rejects a proposition and cannot provide an alternative one.

Dixon (1999) wonders whether exchange rates are ultimately tied down by economic fundamentals, or are free to drift at random on a 'sea of speculation'. The implication of wondering in this way is that speculation in the foreign exchange market cannot be based on fundamentals. This belief is at odds with the available survey and econometric evidence indicating that foreign exchange dealers base their speculative decisions (related to exchange rate forecasting) on fundamentals, technical analysis or a combination thereof. In Moosa (2000) a comprehensive description is presented of decision-making situations involving speculation in the foreign exchange market where the expected exchange rate is a decision variable. Forecasting the unknown decision variable may be based on fundamental models, technical models or even market-based models. Hence, speculation does not necessarily preclude the use, and hence the relevance, of fundamentals. The most successful currency speculator, George Soros, has made his billions by speculating on the basis of fundamental factors. This observation alone is a testimony in favour of the proposition that fundamentals are important. Moreover, 'drifting at random' does not necessarily mean that fundamentals do not matter.

Because of the heterogeneity of foreign exchange market participants, it is not possible to construct a model of exchange rate determination that is represented by a set of equations, let alone a single equation. The heterogeneity of the characteristics and actions of market participants leads to the empirical failure of fundamental models despite the relevance of fundamentals. The importance of fundamentals cannot be judged on the basis of the empirical validity or otherwise of a fundamental model. In a comment on Mark's (1995) finding of the superiority of fundamental models at long horizons, Rogoff (1999) describes Mark's results as implying 'modest empirical connection between exchange rates and macroeconomic fundamentals'. Fundamentals are important and relevant if dealers act upon them and take them into consideration when they decide to buy and sell currencies. By doing so, they cause shifts in the excess demand function, leading to changes in the exchange rate. In this sense, fundamentals are relevant to exchange rate determination.

If the monetary model (or any other model for that matter) is to be valid as reflecting the actual behaviour of exchange rates, then all foreign exchange dealers must be fundamentalists, reacting to changes in three variables only: money supply, output and interest rates (domestic and foreign). They should react to changes in these variables by buying the foreign currency when the domestic money supply rises relative to the foreign money supply, when domestic output grows more slowly than foreign output and when the interest rate differential rises in favour of the domestic currency. And if the coefficient restrictions implied by the monetary model are to be satisfied, then the reaction of foreign exchange dealers to changes in these variables must be quantitatively linked to the income elasticity and interest semi-elasticity of the demand for money functions. Obviously, these conditions cannot be satisfied. No wonder then that various estimates of the monetary model and the portfolio balance model have typically produced wrongly signed, insignificant and numerically implausible coefficients, not to mention poor diagnostics, structural breaks and poor out-of-sample forecasting power.

Ample survey and econometric evidence indicates the existence of fundamentalists. Allen and Taylor (1989, 1990) and Taylor and Allen (1992) provide evidence, based on a survey of some 240 foreign exchange dealers in London, indicating that both technical and fundamental analyses are used. Lui and Mole (1998) conducted a similar survey involving 153 foreign exchange dealers in Hong Kong and found that dealers placed some weight on both technical and fundamental analysis. The econometric evidence is also supportive. Goodhart (1988) puts forward the view that exchange rate misalignment is determined by the balance of the predictions of technical analysts and fundamental analysts. Likewise, Frankel and Froot (1990) use an econometric model to demonstrate that both technicians and fundamentalists play a role in the foreign exchange market. On the basis of a similar model, Moosa and Korczak (2000) find that both fundamentalists and technicians play a role in exchange rate determination, and that fundamentalists play a bigger role.

Fundamentals, therefore, do matter. It is wrong to view the foreign exchange market as a mechanical system with buttons assigned to various fundamentals. It is hazardous to believe that fundamentals do not matter just because pushing a particular button does not drive the foreign exchange market in a particular direction. The process is too complex to be viewed this way. Fundamentals do matter, because they are taken into account when decisions are made to buy and sell currencies. The exchange rate determination puzzle is not a puzzle at all.

2.3   THE PPP PUZZLE

The PPP puzzle is an example of the broader exchange rate determination puzzle, but for some reason it is described by Obstfeld and Rogoff (2000) as a 'very important one'; that is, a very important example of the determination puzzle. However, they do not tell us why it is 'very important', given that there is no reason to believe that relative prices are more important than other macroeconomic determinants of the exchange rate. The puzzle follows from the observation that exchange rates do not move in tandem with relative prices. According to Obstfeld and Rogoff (2000), 'purchasing power has to remain constant across countries over long periods of time in a world with international arbitrage in goods markets'. Characterizing PPP as an arbitrage condition, which is incorrect, seems to be the reason for belief in this puzzle.

Again, the implication here is that PPP is a law of physics, according to which exchange rates are determined by relative prices only. We have already seen that the monetary model of exchange rates, which has PPP as a component linking two national economies, has failed. It must, therefore, seem odd to wonder why PPP fails to explain exchange rate movements, except under conditions of hyperinflation. We have also seen that one of the reasons for the failure of the monetary model, as envisaged by Lane (1991), is the assumption that PPP holds continuously.

To make it sound 'sciency', Obstfeld and Rogoff invoke the concept of 'half-life', which is a measure of the speed at which convergence to the equilibrium condition implied by PPP occurs; that is, the time required for a unit shock to PPP to dissipate by half. They wonder how it is possible that the half-life of real exchange rate innovations can be three to four years, and declare that 'in the presence of trade costs, econometric estimates of the half-life of real-exchange-rate movements may be exaggerated', thus attributing the failure of PPP to transaction costs. Choi et al. (2004) suggest that the solution lies in the use of panel data, on the grounds that 'increasing the number of data points by combining the cross-section with the time-series should give more precise estimates'. The fact of the matter is that the use of panel data is an 'econo-trick' intended to boost the sample size by pooling time series and cross-sectional data. What kind of 'more precise estimates' do we get by pooling time series data from Sweden and Somalia?

The arbitrage view of PPP is that it is a generalization of the law of one price, which states that the price of a commodity should be the same when expressed in a common currency. The condition holds because commodity arbitrage acts as the mechanism that eliminates deviations from equilibrium. When this condition is extended from one commodity (such as gold) to the general price level, we obtain:

$$P = SP* \tag{2.3}$$

where P and $P*$ are the domestic and foreign price levels, respectively, and S is the exchange rate measured as the domestic currency price of one unit of the foreign currency. Equation (2.3) can be written as:

$$S = \frac{P}{P*} \tag{2.4}$$

Thus, as domestic prices rise relative to foreign prices, S will rise (the domestic currency will depreciate) and vice versa. How can equations (2.3) and (2.4) hold for the general price levels, which are measured as indices? Intuitively, a variable that is measured in certain units (the bilateral exchange rate) cannot be equal to the quotient of two variables (the price levels) measured without units.

It makes more sense to write the PPP equation in a functional form as:

$$S = a + b\left(\frac{P}{P*}\right) \qquad (2.5)$$

where $b > 0$. In a testable logarithmic form, the equation becomes:

$$s_t = a + b(p_t - p_t^*) + \varepsilon_t \qquad (2.6)$$

where lower-case letters are used to indicate natural logarithms. By relaxing the assumption of symmetry, that the domestic and foreign prices have equal (absolute) effects on the exchange rate, the PPP model may be written as:

$$s_t = a + b_1 p_t + b_2 p_t^* + \varepsilon_t \qquad (2.7)$$

where $b_1 > 0$ and $b_2 < 0$.

The exchange rate compatible with (or predicted by) PPP can be calculated by considering exchange rates and prices at two points in time, 0 and 1. If PPP holds at these two points in time, then:

$$\frac{S_1}{S_0} = \frac{P_1/P_1^*}{P_0/P_0^*} \qquad (2.8)$$

or:

$$S_1 = S_0\left[\frac{P_1/P_1^*}{P_0/P_0^*}\right] = S_0\left[\frac{P_1/P_0}{P_1^*/P_0^*}\right] \qquad (2.9)$$

Equation (2.9) can be written as:

$$S_1 = S_0\left[\frac{1 + \dot{P}}{1 + \dot{P}*}\right] \qquad (2.10)$$

where $\dot{P}$ and $\dot{P}*$ are the percentage changes in P and $P*$, respectively, between points in time 0 and 1. Equations (2.9) and (2.10) tell us the following: starting from time 0, with an exchange rate, S_0, the exchange rate at time 1, S_1, will differ from S_0 by a factor reflecting domestic and foreign inflation rates between 0 and 1. The underlying idea is that if PPP held during the period between 0 and 1, in the sense that relative inflation is the only factor determining the exchange rate, then deviation from the PPP rate will not be observed. Deviation, however, arises because of the effect of other factors on the exchange rate. In general, the exchange rate consistent with PPP (some sort of an equilibrium exchange rate) may be calculated as:

$$\overline{S}_t = S_0\left[\frac{P_t}{P_t^*}\right] \qquad (2.11)$$

where prices are measured as indices relative to the same base period, 0.

PPP has implications for the real exchange rate, which is defined as:

$$Q = S\left[\frac{P*}{P}\right] \qquad (2.12)$$

This means that:

$$\frac{Q_1}{Q_0} = \frac{S_1}{S_0}\left[\frac{\dfrac{P_1^*}{P_0^*}}{\dfrac{P_1}{P_0}}\right] \qquad (2.13)$$

which gives:

$$(1 + \dot{Q}) = \left[\frac{(1 + \dot{S})(1 + \dot{P}*)}{1 + \dot{P}}\right] \qquad (2.14)$$

where a dot implies the percentage change in the underlying variable between 0 and 1. Equation (2.14) can be simplified to the following:

$$1 + \dot{P} + \dot{Q} + \dot{Q}\dot{P} = 1 + \dot{P}* + \dot{S} + \dot{P}*\dot{S} \qquad (2.15)$$

By ignoring cross-products, which are numerically small, we obtain:

$$\dot{Q} = \dot{S} + \dot{P}* - \dot{P} \qquad (2.16)$$

If PPP is valid, then $\dot{S} = \dot{P} - \dot{P}*$, which gives $\dot{Q} = 0$. The implication of PPP, therefore, is that the real exchange rate is constant, which necessarily means that it is independent of the nominal exchange rate.

Obstfeld and Rogoff (2000) use the following equation to measure the half-life of the real exchange rate:

$$q_t = \alpha + \beta t + \gamma q_{t-1} + \zeta_t \qquad (2.17)$$

where t is time and high values of γ imply long half-lives. It is also possible to measure the speed of adjustment to equilibrium by estimating an error correction model corresponding to equation (2.6), which is written as:

$$\Delta s_t = \alpha + \sum_{j=1}^{m}\beta_j\Delta s_{t-j} + \sum_{j=0}^{m}\delta_j\Delta(p_{t-j} - p_{t-j}^*) + \theta[a - b(p_{t-1} - p_{t-1}^*)] + \zeta_t$$

$$(2.18)$$

Table 2.1   Measures of adjustment to deviations from PPP

Exchange rate	γ	Half-life in quarters	θ
AUD/USD	0.950	13.5	−0.043
	(41.86)		(−1.86)
JPY/USD	0.948	13.0	−0.041
	(39.78)		(−1.71)
GBP/USD	0.919	8.2	−0.097
	(29.65)		(−3.05)
JPY/AUD	0.958	16.2	−0.036
	(48.93)		(−1.81)
JPY/GBP	0.929	9.4	−0.079
	(34.29)		(−2.93)
AUD/GBP	0.952	14.1	−0.049
	(43.22)		(−2.11)

Note: t statistics are placed in parentheses.

where the speed of adjustment to deviations from PPP is measured by the coefficient θ.

Let us see some empirical results based on the estimation of equations (2.17) and (2.18). For this purpose, six exchange rates are used involving four currencies: Australian dollar (AUD), US dollar (USD), Japanese yen (JPY) and British pound (GBP). Quarterly data on the exchange rates and consumer prices were obtained from *International Financial Statistics*. The results, which are reported in Table 2.1, show that γ has high values, implying long half-lives, ranging between 8.2 and 13.5 quarters. θ, which is a measure of the speed of adjustment to deviations from PPP, is either insignificant or very small. For example, in the case of the AUD/GBP exchange rate, 4.9 per cent of the deviation is corrected each quarter, which means that it takes on average 20.4 quarters (just over five years) to eliminate deviation from the equilibrium condition.

Further evidence against PPP is provided by Figure 2.3 where we observe nominal and real exchange rates. Against the predictions of PPP, the real exchange rates are far away from being stable and they are highly correlated with the nominal rates. In Figure 2.4 we can see significant deviations of the actual exchange rates from those predicted by PPP as measured by equation (2.11).

The PPP puzzle is based on a faulty characterization of PPP that it is an arbitrage condition. For example, Obstfeld and Rogoff (2000) say the following:

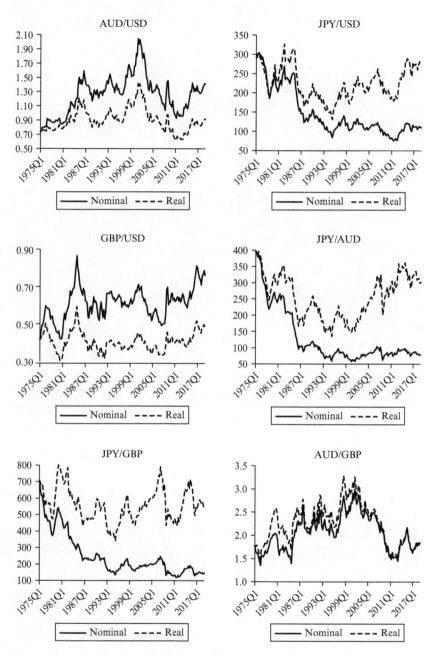

Figure 2.3   Nominal and real exchange rates

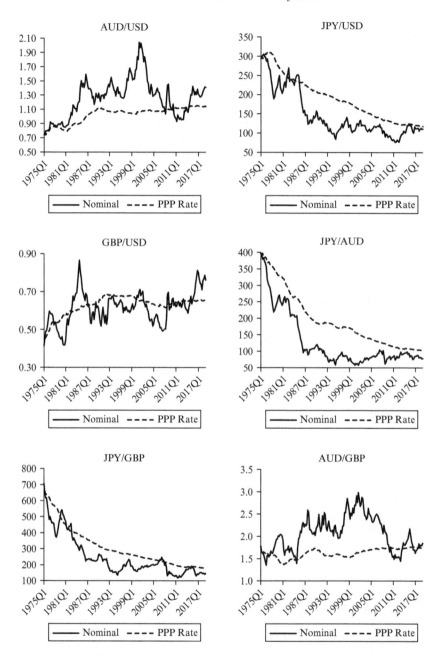

Figure 2.4   Observed and PPP exchange rates

If there are only modest obstacles to short-term price arbitrage across borders, there can be only modest short-term price differentials. In fact, at the consumer level, arbitrage costs are likely to be rather large, and, after all, most goods embody very large nontraded content once they reach consumers at the retail level. But one cannot make this argument for wholesale importers who trade in bulk.

In a way, they suggest that adjustment is faster on the wholesale than the retail level. This is what they say:

> One might think that the slow mean reversion just documented applies primarily to goods with extremely high international trade costs, whereas, at least for goods that are heavily traded, mean reversion in relative international consumer prices might be more rapid. That is not the case, however, as documented most strikingly by Engel (1999).

Their explanation for the failure of PPP is the following:

> Once one allows for pricing to market, however, it does become possible to develop models that can generate large price differentials exhibiting considerable persistence. Leading examples of such models are in Bergin and Feenstra (2001) and Chari, Kehoe, and McGrattan (1998).

Replacing consumer prices with wholesale prices in the PPP equation does not change the results, at least qualitatively. As an example where the data are chosen randomly, consider PPP between Japan and Australia over the period 1975Q1 to 1996Q3. In terms of the coefficients γ and θ, the results are indistinguishable. With consumer prices, $\gamma = 0.906$, compared with $\gamma = 0.896$, both high values implying slow mean reversion. With consumer prices, $\theta = -0.078$, compared to $\theta = -0.060$, both of which are statistically insignificant. Figure 2.5 shows the nominal AUD/JPY rate, together with the corresponding real rates calculated by using consumer and wholesale prices. Both real rates are highly volatile and correlated with the nominal rate. Choosing any other exchange rate over any period will produce similar results, indicating the failure of PPP and the invalidity of the Obstfeld–Rogoff explanation.

The characterization of PPP as an arbitrage condition is inconsistent with the writings of Gustav Cassel (1916) who presented an operational theory of foreign exchange and coined the term 'purchasing power parity'. Cassel, a brilliant economist, did not portray his theory as a condition of equality between the exchange rate and price ratio, neither did he say that only the price ratio affected the exchange rate. However, he did come up with a formula as a pragmatic approximation to what happens under conditions of high inflation or in the long run. He presented an

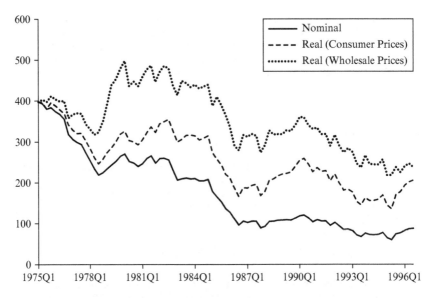

*Figure 2.5   JPY/AUD real exchange rates based on consumer and
              wholesale prices*

operational theory in which the exchange rate is affected by monetary
and non-monetary factors, rather than a mechanistic equality between the
exchange rate and price ratio.

Cassel (1922) described as 'pure dogma' the version of PPP whereby
monetary factors, as proxied by prices, determine the exchange rate exactly.
He rejected the arbitrage view of PPP, which leads to the dogma, and advocated the monetary view, which is obvious in his writings. Cassel (1916) set
out to explain his theory of foreign exchange by viewing the exchange rate
to be 'an expression for the value in the money of one country put upon
the money of another country' such that 'the rate of exchange between the
two countries will be determined by the quotient of the general levels of
prices in two countries'. Since the quantity theory of money stipulates that
the general price level varies, other things being equal, in direct proportion
to the quantity of money (or what Cassel called the 'circulating medium'),
it follows that 'the rate of exchange between the two countries must vary
as the quotient between the quantities of their respective circulating media'
(Cassel, 1916). Cassel's theory is in fact an extension of the quantity theory
of money to the case of an open economy, implying that doubling the
money supply leads to a doubling of the price level, which in turn causes a
proportional rise in the exchange rate.

Bresciani-Turroni (1934) argued that the mechanistic view of PPP as reflected in the arbitrage approach does not hold generally because it ignores other factors. If the price ratio reflects relative monetary conditions, then P and P^* must represent the general price levels which are inevitably measured by some indices. This formulation lacks logical consistency because, as Holmes (1967) succinctly put it, 'the ratio of two arbitrarily weighted commodity price indexes will not equal to any given number'. In this case, Holmes adds, 'no empirical evidence is relevant in determining the truth or falsity of the dogma'.

Cassel's theory is an operational theory, postulating that: (1) monetary factors are the most important long-run determinants of the exchange rate; and (2) other factors (such as trade impediments, transportation costs, capital flows and expectations) play a role in the process of exchange rate determination. According to Gailliot (1970), Cassel's PPP amounts to saying that 'in the long run important changes in the domestic price level have a much greater influence on the exchange rate in the real conditions of international trade'. Holmes (1967) argues that 'the theory Cassel actually expounded contains several non-monetary variables and is presented within a framework which is conceptually similar to an econometric model in which the behavioral equations contain random terms'.

Moosa and Bhatti (1999) present a thorough discussion of Cassel's view of PPP as a functional relation of several variables. The empirical evidence shows that PPP works perfectly under hyperinflation where monetary factors dominate. If PPP is an arbitrage condition, this must mean that commodity arbitrage works better under hyperinflation, which does not make sense. PPP is not an arbitrage condition, in which case the explanation put forward by Obstfeld and Rogoff for the PPP puzzle is wrong. There is no puzzle here: exchange rates are not determined by a law of physics called purchasing power parity.

2.4   THE EXCESS VOLATILITY PUZZLE

The excess volatility puzzle is the observation that exchange rates are excessively volatile relative to macroeconomic fundamentals; it follows naturally from the determination puzzle. Because of the weak link between exchange rates and macroeconomic fundamentals, these fundamentals cannot explain exchange rate volatility. In other words, the determination puzzle is about the inability of macroeconomic fundamentals to explain the level of the exchange rate, whereas the excess volatility puzzle is about the inability of fundamentals to explain volatility, or period-to-period changes.

To start with, macroeconomic fundamentals are not necessarily less

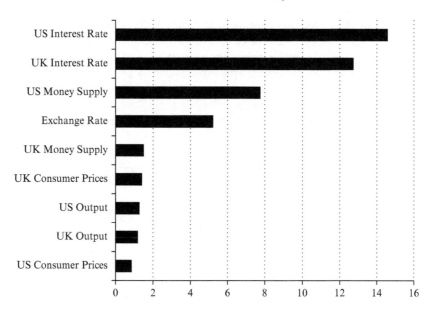

Figure 2.6   Standard deviation of percentage change

volatile than exchange rates. In Figure 2.6 we observe volatility of exchange rates and macroeconomic variables measured as the standard deviation of the percentage change in each variable, using data on the GBP/USD exchange rates over the period 1975:1 to 2019:1, which are the same data used earlier to estimate the monetary model. The GBP/USD exchange rate is significantly more volatile than consumer prices and output in both countries as well as the United Kingdom (UK) money supply. The exchange rate is less volatile than the US money supply (due mainly to the big jumps caused by quantitative easing) as well as the two interest rates. In Figure 2.4, which shows the exchange rate behaviour predicted by PPP, we can see that the lack of volatility in consumer prices produces a very smooth kind of behaviour in the PPP exchange rate. However, the observed rates are much more volatile than the PPP rates because exchange rates are determined by more than relative prices.

Economists have attempted to explain the excess volatility puzzle. Flood and Rose (1999) argue that the observation that exchange rate volatility differs systematically in the apparent absence of corresponding differences in economic volatility is hard to understand in linear macroeconomic models. Hence, they explore a potential explanation in non-linear models with multiple equilibria, proposing a non-linear portfolio balance equation to represent the changing market structure as the exchange rate regime changes. They use the model to explain the increase in exchange rate volatility as the exchange rate regime changes from fixed to floating exchange rates. However, they do not attempt to demonstrate the adequacy of the model for explaining the difference between the volatility of the exchange rate and that of macroeconomic variables in the post-1973 era. Frankel and Dornbusch (1988) argue that exchange rates must be reacting to something other than fundamentals such as factors that are unknown to economists (magic or aliens?) or to irrelevant noise. The same story is told by Williams et al. (1998), who explain exchange rate volatility in terms of some factors derived from asset market variables, which they call 'virtual fundamentals' as opposed to 'traditional fundamentals'.

A simpler explanation for this puzzle, which is not a puzzle, can be found by going back to basics, the basics of supply and demand in the foreign exchange market. It can be demonstrated that the heterogeneity of market participants leads to random and staggered shifts in the excess demand function, causing the observed random-like behaviour and volatility of exchange rates. In Figure 2.7 it is shown that the exchange rate moves erratically as the excess demand function shifts from E1 to E2, and so on. The aggregate excess demand function shown in Figure 2.7 is made up of

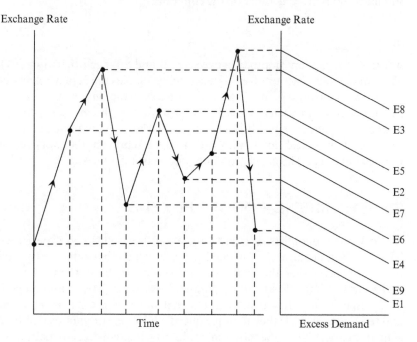

Figure 2.7   Volatility caused by erratic shifts in the excess demand function

the excess demand functions of individual and groups of heterogeneous market participants. What happens to the aggregate excess demand function is a representation of the net aggregate change in the excess demand of individual and groups of participants. The heterogeneity of participants means that at any point in time these participants and groups of participants have different beliefs, views, sentiments and expectations. Hence, they are likely to react differently to new developments: some want to buy (thus raising excess demand) while others want to sell (thus reducing excess demand). The net effect of their actions causes a shift in the aggregate excess demand function by a certain amount in a certain direction at a certain point in time. It is the heterogeneity of market participants that causes exchange rate volatility. Moosa (2002b) elaborates on the sources of heterogeneity of traders with respect to the criteria they use to generate buy and sell signals.

Figure 2.8 displays some simulation results of how exchange rates move over time in reaction to the buy and sell decisions of heterogeneous market participants. The underlying assumption is that traders are of four different kinds (say, fundamentalists, technicians, contrarians and noise traders) whose actions give rise to erratic changes in the exchange rate. The simulated rates are generated by the equation:

$$S_t = S_{t-1} + \frac{1}{4} \sum_{j=1}^{4} \varepsilon_{j,t} \tag{2.19}$$

where ε is a random number between -10 and 10, such that $S_0 = 100$. The simulated behaviour of exchange rates resembles the actual behaviour observed in historical time series. The excess volatility puzzle can be explained easily in terms of the fact that traders in the foreign exchange market are heterogeneous. It is a puzzle only when the unrealistic assumptions of neoclassical economics are used to represent the working of financial markets. The excess volatility puzzle is not a puzzle.

2.5   THE MEESE–ROGOFF PUZZLE

In 1983 two economists, Richard Meese and Kenneth Rogoff, published what has become a frequently cited paper in which they interpreted their results to mean that the random walk could not be outperformed by exchange rate models in out-of-sample forecasting (Meese and Rogoff, 1983). Specifically they demonstrated that none of the macroeconomic and time series models they used produced a lower mean square error (and similar metrics) than the random walk, which predicts zero period-to-period changes in the exchange rate. Their findings stimulated significant

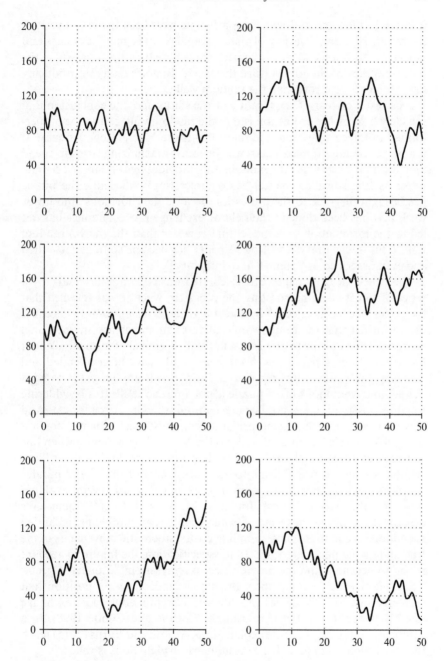

Figure 2.8   Simulated exchange rate movements

research in the area, and numerous attempts have been made to overturn the results by using a variety of data, sample periods, methodologies and model specifications. Most of these attempts have been unsuccessful in the sense that they could not overturn the Meese–Rogoff results by producing lower forecasting errors than the random walk.

As a result of fear of the tyranny of the status quo, the conclusion that is widely held by the profession is that the random walk cannot be outperformed in forecasting exchange rates: this is the Meese–Rogoff puzzle. It is a puzzle because it makes no sense for profit-maximizing firms to spend money on forecasts when the random walk provides free and more accurate forecasts (the so-called market-based forecasting). Allegedly, the puzzle has brought disgrace to the profession because the enormous amount of work that has been done in the field of exchange rate economics has not led to the formulation of a model that is better than the (naive) random walk. This is why the Meese–Rogoff paper has become so frequently cited and even described as 'seminal' and 'influential'.

The Meese–Rogoff paper was celebrated on its 25th anniversary by a series of papers commemorating the occasion, when it was revealed that the paper had been rejected by the *American Economic Review* because the editor felt that the results would offend and embarrass any potential referee. The fact of the matter is that nothing is seminal or influential about the Meese–Rogoff paper, and no referee should have been offended and embarrassed by the results reported in the paper. If anything, the paper is flawed, and what looks like a puzzle is not a puzzle at all. It is bewildering why this observation has not been recognized when it is crystal clear. And it is flabbergasting that some brilliant economists feel ashamed for not being able to beat the random walk (in the Meese–Rogoff sense) when this is a natural outcome, the rule rather than the exception. Those brilliant economists have instead fallen into the murky water of the alleged puzzle.

Believing in the puzzle, economists have put forward several explanations for the Meese–Rogoff findings. Meese and Rogoff themselves explained the puzzle in terms of some econometric problems, including simultaneous equations bias, sampling errors, stochastic movements in the true underlying parameters, model misspecification, the failure to account for non-linearities, and the proxies used to represent inflationary expectations. Many economists support the model inadequacy proposition that exchange rate models do not provide a valid representation of exchange rate behaviour in practice (for example, Cheung and Chinn, 1998). In a comprehensive study of these explanations, Moosa and Burns (2015) reach the conclusion that none of the econometric explanations is valid.

The main reason underpinning, and the root cause of, the Meese–Rogoff puzzle has been overlooked in the literature. Assessing forecasting accuracy exclusively by the magnitude of the forecasting error (which is what Meese and Rogoff did) may explain why the random walk cannot be outperformed. In fact, we should expect nothing other than the failure of exchange rate models to produce smaller forecasting errors than the random walk. When forecasting accuracy is assessed by a broader range of metrics, the Meese and Rogoff results can be overturned with considerable ease.

More puzzling than the puzzle are the claims that the Meese–Rogoff results are yet to be overturned comprehensively, and that they indicate a serious weakness in the field of international monetary economics. For example, Abhyankar et al. (2005) describe the Meese–Rogoff findings as a 'major puzzle in international finance'. Evans and Lyons (2005) note that the Meese–Rogoff finding 'has proven robust over the decades' despite it being 'the most researched puzzle in international macroeconomics'. Fair (2008) describes exchange rate models as 'not the pride of open economy macroeconomics', and contends that the 'general view still seems pessimistic'. Engel et al. (2008) summarize the current state of affairs by stating that the 'explanatory power of these models is essentially zero'. Frankel and Rose (1995) argue that the puzzle has a 'pessimistic effect' on the field of exchange rate modelling in particular and international finance in general. Bacchetta and van Wincoop (2006) describe the puzzle as 'most likely the major weakness of international macroeconomics'. Neely and Sarno (2002) consider the Meese–Rogoff conclusion to be a 'devastating critique' of the monetary approach to exchange rate determination and to have 'marked a watershed in exchange rate economics'.

Flood and Rose (2008) emphasise the point that the Meese–Rogoff results are 'devastating for the field of international finance', going so far as claiming that 'the area [international finance] fell into disrepute' and that 'the area is not even represented on many first-rate academic faculties'. Thus an apparent bewilderment is widespread as to why exchange rate models cannot outperform the random walk, leading to dramatic claims about the miserable state of international finance and international monetary economics, which allegedly have fallen into disrepute. These claims are a gross exaggeration and an unnecessary dramatization of a normal state of affairs. Even economists who actually overturned the Meese–Rogoff results by using alternative measures of forecasting accuracy portrayed their results so modestly as to be aligned with the status quo, thereby perpetuating the myth of the puzzle and the alleged historical significance of the Meese–Rogoff work. It is no exaggeration to say that those economists who have ridden the bandwagon make the Meese and Rogoff work look as though it were in the same league as the work of Grigori Perelman on the Poincaré conjecture. One of the few papers

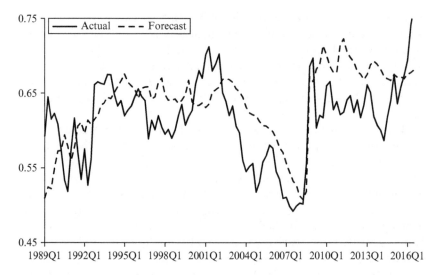

Figure 2.9   Out-of-sample forecasts (GBP/USD)

that challenge the Meese–Rogoff methodology and conclusions without making any apology is that of Moosa and Burns (2014).

Let us at this stage consider some empirical results where the out-of-sample forecasts are generated from the monetary model estimated earlier for the GBP/USD exchange rate. The forecasts are generated recursively over the period 1989:1 to 2016:3. The actual and forecast values are depicted in Figure 2.9, where it can be seen that the forecasting error (the difference between forecast and actual values) can be massive, but the model does rather well in following the direction of exchange rate movement over time. Table 2.2 reports measures of forecasting accuracy based on the magnitude of the forecasting error, including the mean absolute error (MAE), mean square error (MSE), root mean square error (RMSE) and Theil's U (the ratio of the RMSE of the model to that of

Table 2.2   Measures of forecasting accuracy of the monetary model

Measure	Monetary model	Random walk
MAE	7.53	3.59
MSE	76.47	23.20
RMSE	8.74	4.81
Theil's U	1.81	1.00
Direction accuracy	0.53	0.00

the random walk). Obviously, the model is inferior to the random walk in terms of MAE, MSE, RMSE and U. However, it is far superior in terms of direction accuracy, as 53 per cent of the forecasts predict the direction of change correctly, whereas the random walk (without drift) predicts none because it always generates no-change forecasts. Moosa (2014) has shown that predicting the direction correctly is more important for profitable forecasting-based trading than the magnitude of the error. Intuitively, we should expect any model to outperform a dumb model such as the random walk because the random walk without drift tells us that the best forecast is a no-change, while the random walk with drift implies that the exchange rate always rises or falls, both of which are gross misrepresentations of the observed behaviour of exchange rate.

The Meese–Rogoff results do not represent a puzzle, but rather a natural outcome. We should expect nothing but that exchange rate models cannot outperform the random walk in terms of the magnitude of the forecasting error, particularly over short forecasting horizons and when high-frequency data are used. Kilian and Taylor (2003) raise the question in the title of their paper as to why it is so difficult to beat the random walk, a question that can be answered intuitively. They go on to suggest that beating the random walk in terms of the RMSE is 'too strong a criterion for accepting a model'. Engel (1994) argues that beating the random walk in terms of the magnitude of error is not an appropriate benchmark because it will always have a very small error, making it difficult (if not impossible) to beat on this basis.

If the underlying exchange rate (or any financial price) is relatively stable, the forecasting error of the random walk will be small. As the exchange rate becomes more volatile, the forecasting error of the random walk grows bigger, but so does the forecasting error of the model. If we start from a situation of a stable exchange rate where the forecasting error of the random walk is smaller than that of the model, then as long as the error of the random walk does not grow faster than that of the model, the model will always produce a higher root mean square error. By using simulated data to account for a wide range of volatility, Moosa (2013) demonstrates that as volatility rises, the forecasting error of any model rises more rapidly than that of the random walk. Likewise, Moosa and Vaz (2015) demonstrate, by using two stock price models, that as price volatility rises, the RMSE of the random walk rises but the RMSE of the model rises more rapidly.

Forecasting accuracy should be assessed by reference to the purpose for which forecasts are generated and used. In the real world, exchange rate forecasts are used as an input in the financial decision-making process, which means that forecasting accuracy should not be assessed by measures that only take into account the magnitude of the forecasting error. The ultimate test of forecasting power is the ability to make profit by trading on the basis of the forecasts, hence an important criterion is profitability. The critical question is whether or not the Meese–Rogoff results are robust when forecasting accuracy is assessed by measures that do not rely exclusively on the magnitude of the forecasting error. Moosa and Burns (2013) demonstrate that the Meese–Rogoff results are not robust in this sense. Intuitively, we should expect the monetary model (or any other model) to outperform the dumb random walk, but not in terms of the root mean square error and similar metrics.

The Meese–Rogoff puzzle has survived the test of time because economists working in this field (and economists in general) demonstrate an incredible lack of resolve in challenging established ideas. This is confirmation bias at its best: if you challenge an established idea, your paper will be rejected. Since it has become more important to publish papers than to reveal the truth, it is tantalizing to report results that confirm the Meese–Rogoff puzzle. The field is in bad shape, not because exchange rate models cannot outperform the random walk in terms of the RMSE, but because of the lack of will to challenge well-established but faulty notions such as the Meese–Rogoff puzzle. Economic and financial models in general are not that great in terms of explanatory and predictive power, but they are not as bad as not being able to outperform the random walk. The Meese–Rogoff puzzle is not a puzzle at all.

2.6   THE FORWARD BIAS PUZZLE

The forward bias (or forward premium) puzzle is the observation that the forward exchange rate cannot predict the spot rate in accordance with the unbiased efficiency hypothesis (UEH), which is a component of uncovered interest parity (UIP). The underlying idea is that even though the forward market captures market expectations of future movements in exchange rates, it systematically predicts exchange rate movements in the wrong direction. The fact of the matter is that the forward rate has nothing to do with forecasting and that it is determined by a cost of carry relation called covered interest parity (CIP). One can only wonder about the rationale for the heroic statement that the forward rate captures market expectations. This is the real puzzle.

The forward rate is simply the spot rate adjusted for a factor that reflects the interest rate differential. Thus the relation between the spot and forward rates is a contemporaneous definitional equation that represents covered interest parity, which is an arbitrage or a hedging condition that must hold by definition and by necessity, irrespective of expectations. Yet, Obstfeld and Rogoff (2000) apologize to readers for not addressing the forward premium puzzle, because 'it is a pure finance question rather than a macroeconomic puzzle'; or perhaps they do not want to venture into dealing with this 'perplexing' issue.

UIP, which is obtained by combining CIP with UEH, is written as:

$$\Delta s_{t+1} = i_t - i_t^* \tag{2.20}$$

where Δs_{t+1} is the expected change in the exchange rate and $i_t - i_t^*$ is the interest rate differential. CIP is written as:

$$f_t - s_t = i_t - i_t^* \tag{2.21}$$

where f and s are the logarithms of the forward and spot rates, respectively. It follows that UEH is given by:

$$\Delta s_{t+1} = f_t - s_t \tag{2.22}$$

In a testable form, equation (2.22) is written as:

$$\Delta s_{t+1} = \alpha + \beta (f_t - s_t) + \varepsilon_t \tag{2.23}$$

Empirical studies of UIP are typically based on the estimation of equation (2.23), where the expectation is that $\beta = 1$. This equation has been estimated for a variety of currencies and time periods, generally reporting that β is insignificant and closer to -1 than $+1$. Sarno (2005) suggests that the negative value of β is the central feature of the forward bias puzzle, making the typical mistake of describing CIP as a 'reasonably mild assumption', when in fact it is a truism, a definitional equation used by bankers to calculate the forward rates they quote to their customers.

As usual, some fancy econometric explanations have been suggested to resolve this puzzle. One explanation is that when the regression equation does not allow for a risk premium, OLS would yield biased and inconsistent estimates of β. For example, Barnhart et al. (1999) suggest that most common tests of UIP are non-informative in the presence of an omitted risk premium. McCallum (1994) notes that a negative slope coefficient may be produced by the simultaneity induced by a monetary policy reaction function where the interest rate differential is set in order to avoid large exchange rate fluctuations and to smooth interest rate movements. Chinn and Meredith (2004) extend the analysis of McCallum (1994) to tighten the link between monetary policy and the behaviour of deviations from

UIP. Economists are in love with complex explanations that make no sense when simple explanations make more sense. For example, how can a country on its own determine the interest rate differential as McCallum claims?

The puzzle is a puzzle because of the empirical failure of the UEH when it should be the other way round: that is, finding supportive evidence for the UEH. Aggarwal and Zong (2008) argue that 'in theory the forward rate should be an unbiased forecast of the future spot rate, but this hypothesis has little empirical support'. Hansen and Hodrick (1980) reject the UEH by using data covering the 1970s and 1920s, concluding that 'the hypothesis is suspect for several currencies', although they employ a 'new and asymptotically more powerful estimation technique than ordinary least squares'. They attribute the failure of UEH to the use of large sample approximations to calculate the probabilities associated with test statistics without explicit knowledge of how large the sample size must be before the approximations become valid. Aggarwal et al. (2009) find that even after accounting for non-stationarity, non-normality and heteroscedasticity, using parametric and non-parametric tests on data for over a quarter of a century, forward rates are 'generally not rational forecasts of future spot rates'. They seem to forget that econometrics cannot solve a puzzle that does not exist.

Most economists tend to explain the failure of the UEH in terms of the irrationality of expectations and the presence of a risk premium. The results presented by Moosa (2004) and others support the presence of a time-varying risk premium, but the inclusion of a risk premium does not lead to any improvement in forecasting accuracy. As for the rationality of expectations, it has by now been established that the idea of rational expectations in the foreign exchange market is bizarre, to say the least. Little evidence has been produced for rational expectations in the foreign exchange market by studies based on both survey data and the demand-for-money approach (Ito, 1990; Davidson, 1982; Harvey, 1999; Moosa, 1999, 2002a). Other (sophisticated) explanations for the failure of unbiased efficiency include the peso problem, central bank intervention, transaction costs, political risk, foreign exchange risk, purchasing power risk, interest rate risk and the effect of news (see Moosa, 2000, for details). However, a simple and plausible (and perhaps the only) explanation is that of covered interest parity (CIP) because the CIP condition implies that the spot and forward rates are related contemporaneously, which makes the lagged relation representing the UEH misspecified.

Yet, economists have persistently used the forward rate as a forecaster and made it even worse by using the random walk (that is, the lagged spot rate) as a benchmark for measuring forecasting accuracy. The forward rate is a dumb forecaster, no different from the random walk. In Figure 2.10

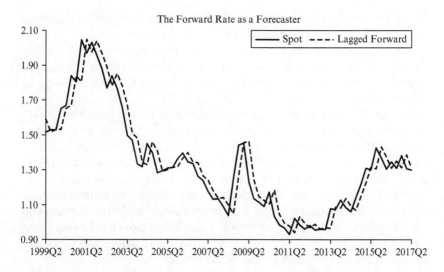

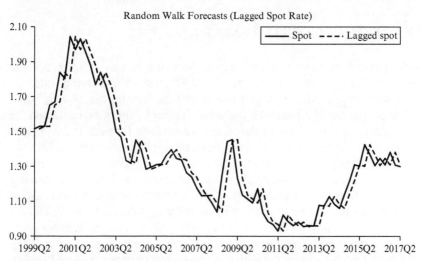

Figure 2.10   Forward and random walk forecasts (AUD/USD)

we observe the forecasts generated by the forward rate, compared to those generated by the random walk (the lagged spot rate). We can see why the forward rate is a dumb forecaster as the forecast turns after the actual value. This means that the 'forecastee' forecasts the forecaster, and not vice versa. It is also obvious that the forecasts generated by the forward rate are identical to the forecasts generated by the random walk, which casts doubt on the common and faulty practice of using the forward rate as a forecaster and the random walk as a benchmark for measuring forecasting power. The forecaster and benchmark must be independent, as demonstrated by Moosa (2015). It remains to be said that those who claim ability to outperform the random walk by using the forward rate as a forecaster will never show you a graph like Figure 2.10 because it is embarrassing, to say the least.

The forward bias puzzle is based on belief in the UEH (and hence, UIP) as a law of physics, when in fact it is misspecified and built on the flawed idea that the forward rate can be used to forecast spot rate. The failure of UIP is not a transitory phenomenon because at one time it was in a 'crisis', as Flood and Rose (2002) put it; rather, it is designed and destined to fail because it is flawed. This faulty idea has been extended to futures markets. Unlike academic economists, practitioners do not think that forward and futures prices have anything to do with forecasting (more will be said about this issue in Chapter 7). For some reason, academic economists keep talking about the forward bias puzzle. What puzzle?

2.7   CONCLUDING REMARKS

The puzzles of international finance discussed in this chapter are the exchange rate determination puzzle, the PPP puzzle, the exchange rate volatility puzzle, the Meese–Rogoff puzzle and the forward bias puzzle. None of these puzzles is a puzzle in the sense that they cannot be explained. In fact, simple and plausible explanations are available for each and every one of them. The problem is that economists do not like simple explanations.

The exchange rate determination puzzle is considered to be a puzzle because of the inadequacy of macroeconomic models for explaining observed behaviour of exchange rates. It is a puzzle why economists aspire to a model that can be used to quantify precisely the effects of all relevant variables on the exchange rate. The finding that these models have low explanatory power does not mean that fundamentals do not matter. They do matter, because they are taken into account by currency traders, but they do not matter to the extent that they can explain exchange rate movements precisely over time. It is more of a puzzle that the PPP puzzle is considered to be a puzzle. If a collection of macroeconomic variables cannot explain exchange rate movements adequately, why do economists expect exchange rates to be explained by only one of these variables: relative prices?

The excess volatility puzzle is not a puzzle because if macroeconomic variables cannot explain the level of the exchange rate, it follows that they cannot explain exchange rate volatility. These models cannot do a good job by forecasting exchange rates out of sample, but this does not justify the claim that the inability of exchange rate models to outperform the random walk is a puzzle. Exchange rate models do outperform the random walk in terms of directional accuracy and, consequently, in terms of the profitability of forecasting-based trading. As for the forward bias puzzle, the expectation that the forward rate can be used to generate accurate forecasts for the spot rate is bizarre, because the forward rate has nothing to do with forecasting. Economists claiming that this is a puzzle need an injection of a big dose of reality.

3. Puzzles in international economics and macroeconomics

3.1 THE HOME BIAS IN TRADE PUZZLE

The home bias in trade (as opposed to the home bias in equity) puzzle is the observation that international goods markets appear to be far more segmented than is commonly believed and that trade among regions within the same country is stronger than trade among countries. According to Friberg et al. (2011), market segmentation is indicated by a disproportionate market share for domestic products, which is conspicuous in goods markets. In other words, home bias is the tendency of consumers to differentiate between domestic and imported goods, preferring to purchase the former. A vast number of empirical studies report a large degree of home bias, while many theoretical studies assume its presence (Evans, 2001).

Early evidence for goods market segmentation was produced by McCallum (1995), who used a gravity model that controls for distance, trading partner sizes and a small number of other factors. He found that in 1988 trade among Canadian provinces was 20 times greater than trade among Canadian provinces and individual United States (US) states. Subsequently, Helliwell (1998) used data for the period 1993–96 and found that unexplained home bias had fallen to a factor of 12, which is still substantial. Wei (1998) and Evans (1999) used indirect methods to test home bias for other Organisation for Economic Co-operation and Development (OECD) country pairs. Wei suggests that the average bias may be as low as 2.5, while Evans finds values falling between those of Wei and Helliwell. Van Wincoop (2000) argues that McCallum's results give an exaggerated impression of home bias in global trade because the bias is calculated from the perspective of the small country, Canada. Anderson and Van Wincoop (2003) identify a number of reasons why McCallum's estimates may be upward biased, particularly the omission of multilateral resistance variables.

Obstfeld and Rogoff (2000) explain home bias in trade in terms of added border costs (such as tariffs and non-tariff barriers) and foreign exchange risk. In general, they believe that trade costs, together with high elasticities of substitution in consumption, can explain substantial home biases in trade. Indicative of the importance of the exchange rate factor is that Rose (2000) found countries with currency unions to trade about three times as much with each other as countries with separate currencies. This point has been made repeatedly in empirical studies showing that exchange rate volatility has an adverse effect on international trade (for example, Peree and Steinherr, 1989; Bini-Smaghi, 1991; Savvides, 1992; Chowdhury, 1993; Doganlar, 2002; Clark et al., 2004; Mukherjee and Pozo, 2011; Khan et al., 2014).

Mika (2017) examines home bias with respect to trade in goods and services within the European Union by using the gravity model to find that the trade-reducing effect of borders is 'sizeable'. While she admits that 'it is unsurprising that countries find it easier to engage in domestic trade than international trade', she suggests that 'past studies have shown that the degree to which international borders hinder trade is greater than expected'. Friberg et al. (2011) attribute home bias in trade to preference for home goods and to trading costs, which in turn can be reflected in higher prices or weaker distribution networks for imported goods. They explore the contribution to home bias of these factors, using a structural model of demand for wine sales in New Hampshire in the United States, and find that preferences rather than trade costs explain home bias among the available brands.

Evans (2001) mentions, as sources of home bias, trade barriers that make imports prohibitively expensive, and the inherent distrust of foreign products. She finds that the apparent tendency to purchase domestic rather than imported goods arises almost entirely from pure locational factors. She also finds that if a firm establishes and sells from a subsidiary located in the foreign country, its local sales are nearly on a par with those of domestic firms in that market. She concludes that 'foreign-ness' in and of itself does not appear to impede purchases of imported goods. Turrini and Van Ypersele (2002) argue that even between perfectly integrated and similar countries, the legal systems differ, so that legal costs are higher when business is done abroad.

Based on the studies of home bias in trade, this observation is considered as a puzzle either because home bias should not be present at all, even though theory and empirical evidence support the findings, or because it is present but to an extent that is larger than expected or commonly believed. But what is the source of this expectation or common belief? Perhaps it is the feeling that in a globalized world, markets should not be segmented, even though the empirical evidence shows disagreement on the magnitude of home bias. This is a typical situation where a prior belief is rejected by an empirical test, leading to the perception of a puzzle.

The empirical results are typically based on the gravity model of trade, which is perhaps why they should not be taken at face value and why they vary significantly from one study to another. The variability of the results is not surprising, as it is typical that econometric models produce a mixed bag of results. The gravity model, which relates the volume of trade to economic size (measured by gross domestic product, GDP) and distance, commands a lot of respect. Sampson et al. (2016) describe the gravity model as 'the most reliable empirical relationship in international economics'. This view is shared by many economists; for example, Chaney (2013) makes the observation that 'the gravity equation in international trade is one of the most robust empirical findings in economics'. Sampson et al. (2016) refer to 'hundreds of data-based studies' showing the robustness of this relationship across many countries, industries, time periods and multiple specifications (see Head and Mayer, 2014, for a survey). Results obtained from the International Monetary Fund's (2016) gravity model of the United Kingdom (UK) indicate that it is a good predictor of the level of trade, in both goods and services.

However, the gravity model is by no means flawless, or as precise as the gravity model in physics. Economists disagree on the specification of the model (for example, logarithmic versus exponential) and the estimation method. Santos Silva and Tenreyro (2006) argue that estimating the equation by ordinary least squares (OLS) can lead to significant biases, and this is why they suggest the alternative of estimating the exponential form of the equation by using the Poisson pseudo-maximum likelihood estimation method. In its extended form, which contains other variables, the model is subject to the Leamer (1983) critique that the results derived from cross-sectional regressions are highly sensitive to the selected set of explanatory variables. Young and Holsteen (2017) suggest that control variables, which vary from one model to another, are a common source of uncertainty and ambivalence. A big list of control variables is effectively the ammunition needed for indulging in data mining.

Take, for example, the gravity model estimated by the International Monetary Fund (2016) for the UK. It contains eight explanatory variables: the product of GDPs, partner population, distance, European Union (EU) membership, European Free Trade Association (EFTA) membership, common language, colonial linkages and common border. Other potential explanatory variables include common legal systems, common currencies, cultural ties, membership of North American Free Trade Area (NAFTA), membership of the World Trade Organization (WTO), as well as numerous variables representing treaties and alliances. In the model used by Mika (2017) to examine the puzzle, exports from one country to another depend on a home dummy (to reveal the extent of home bias), the product of GDPs, population, distance, common language, common border, EU membership, eurozone membership and remoteness.

Another point that produces differences in the results pertains to alternative measures of internal distance, which is highlighted by Jošić and Jošić (2016) as they demonstrate how internal distance measurement affects home bias in trade. Their results indicate that sub-unit-based weighted measures perform better in the assessment of Croatia's internal distance than area-based measures and those based on relation to neighbouring countries. They corroborate the theoretical assumptions pertaining to the impact of geographical distance of countries and transport costs on bilateral trade flows. On the other hand, Worstall (2017) suggests that what matters is not geographical proximity but transport proximity.

Let us, for the sake of argument, suppose that the results derived from the gravity model are fine, all showing evidence for home bias with different magnitudes. Other plausible explanations for home bias include border costs that make foreign goods more expensive, high elasticities of substitution in consumption, foreign exchange risk, countries finding it easier to engage in domestic trade than international trade, preferences for home goods, weaker distribution networks for imported goods, inherent distrust of foreign products, and the possibility that legal costs are higher when business is done abroad. If this is the case, why is this a puzzle? Is it a puzzle because the empirical results supporting what is claimed to be a theoretically sound proposition (that home bias should not be present) turn out to be different from what is expected or commonly believed?

The fact of the matter is that preference for home goods is not a universal observation. The US Civil War was triggered by the North's action of imposing tariffs on the equipment imported by the South from Europe. Imported goods may or may not be more expensive than similar domestic goods. Consumers in a country that does not manufacture cars will, by necessity, reveal 'preference' for foreign cars. In the Middle East, local Arabian lamb is preferred to imported (primarily Australian) lamb, even though it is more expensive. In some countries the consumption of more expensive imported goods is a sign of prestige, which is why the rich have a preference for foreign goods while the poor prefer the more affordable domestic goods. Preference for national as opposed to foreign airlines depends on price and the quality of service; no one is 'patriotic' enough to use the national airline when a foreign airline offers a better deal. The citizens of some countries whose airlines do not serve alcohol prefer foreign airlines that do (Saudis and Kuwaitis may prefer Emirates to Saudi Airlines and Kuwait Airways for this reason).

In general terms, preference for domestic or foreign goods is a matter of choice, depending on relative prices, income, taste and availability. In one country, some consumers go for imported goods while others go for domestic goods. The best way to measure preferences for domestic or

Table 3.1   Ratio of imports to consumption

Country	2017		2018	
	Constant 2010 USD	Current local currency units	Constant 2010 USD	Current local currency units
Australia	0.30	0.27	0.31	0.28
Brazil	0.13	0.14	0.17	0.14
Egypt	0.41	0.30	0.46	0.31
France	0.43	0.41	0.43	0.42
Japan	0.21	0.22	0.22	0.24
Kuwait	0.79	0.69	0.74	0.71
Qatar	0.93	0.90	–	0.91
Russia	0.29	0.29	0.29	0.31
Spain	0.39	0.41	0.40	0.42
UK	0.39	0.38	0.39	0.38
US	0.21	0.18	0.22	0.19

foreign goods is to use the linearized version of Deaton and Muellbauer's (1980) Almost Ideal Demand System (AIDS) whereby the budget shares of domestic and imported goods are functions of prices and incomes (see, for example, Moosa and Baxter, 2002). If data availability is not a problem, this will show that preference differs from one country to another, which means that home bias should not be generalized.

A simple, but realistic, measure of preference for home goods is the ratio of imported goods and services to consumption expenditure on goods and services. Based on data obtained from the World Bank, Table 3.1 shows some results for 2017 and 2018. We can see that two oil-exporting countries show significantly higher ratios of imports to consumption than other countries, for a simple reason: they can afford imported goods but they cannot produce them. In all other countries, more domestic than imported goods are purchased. After all, it may not be a matter of choice. The puzzle of home bias in trade is not a puzzle, it is a phenomenon that may or may not be observed.

3.2   THE HOME BIAS IN EQUITY PORTFOLIO PUZZLE

The home bias in equity portfolio puzzle is the observation that, despite the perceived benefits of international diversification, investors seem unwilling to exploit these benefits, opting instead to invest predominantly in domestic assets. In other words, it is the observed behaviour of investing heavily in domestic assets instead of diversifying portfolios internationally. Investors exposed to home bias tend to allocate a relatively large fraction of their wealth to domestic securities, even though conventional wisdom tells us that internationally diversified portfolios are more efficient in terms of risk and return. Several explanations for this phenomenon have been put forward, but economists seem to believe that these explanations have not been proven empirically (for example, Constantinos, 2010).

For some reason, economists do not question the benefits of international diversification, even though the empirical evidence is mostly based on work carried out in the 1960s and 1970s when markets were segmented and returns weakly correlated, which produced effective diversification. At that time, cross-country stock returns were weakly correlated because markets were segmented and capital controls (as well as other impediments) were imposed to restrict capital outflows and foreign ownership of domestic stocks. Although the scope for international diversification was limited (because of impediments to diversification), it was intuitive to suggest that diversification across countries was useful, in the sense of providing better risk–return combinations.

Harry Markowitz (1952) was the first economist to identify the benefits of investing in a portfolio of assets rather than just one asset. Grubel (1968) extended Markowitz's portfolio theory, suggesting that portfolios should be diversified internationally on the grounds that return correlations are lower among international markets than within domestic markets. Likewise, Levy and Sarnat (1970), Grubel and Fander (1971), Solnik (1974), Lassard (1976) and Biger (1979) have demonstrated that international diversification provides US investors with lower risk for a given level of expected return. The prime implication of international portfolio diversification is that if the set of available assets is expanded to include foreign assets, the resulting portfolio will be more efficient in terms of risk and return.

Some advocates of international diversification argue that diversification into emerging markets can be useful. For example, Conover et al. (2002) suggest that emerging equity markets are a worthy addition to a US investor's portfolio of developed market equities. Specifically, they found portfolio returns to be higher by approximately 1.5 percentage points a year when emerging country equities were included in the portfolio. A similar idea is put forward by Russell (1998), who states that 'even the relatively risky practice of investing in emerging markets has been viewed, by some, as a sound investment strategy for individuals'. Goetzmann et al. (2005) contend that globalization has led to a higher level of return correlation among developed markets, consequently limiting the benefits of diversification when only developed markets are considered. However, they argue, the benefits of international diversification can be realized by investing in emerging markets. Merkellos and Siriopoulous (1997) found that despite increasing international integration, opportunities for diversification in smaller and less-studied European stock markets still exist. Ang and Bekaert (2002) show that, despite the risk of time-varying correlation, the benefits of international diversification are still significant.

The puzzle of home bias in equity portfolio is that investors shy away from international diversification, even though barriers and costs in international investments have fallen dramatically. French and Poterba (1991), Cooper and Kaplanis (1994) and Tesar and Werner (1995) observe strong home bias in investors' behaviour. Gorman (1998) argues that the typical US pension plan remains underexposed to international equity, and recommends more to be allocated to international securities. Wright and McCarthy (2002) demonstrate the lack of international diversification by Australian investors, arguing that they perceive foreign markets as risky, and casting doubt on the ability of investors to realize the benefits of international portfolio diversification by purchasing shares in multinational corporations. Baxter and Jermann (1997) argue that 'while recent years have witnessed an increase in international diversification, holdings of domestic assets are still too high to be consistent with the theory of portfolio choice'. They also wonder why this is happening despite the integration of capital markets.

The most common explanations for the home bias phenomenon are asymmetric information, non-traded goods, inflation hedging, costs of and barriers to foreign equity trading, and the costs/benefits of international diversification. Asymmetric information and investors' belief provide a reasonable explanation for the home bias puzzle. French and Poterba (1991) suggest that investors are optimistic about beating their domestic markets, but not foreign markets. They perceive foreign markets as involving more risk because of the lack of information as well as different rules and regulations, accounting standards and disclosure requirements. By using a simple noisy rational expectations model, Gehrig (1993) shows that even in equilibrium, investors remain incompletely informed, suggesting that foreign assets seem to be riskier than domestic assets even without foreign exchange risk. Brennan and Cao (1997) use a model of equity portfolio flows that is based on information differentials among domestic and foreign investors, under the assumption that domestic investors are more informed than foreign investors about the domestic market. Even if inflation can be hedged by holding stocks, domestic inflation is unlikely to be hedged by holding foreign stocks.

Another possible explanation of the home bias puzzle is that the presence of non-tradable goods makes investors biased to domestic assets. Serrat (1996) argues that market participants hedge the consumption risk of non-tradable goods by investing in home tradable goods. The desire to hedge inflation is yet another explanation for the puzzle, whereby investors prefer to hold domestic assets in order to hedge domestic inflation risk. Solnik (1978) suggested that investors try to hedge property costs and not general inflation by investing in domestic securities, particularly those issued by real estate companies. Taxes, transaction costs and other barriers to equity trading provide disincentive for investing in foreign markets. By using a simple overlapping generations model, Carmichael and Coën (2003) show that in a world with no barriers to international investment, the introduction of a very small transaction cost can generate home bias in portfolio holdings.

Perhaps the ultimate reason for home bias, which explains the puzzle, is that international diversification does not pay off or that it is not effective in reducing risk. Gorman and Jorgensen (2002) suggest that it is difficult in practice to capture the theoretical gains from international diversification. Their results indicate that a 100 per cent domestic portfolio performs as well or better than the tangency portfolios when expected returns and the covariance parameters are estimated by the Markowitz approach and the Bayes–Stein tangency 'shrinkage' algorithm. They conclude that home bias is not irrational, as it can be justified by the inability of investors to benefit from international diversification.

Kalra et al. (2004) find that the benefits of international diversification are much smaller than previously thought. Their findings suggest that only a small allocation of 10 per cent to international securities may be justified and that even the slight advantage of international diversification may disappear when taxes are incorporated in the evaluation. They also argue that to maintain the intended diversification, periodic rebalancing of the portfolio is necessary to keep the weights of the domestic and foreign components at target levels as suggested by Rowland (1999) and Laker (2003). However, international investment (particularly in developing markets) involves non-trivial transaction costs that need to be considered when estimating portfolio performance. It follows that, in the presence of periodic rebalancing and associated transaction costs, international diversification may not pay off.

In finance, there is no free lunch. While international diversification may boost risk-adjusted return, the costs involved in the operation may be significant, even overwhelming. The costs incurred as a result of international diversification go beyond the transaction costs associated with rebalancing or the initial acquisition of foreign assets. For example, Swedroe (2010) wonders if international diversification is worth the costs, identifying the incremental costs of international investing as higher fund expenses, greater trading costs and issues related to foreign tax credits. In addition to transaction costs, Yuan (2004) identifies various kinds of risk, including foreign exchange risk, settlement risk, and legal and regulatory risk, as well as country risk and political risk (exposure to these kinds of risk may be viewed as costs resulting from international diversification). Asness et al. (2010) identify as costs of international diversification exchange fees and time lags between countries in different time zones, arguing that 'many more reasons like this can increase an investor's cost'. It is very likely, then, that the costs of international diversification outweigh its benefits.

By using a hedging approach to international diversification, Moosa and Al-Deehani (2009) test the proposition that international diversification is effective in reducing risk. They analyse more than 100 portfolios involving developed and emerging markets, showing that correlations are not adequately low to produce effective diversification when long positions are taken. In a few cases involving developed markets only, correlations are so high that taking opposite positions (long and short) produces effective diversification. In general, however, they cast serious doubt on the effectiveness of international diversification in reducing risk.

Why is it that those obsessed with the presence of the home bias in equity portfolio puzzle reject these explanations as being implausible? In Chapter 4 the equity premium puzzle will be examined where we will find out that investors, particularly 'down-to-earth' investors, shy away from investing in domestic stocks despite the availability of a massive premium, simply because they view stock markets as risky. An investor who rejects a massive premium (over fixed income securities) in the domestic market is unlikely to be attracted to foreign stock markets because of the availability of better risk–return combinations. Furthermore, the risk–return trade-off does not apply to foreign exchange risk, political risk and country risk.

3.3 THE FELDSTEIN–HORIOKA PUZZLE

The Feldstein–Horioka (FH) puzzle is the observation that national saving and investment rates (measured as the ratio of saving and investment to GDP, respectively) are highly correlated, implying low capital mobility. This puzzle has arisen out of the work of Feldstein and Horioka (1980), who found domestic investment and saving rates to be highly correlated. This finding was largely confirmed, *inter alia*, by the cross-sectional studies of Feldstein (1983), Feldstein and Bachetta (1991), Tesar (1991) and the time series studies of Alexakis and Apergis (1992), Tesar (1993) and Afxentiou and Serlitis (1993).

High correlation between domestic saving and investment rates is perceived to be a puzzle because it implies low capital mobility, implying that countries do not resort to foreign savings to finance domestic investment, which means that the latter is constrained by the inadequacy of domestic savings. It is considered a puzzle because the results of empirical testing do not confirm a prior belief, the belief that capital must be highly mobile in the age of globalization. What about the possibility that capital is indeed immobile for the same reasons that lead to preference for investing in domestic markets? What about the other possibility that the FH test is faulty? And what about the validity of the assumption that individuals and firms in one country have access to foreign savings and that they tend to expose themselves to foreign exchange risk, political risk and country risk by tapping foreign savings?

Capital mobility depends on the absence or inadequacy of exchange controls, or the failure to implement them fully. It also depends on the availability of institutions (most notably, international banks) that engage in and encourage capital movement, and thus act as a catalyst to capital mobility. Given these qualifications, it is no wonder that capital mobility was extremely limited in the immediate post-war period. But ever since the late 1950s and early 1960s, capital controls have been abolished progressively and the growth of institutions engaged in capital movements has been remarkable, providing an environment that is conducive to high capital mobility. Factors contributing to capital mobility also include the growth of multinational corporations, the development of new financial instruments, lower information costs and the general trend towards financialization. An indicator of capital mobility is the (perhaps justifiable) complaint of central bankers that they have lost their autonomy (Goodwin and Grennes, 1994), and the ineffectiveness of intervention in the foreign exchange market, which is due to the limited amount of resources available to central banks relative to the sheer size of trading volume.

It is therefore intuitive to think that capital mobility has been on the rise, except perhaps for the interruption caused by the global financial crisis when some countries reintroduced capital controls. Frankel and MacArthur (1988) list the following stylized facts: (1) the degree of capital mobility is high; (2) it is higher for industrial countries; and (3) it has been rising since the 1950s and particularly since 1973. If these stylized facts are readily observed, why do we need an econometric test to confirm what we can see, given that empirical work is invariably unreliable and that econometric testing could tell us anything?

While observing capital mobility should be the ultimate test to find out whether capital is mobile or immobile, two problems are associated with this 'test'. The first pertains to the benchmark used to judge the degree of capital mobility (for example, is it $2 trillion or $5 trillion?). The second problem is that observing capital flows gives us an idea about the actual mobility of capital, not potential mobility, which is unobservable.

The theoretical rationale for the Feldstein–Horioka equation, relating the domestic investment rate to the domestic saving rate, is that perfect capital mobility drives a wedge between saving and investment, as savers would face the same (world) interest rate. If, on the other hand, capital mobility is low, a wedge will be driven between the domestic and foreign costs of borrowing. It follows that saving and investment will be highly uncorrelated when capital is mobile, and vice versa. In a cross-sectional regression of the domestic investment rate on the domestic saving rate, Feldstein and Horioka found that the coefficient on the explanatory variable was not significantly different from unity, which implies low capital mobility.

Economists have attempted to solve the FH puzzle by using models that predict both high correlation and high mobility. Alternatively, they put the blame on some econometric loopholes in the Feldstein–Horioka work, including: (1) the endogeneity of the saving rate; (2) missing variables; (3) the use of averages; and (4) non-stationarity of the variables. They have also attempted to solve the puzzle by questioning two aspects of the data, most notably the sample period and country size. Although some of these studies produced results showing lower saving–investment correlations than those obtained by Feldstein and Horioka, the bulk of the available evidence supports their finding as a robust empirical regularity.

One explanation rests on the proposition that the endogeneity of saving leads to biased estimates. If the investment and saving rates are driven by another factor or factors, strong correlation will be observed between them even though they are unrelated. Obstfeld (1986), for example, argues that these influencing factors could be the growth rate of the economy and a measure of income distribution, neither of which were considered by Feldstein and Horioka. In terms of conventional econometric problems, this argument implies misspecification in the form of omitted variables and/or simultaneous equation bias, both of which affect the statistical properties of the estimated coefficient. Other economists use the country size argument to illustrate the problem of endogeneity (for example, Harberger, 1980; Murphy, 1984). This argument goes as follows: a fall in the saving rate of a large country would lead to a rise in interest rates and, consequently, to a fall in investment in these countries. Baxter and Crucini (1993) and Tesar (1991) investigated the effect of size and found correlations to be higher for larger countries.

Another argument that has been used to cast doubt on the Feldstein–Horioka results, and to solve the puzzle, is the policy response argument proposed by Fieleke (1982) and Tobin (1983) who suggested that saving and investment appear to be positively correlated because governments try to reduce a current account imbalance via fiscal policy. Dar et al. (1994) address two problems associated with the Feldstein–Horioka model: (1) the use of averages; and (2) the failure to allow for country-specific differences with respect to size, structure and institutions, which, they argue, are relevant to the policy implications of capital mobility. Still, their results indicate low capital mobility in the Group of Seven (G7) countries. It seems that economists have been trying every trick to overturn the FH results, just to confirm a prior belief, which sounds familiar.

Bayoumi (1990) argues that high correlation between saving and investment may be due to endogenous behaviour in response to unanticipated shocks and government policy. Other relevant variables include productivity, population growth, labour immobility and the existence of non-traded goods. For example, Engel and Kletzer (1989) present a model, based on the distinction between traded and non-traded goods, that predicts positive correlation between saving and investment. Other models that produce similar results are those of Obstfeld (1986) and Baxter and Crucini (1993). Some economists question the sample period used by Feldstein and Horioka (1960–74), when capital controls were widespread. For example, US time series data of the 1980s show significantly lower correlations than data covering the 1970s (Rivera-Batiz and Rivera-Batiz, 1994).

The 'usual suspects' of non-stationarity, unit root and cointegration have also been used to solve the puzzle, as in Bodman (1995). By allowing for omitted variables, such as output and fiscal deficit, he obtained significant cointegrating vectors in which the coefficient on saving is significantly less than unity. His results are based on the notorious Johansen test, which is not to be trusted as it produces the results anyone can wish for (Moosa, 2017a). Econometrics in general provides the means whereby the results that confirm a prior belief can be obtained, but playing around with model specification and estimation method is not the way to solve this or any puzzle.

Other economists have tried to solve the puzzle by arguing that saving–investment correlation is not a proper measure of the degree of capital mobility and market integration. For example, Goldstein et al. (1991) argue that 'the degree of integration of international capital markets is captured better by rate-of-return differentials (appropriately defined) than by the scale of capital flows'. A similar assertion is made by Frankel and MacArthur (1988), who argue that measures of capital mobility that are based on deviations from international parity conditions (covered interest parity, CIP; uncovered interest parity, UIP; and real interest parity, RIP) are superior to saving–investment correlations because the former require no assumption about the endogeneity of saving, nor about the sensitivity of investment to real interest rates. This argument takes us nowhere, because the empirical validity of UIP and RIP is questionable due to the failure of the unbiased efficiency hypothesis, UEH, as pointed out in Chapter 2. Frankel and MacArthur (1988) advocate the use of CIP as a measure of capital mobility, which is convenient because CIP is easy to pass. However, CIP is not a testable hypothesis and it is not a macroeconomic relation (Moosa, 2017c). The choice of CIP as a criterion for measuring capital mobility is motivated by the desire to solve the puzzle by reconciling formal empirical evidence with casual observation. This is not exactly a quest for the truth, but rather the desire to demonstrate that capital is mobile.

Tests based on monetary autonomy and the effectiveness of sterilization can be used for the same purpose. Measures of capital mobility are also based on indices of capital controls, asset diversification, political risk and the onshore–offshore nominal interest differential. Consumption patterns can be used for the same purpose (for a description of these measures and some results on the consumption approach, see Al-Jassar and Moosa, 2020). These tests invariably produce mixed results, which is convenient because one tends to report results that support of capital mobility if one believes that Feldstein and Horioka have indeed discovered a puzzle, and unsupportive results if one wants to dismiss the puzzle as an artefact.

It is not entirely clear what economists mean by 'capital' when they refer to capital mobility. Frankel (1993) makes this point clear by asserting that 'the aggregation together of all forms of capital has caused more than the usual amount of confusion in the literature on international capital mobility'. It is possibly the case that economists reaching the opposite conclusions about capital mobility might consider different concepts of capital. For example, the word 'capital' may imply micro as opposed to macro capital, net as opposed to gross capital, portfolio or financial as opposed to physical capital, and short-term as opposed to long-term capital. Perhaps capital is mobile in one form but immobile in another from.

Dooley et al. (1987) present two definitions of capital mobility. The first, which refers to real or physical capital, is that it is 'the condition under which expected differentials yields on physical capital in different countries are eliminated by net saving flows as conventionally measured by current account imbalances'. The second definition, which refers to financial capital, is that it is 'the tendency of investors to equalise expected rates of return on a subset of liquid, short-term, default-free financial assets denominated in different currencies or issued by the residents of different countries'. It is certainly the case that capital in the second sense is more mobile than capital in the first sense. Indeed, they demonstrate that the mobility of financial capital does not mean mobility of physical capital, except when the two kinds of capital are highly substitutable. Thus, Dooley et al. (1987) solve the puzzle by arguing that high saving–investment correlations imply low mobility of physical capital, but that does not alter the fact that financial capital is highly mobile.

The distinction between financial capital and physical capital leads to another distinction, between short-term and long-term capital. Since physical capital tends to be long-term in nature, while financial capital is short-term in nature, it is arguable that saving–investment correlation is a measure of the mobility of long-term capital. Then comes the distinction between gross and net capital flows. While capital moves in all directions, it could be the case that net capital flows are insignificant, and that Feldstein and Horioka were concerned with net capital movements. This is because net capital flows, which constitute the financial counterpart to the transfer of real resources through payment imbalances, arise only when saving and investment are not matched within individual countries. On the other hand, gross capital flows can be mutually offsetting across countries. Last but not least, distinction can be made between observable actual and unobservable potential capital flows.

So, one way to solve the puzzle is to put forward the following proposition. On a net basis, domestic investment is financed by domestic saving without borrowing from abroad. This, however, does not indicate insignificant capital movement, but rather that the net balance of capital flows is close to zero. Indeed, countries may not find it optimal or desirable to pursue policies leading to persistent current account imbalances. As a result, a limit will be set on how much national saving can diverge from national investment, and hence the apparent high correlation.

Let us return to the proposition that capital is mobile but the Feldstein–Horioka test cannot pick it up. Imagine that while driving your car one day, the petrol gauge gives a reading indicating that your tank is empty. Your immediate reaction would be to stop at the first petrol station on your way and fill up the tank. When you start your car again, the gauge still gives a reading of zero. Assuming that your tank does not have a big hole, your immediate reaction is that there must be something wrong with your gauge, not that your tank is empty. This view is reinforced when you drive for another 30 miles without the car stopping. The analogy to be derived from this example is that indicators of high and increasing capital mobility are plentiful. If a formal econometric test shows that capital is immobile, or that capital mobility has been declining, then there must be something wrong with this test: it is not that capital is immobile. A casual examination of the relevant figures shows that capital is highly and actually (not only potentially) mobile, including international bank lending, securities transactions with foreigners, the value of global cross-border transactions in equities, and foreign direct investment.

So, is there a puzzle here? The answer is 'no'. We know that capital mobility has increased significantly, as indicated by the rapidly growing indicators of the internationalization of finance. We also know that capital mobility is imperfect because of home bias. And we know that capital mobility differs from one country to another and from one concept of capital to another. So, what is the big deal about a finding that a simple saving–investment equation estimated with cross-sectional data for a set of diverse countries does not confirm the observation that capital is mobile but not perfectly mobile? The problem is that economists trust numbers coming out of a computer more than common sense. This is why the FH puzzle, which is not a puzzle at all, has arisen and persisted.

3.4   THE INTERNATIONAL CONSUMPTION CORRELATION PUZZLE

The international consumption correlation puzzle, also called the Backus–Kehoe–Kydland puzzle or the BKK puzzle (Backus et al., 1992, 1995), is the observation that consumption is much less correlated across countries than output. This puzzle is related to the Feldstein–Horioka and the home equity bias puzzles. The underlying idea is that consumers can use foreign capital markets to smooth consumption, which works only if the market means of consumption 'smoothing' (debt and equity trade) are operative across borders. In this context, the term 'smoothing' refers to counterbalancing the ups and downs of household consumption by exporting and importing consumption goods, respectively.

In an Arrow–Debreu economy (that is, an economy with a complete set of state-contingent markets), country-specific output risks should be pooled and domestic consumption growth should not depend heavily on country-specific income shocks. In other words, the ability of agents to exchange goods without transaction costs should lead to limited dependence of domestic consumption on domestic output. Accordingly, consumption should be more strongly correlated across countries than output.

The puzzle was born when Backus et al. (1992) found that consumption is much less correlated across countries than output. When they calculated the correlation of HP-filtered consumption and output for 11 advanced countries relative to the US, they found the average consumption correlation to be 0.19, whereas the average output correlation was 0.31. Obstfeld and Rogoff (2000) report average correlation of OECD countries with world consumption (35 benchmark countries) of 0.43, whereas the average output correlation with world benchmark is 0.52. For convenience, and to claim a puzzle, nothing is said about the statistical significance of the difference between 0.43 and 0.52 (unlikely to be significant).

As always, some attempts have been made to solve the puzzle. For example, Stockman and Tesar (1995) suggest two means of breaking the link between prices and quantities, which makes it difficult for households to smooth consumption by trade: non-traded goods and taste shocks. Other explanations of the consumption correlation puzzle emphasize a variety of market imperfections and, therefore, transaction costs. For example, empirical evidence indicates that financial markets promote risk-sharing more effectively within a country than between countries, which hinders cross-border consumption smoothing. Perhaps one explanation for the puzzle is that capital is not as mobile as it is thought to be.

Let us look at some facts and figures derived from a sample of annual data on GDP and consumption in 33 countries and four benchmarks against which correlations are measured (US, EU, OECD and the world). The data sample, obtained from the World Bank, covers the period 1970–2016. Correlations are measured between the first logarithmic differences (representing growth rates) of GDP and consumption. Figure 3.1 reports the difference between GDP and consumption correlations using the four benchmarks (that is, correlation between the GDP of the underlying country and that of the benchmark, minus correlation between the consumption of the underlying country and that of the benchmark). The differences are predominantly positive, implying that GDPs are more strongly correlated than consumptions. This is a qualitatively similar result to that obtained by Obstfeld and Rogoff (2000) and Backus et al. (1992).

What matters, however, is not the numerical value of the correlation difference but rather its statistical significance. Table 3.2 shows the Z statistics for the significance of the difference between GDP and consumption correlations for each of the benchmarks. When the US is the benchmark, the difference is statistically significant in four cases only: Canada, Ecuador, Luxembourg and Malaysia.

In terms of averages, Table 3.3 shows average correlations for the 33 countries against the benchmarks with the t statistics for the difference between two means (mean GDP correlation and mean consumption correlation). We can see that the mean difference is statistically significant only when the US is the benchmark. However, averages in this case are as useful as averages of telephone numbers.

On a bilateral basis of all country combinations, the finding of higher output correlation than consumption correlation is maintained. Out of a total of 648 pairs of countries and benchmarks, output correlation is stronger than consumption correlation in 497 cases, compared to 151 cases

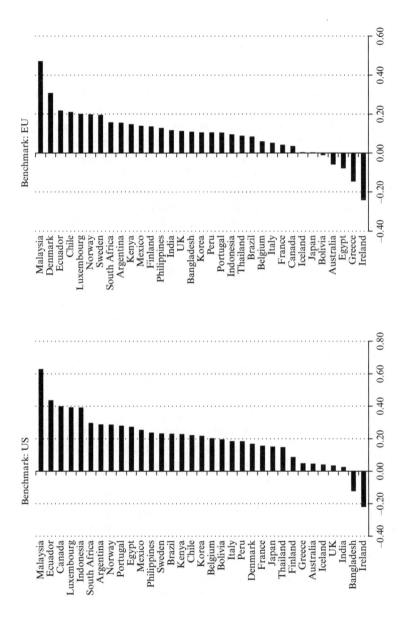

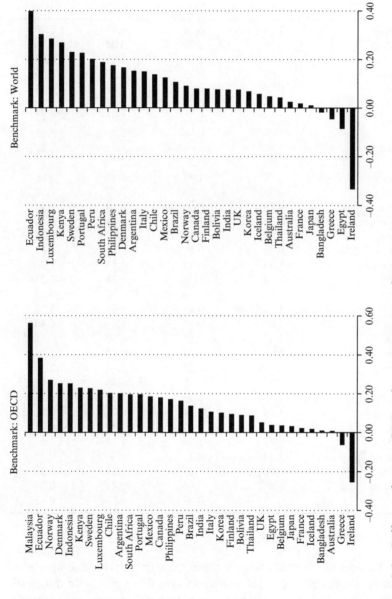

Figure 3.1   Difference between GDP and consumption correlations

*Table 3.2   Z statistics for the difference between GDP and consumption
              correlations*

	US	EU	OECD	World
Argentina	1.34	0.74	0.92	0.70
Australia	0.19	−0.30	0.00	0.10
Bangladesh	−0.60	0.53	0.05	−0.09
Belgium	1.07	0.85	0.37	0.50
Bolivia	0.88	−0.05	0.40	0.38
Brazil	1.06	0.42	0.66	0.58
Canada	3.02*	0.32	1.61	0.82
Chile	1.06	0.98	0.95	0.68
Denmark	1.18	2.07*	1.82	1.20
Egypt	1.26	−0.37	2.79*	−0.37
Ecuador	2.20*	1.01	1.77	1.86
Finland	0.45	0.25	0.67	0.59
France	0.88	0.89	0.24	0.10
Greece	0.23	−1.07	−0.41	−0.24
Iceland	0.42	0.00	0.12	0.31
India	0.09	0.57	0.61	0.33
Indonesia	1.93	0.41	1.15	1.39
Ireland	−1.28	−1.56	−1.54	−2.03*
Japan	0.86	0.00	0.32	0.08
Italy	1.04	0.86	1.15	1.22
Kenya	1.02	0.76	1.13	1.40
Korea	1.33	0.55	0.60	0.37
Luxembourg	2.01*	1.34	0.47	1.62
Malaysia	2.94*	2.29*	2.74*	2.10
Mexico	1.17	0.70	0.48	0.67
Norway	1.53	0.99	1.52	0.50
Philippines	1.14	0.61	0.78	0.81
Peru	0.89	0.47	1.37	0.93
Portugal	1.41	1.06	1.25	1.44
South Africa	1.34	0.73	0.90	0.97
Sweden	−0.98	1.29	1.25	1.36
Thailand	0.66	0.44	0.47	0.20
UK	0.31	0.93	0.53	0.62

Note: * Significant at the 5% level.

when the opposite is true. Thus, the finding that output correlation exceeds
consumption correlation is not a universal law, although it is the dominant
state of affairs. But this should be expected rather than considered a puzzle.
GDPs are correlated because of trade linkages in a globalized world. When

Table 3.3   Average correlations for 33 countries against four benchmarks

	US	EU	OECD	World
GDP correlation	0.29	0.40	0.39	0.41
Consumption correlation	0.09	0.31	0.26	0.30
t-statistic	2.84*	1.20	1.69	1.70

Note: * Significant at the 5% level.

the US economy slows down, imports from China decline, causing a slowdown of the Chinese economy, which leads to lower imports of raw materials from Australia and a slowing down of the Australian economy.

For consumption to slow down proportionately, the marginal propensities to consume (MPCs) across countries must be equal or close, but they are not. Figure 3.2 shows the difference between the MPC of each country in the sample and that of the US. The big variation explains why consumptions are predominantly less strongly correlated than outputs. In Table 3.4 we can see some examples of how correlation difference is related to differences in MPCs. The difference between the MPC of Iceland and the US is small, and it is associated with a small difference in correlation; this is also true for Finland. For Korea, Ireland, Sweden and Luxembourg, the difference in correlation is big, and it is associated with a big difference in the MPCs.

These propositions can be verified by simulation. Consider two countries, 1 and 2 with outputs of y_1 and y_2, and consumptions of c_1 and c_2. The growth rate of y_1 depends on the growth rate of y_2, such that $\Delta y_{1,t} = \alpha \Delta y_{2,t} + \varepsilon_t$ and $\Delta y_{2,t} = \beta \epsilon_t$. It follows that $\Delta c_{1,t} = b_1 \Delta y_{1,t} + \omega_t$ and $\Delta c_{2,t} = b_1 \Delta y_{2,t} + e_t$, where b_1 and b_2 are the marginal propensities to consume and ε, ϵ, ω and e are random numbers generated from a uniform distribution. Simulations are run to generate 20 values of GDP and consumptions correlations under two scenarios: equal MPCs ($b_1 = b_2 = 0.6$) and unequal MPCs ($b_1 = 0.9$ and $b_2 = 0.1$). The simulation results are presented in Figure 3.3. When MPCs are equal, the difference between GDP correlations and consumption correlations is small, but when the difference between MPCs is big, the difference between correlations becomes big. We can also see that GDP correlation is predominantly higher than consumption correlation.

In Figure 3.4 we observe simulated time paths of GDP and consumptions under the two scenarios of equal and unequal MPCs. When the MPCs are equal at 0.6, consumption in both countries follows GDP but growing more slowly. Correlation between c_1 and c_2 is conspicuous. However, when

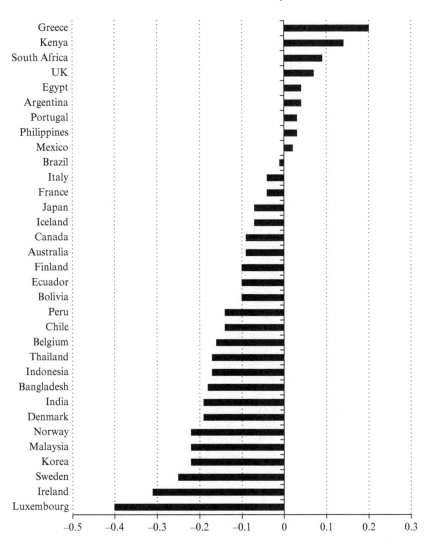

Figure 3.2 Difference in MPCs (versus the US)

MPCs are unequal at 0.9 and 0.1, c_2 does not respond to growth in y_2, whereas c_1 responds strongly to growth in y_1 because of the high MPC. We can see that while GDPs are highly correlated, consumptions are not.

The alleged puzzle is that output is more strongly correlated than consumption. This is not always the case, which means that it is not a universal rule. Furthermore, the difference in correlation may not be

Table 3.4   Examples of how correlation difference is related to MPC difference

	Correlation difference (absolute)	MPC difference (absolute)
Iceland	0.04	0.07
Finland	0.09	0.10
Korea	0.22	0.22
Ireland	0.22	0.31
Sweden	0.23	0.25
Luxembourg	0.39	0.40

statistically significant, but that is never mentioned in the studies glorifying the alleged puzzle. Outputs are highly correlated because of trade linkages; no sophisticated model is needed to realize that. Consumptions may or may not be as strongly correlated as outputs, depending on the marginal propensities to consume. What puzzle is the international consumption correlation puzzle?

3.5   CONCLUDING REMARKS

In this chapter we examined four alleged puzzles: the home bias in trade puzzle, the home bias in equity portfolio puzzle, the Feldstein–Horioka puzzle and the international consumption correlation puzzle. None of these puzzles is a puzzle.

The home bias in trade puzzle is allegedly a puzzle because people in one country prefer to consume domestic goods and services. As for services, it sounds odd that someone would take a three-hour flight to go to his favourite barber somewhere across the border. This is a puzzle only because the empirical results, typically based on the gravity model, turn out to be different from what is expected or commonly believed. Perhaps what is commonly believed is wrong. If what is commonly believed must be right, why bother testing the theory? The same goes for the home bias in equity portfolio puzzle, which is why people do not invest in foreign stock markets to realize the benefits of international diversification. Well, that is because investors are typically risk-averse, and by not investing in foreign markets they avoid foreign exchange risk as well as country risk and political risk. Then why is it that firm belief in the benefits of international diversification persists?

The Feldstein–Horioka puzzle is the observation that national saving

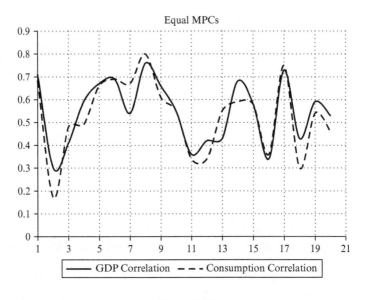

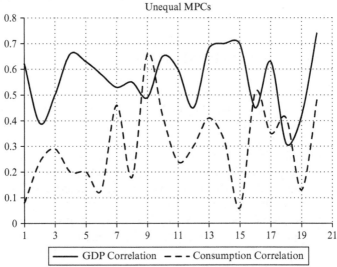

Figure 3.3   Simulated correlations

and investment rates are highly correlated, implying low capital mobility.
They are not supposed to be highly correlated, because people in one country can and do borrow from people in another country to 'smooth' their
consumption. Has anyone heard of anyone residing in Australia borrowing

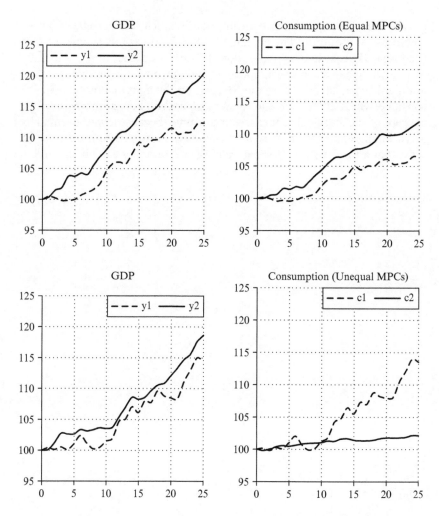

Figure 3.4   Simulated GDP and consumption with equal and unequal MPCs

from a Japanese bank to buy a new car in Australia? Why is it that capital is perceived to be mobile, then when a test shows that capital is immobile the results represent a puzzle? The underlying assumptions are that the test is valid and that capital must be mobile. If this is the case, why bother testing capital mobility? It is a puzzle why economists do not believe what they see with their own eyes, believing instead that their models represent the facts on the ground.

Last but not least, we have the international consumption correlation puzzle, the observation that consumption is much less correlated across countries than output. The explanation for this puzzle is simple: output is correlated because of globalization. When China goes down, Australia goes down. Changes in consumption resulting from changes in output are not highly correlated because they depend on the marginal propensities to consume, which differ from one country to another. For those who hate the concept of the marginal propensity to consume (because it was invented by Keynes), this explanation does not make sense. However, it makes intuitive sense that anyone without formal training in economics can understand.

4.   Puzzles in finance

4.1   THE CAPITAL STRUCTURE PUZZLE

The choice of capital structure, which is one of the most important topics in corporate finance, started with the work of Modigliani and Miller (1958), the cornerstone of capital structure theory. They inspired the development of the trade-off theory, the pecking order theory and the agency cost theory, which suggest various determinants of capital structure. The capital structure puzzle takes two related forms: (1) no agreement on what determines the capital structure (that is, the choice between debt and equity financing or, equivalently, the debt–equity ratio); and (2) the absence of a robust relation between the debt–equity ratio (leverage) and taxes, even though the very reason for raising debt capital is that interest payments are tax deductable.

Myers (1984) highlights the importance of the capital structure puzzle, in its first form, by saying 'we don't know' in response to the question of how firms choose their capital structures. He adds the following:

> We know very little about capital structure. We do not know how firms choose the debt, equity or hybrid securities they issue. We have only recently discovered that capital structure changes convey information to investors . . . our theories don't seem to explain actual financing behavior, and it seems presumptuous to advise firms on optimal capital structure when we are so far from explaining actual decisions.

He also highlights the puzzle in its second form by referring to 'an important gap in modern finance theory on the issue of corporate debt policy' (Myers, 1977). This is what he says about the puzzle in its second form:

> The theory should be able to explain why tax savings generated by debt do not lead firms to borrow as much as possible, and it should explain the phrase 'as much as possible'. It should explain why some firms borrow more than others, why some borrow with short-, and others with long-maturity instruments, and so on.

One reason why the puzzles of economics and finance arise is that a theory is not confirmed by empirical testing as the test results turn out to be all over the place (which is the rule rather than the exception). In the case of the capital structure puzzle, the situation is even worse because more than one theory has been put forward to explain capital structure. Each one of these theories can be easily confirmed or rejected by empirical work, which is typically based on what I call 'stir-fry regressions'; that is, regression equations constructed by lumping together a large number of variables that represent unrelated hypotheses (Moosa, 2012, 2017a). Furthermore, these theories contain similar variables with different predictions for the signs of the estimated coefficients. The first form of the puzzle arises because of the variability and inconsistency of empirical results with respect to the determination of a robust set of explanatory variables. In its second form, the puzzle arises because of inconsistent results with respect to the variable of interest, taxation.

The problem of the sensitivity of estimated coefficients to model specification arises in studies of capital structure because no single theoretical model can be used to select an explicit set of explanatory variables to be included in the corresponding empirical model. Huang and Ritter (2005) correctly argue that no single theory of capital structure is capable of explaining the time series and cross-sectional patterns that have been documented. Likewise, Frydenberg (2008) points out that neither the pecking order theory nor the trade-off theory provides a complete description of empirical observations or explains why some firms prefer equity while others prefer debt. Titman and Wessels (1988) and Harris and Raviv (1991) argue along similar lines, pointing out that the choice of explanatory variables in the analysis of cross-sectional variation in capital structure is fraught with difficulty. A consequence of this state of affairs is that researchers are tempted to try various combinations of the explanatory variables and report the ones they like, typically the ones that produce 'good' results that tell a publishable story and/or confirm prior beliefs. This (mal)practice is quite common in the field of corporate finance. Al-Najjar and Hussainey (2011) find that changing the definition of capital structure may result in changing the sign and significance of the coefficients on potential determinants of capital structure. Instead of thinking that this is a puzzle, because the empirical results vary significantly from one study to another, it would be a puzzle if the results were consistent.

By using data on capital structure, Moosa (2012) demonstrates that 'stir-fry regressions' constitute a 'con job' because they can be used to prove or reject almost anything. Specifically, he shows that: (1) the sign and significance of an estimated coefficient change with the selected set of explanatory variables; (2) adding more explanatory variables changes the sign and significance of a coefficient on a variable that is already included in the equation; (3) it is possible to change coefficients from significantly positive to significantly negative, and vice versa; (4) obtaining desirable results can be achieved by introducing various forms of non-linearities (predominantly partial and selective logarithmic transformation); and (5) it is possible, by changing model specification, to support either of two competing theories (trade-off versus pecking order).

Evidence on the determination of capital structure is a mixed bag, and so it should be. Prasad et al. (2001) survey a large volume of literature on capital structure, concluding that the evidence on trade-off versus pecking order theories remains inconclusive. Booth et al. (2001) argue that it is difficult to distinguish between trade-off and pecking order models because the variables used in one model are also relevant in the other model. Adair and Adaskou (2015) test the predictions of trade-off theory and pecking order theory and find that the estimated effects on leverage of profitability and growth opportunities support the latter, and that the estimated effects of age and size do not provide conclusive evidence for either of the two theories. Chen (2004) argues that neither the trade-off theory nor the pecking order theory provides convincing explanations for the capital choices of Chinese firms.

Result variability is the rule rather than the exception in studies of capital structure (see, for example, Voulgaris et al., 2002; Noulas and Genimakis, 2011; Feidakis and Rovolis, 2007; Nunkoo and Boateng, 2010). Li et al. (2009) use a sample of 417068 firm-year observations over the period 2000–2004 to test the importance of nine explanatory variables: size, profitability, tangibility, asset maturity, industry concentration, industry leverage, state ownership, foreign ownership and marketization (classified into firm characteristics, ownership variables and institutional variables). The results show that state ownership is positively associated with leverage (long-term debt), while foreign ownership is negatively associated with all measures of leverage. Other conclusions are derived on the effect of firm-specific factors. Five different model specifications are estimated: a full specification (all variables), firm characteristics only, ownership variables only, institutional variables only and ownership/institutional variables. The diversity and inconsistency of the results can be demonstrated with just a few examples out of many:

1. For total leverage, industry concentration is highly significant in the full specification but not so in the specification that has firm characteristics only.
2. For short-term debt, size is highly significant in the full specification but not so in the specification that has firm characteristics only. The same goes for industry concentration. Marketization is insignificant

when only institutional variables are included in the model but becomes significant when ownership variables are added.

3. In a model designed to explain the probability of raising long-term debt, asset maturity is significant when firm characteristics only are used but not so in the full specification. It is exactly the other way round for industry concentration.

4. When the equations are estimated with fixed effects, industry concentration, state ownership and marketization are highly significant when the model includes ownership and institutional variables only, but not so in any of the other model specifications.

So, what are we supposed to believe, and how can we derive robust inference from these results? The answer is that since we do not know what to believe, we cannot derive robust inference. The same problem can be observed in Liu et al. (2009), who present a mixed bag of results that differ only with respect to the inclusion or otherwise of a constant term and the number of explanatory variables. With results of this kind we cannot identify the factors determining capital structure with any degree of robustness. It is not a puzzle, and we have to accept the simple fact that identifying the factors determining capital structure is not an exact science.

The sensitivity of the results is illustrated by Moosa (2017a) based on a cross-sectional data set covering observations on the determinants of capital structure for 614 United States (US) shareholding companies. It is demonstrated that the results change with the choice of explanatory variables and how they are measured. It is also shown that it is possible, with the help of 'stir-fry regressions', to support either of two competing theories: the trade-off theory and the pecking order theory. After all, Myers (1984) designed his study as a one-on-one competition of the static trade-off and pecking-order theories. By estimating ten equations containing different combinations of the variable, it turns out that the trade-off theory beats the pecking order theory on five occasions, while the opposite is true on the other five occasions. This con job enables the researcher to prove anything and to reinforce or refute the puzzle in its first form.

Let us now turn to the puzzle in its second form. Again, mixed results have been obtained about the role of taxation such that those who do not subscribe to one view reject the results supporting that view, and vice versa (DeAngelo and Masulis, 1980; Alworth and Arachi, 2001; Bernasconi et al., 2005; Gill and Mathur, 2011; Kunieda et al., 2012; Buettner et al., 2008). The puzzle is that firms put limits on borrowing even though debt financing confers tax savings. The main reason why firms use debt financing is identified by Al-Nakeeb (2017), who attributes the astronomical growth of debt to a biased tax system that favours debt over equity financing;

accordingly, he presents a solid case for taxing interest transactions. The reasons why firms do not use 100 per cent debt financing are that it gives a bad impression to potential investors, and puts the firm in a vulnerable position as it is exposed to the risk arising from unanticipated changes in interest rates. Mortgage holders are always advised to pay more, pay more frequently and pay all if windfall income materializes. Financing decisions are actually signalling devices, conveying information to investors about the firm's business risk and profitability. Thus, it is only logical that firms try to strike some sort of balance between debt and equity financing. It is not a puzzle to not find a formula or a model that tells us what the balance looks like. And it is unwise to aspire for a model that captures behaviour across firms.

Myers (1977) acknowledges the availability of a 'variety of ideas' that have been put forward to explain the connection between leverage and tax. Modigliani and Miller (1963) note that firms maintain 'reserve borrowing capacity', suggesting that the incremental tax advantage of borrowing declines as more debt is issued and interest tax shields become less certain. They also note that the difference between tax rates on capital gains and those on regular income reduce the theoretical tax advantage of corporate borrowing. Miller (1977) has presented a model in which the advantage of debt financing disappears entirely. Furthermore, limits to corporate borrowing can be explained in terms of credit rationing by banks and other financial institutions. Managers may wish to avoid high debt ratios in an attempt to protect their jobs and stabilize their personal wealth. Bankruptcy costs (the transaction costs of liquidation or reorganization) are likely to discourage borrowing, although Warner (1977) wonders whether these costs are large enough to be significant. Robichek and Myers (1966) argue that the cost of financial distress is incurred when the firm comes under the threat of bankruptcy, even if bankruptcy is avoided eventually.

Unlike the previous explanations, Myers (1977) presents a new approach that does not rely on any of the ideas mentioned above. He explains why it is rational for firms to limit borrowing, even in the presence of a genuine tax advantage to corporate borrowing and even if capital markets are strictly perfect, efficient and complete. Vasiliou and Daskalakis (2009) argue that behavioural finance provides better explanations for financial managers' opinions and behaviour, and that the relation between capital structure and stock prices seems to be explained in a better way by following the behavioural finance approach. Baker et al. (2004) classify their research on behavioural finance into the irrational investors approach and the irrational managers approach, and explain why managers decide to refrain from issuing new stock.

So, what is the verdict? The capital structure decision is tested by estimating an equation of the form $L = f(X_1, X_2, \dots, X_n)$ where L is the leverage ratio and X_i is an explanatory variable. In its first form, the puzzle is a puzzle because the estimates do not produce consistent results, neither do they provide solid support for one theory against another. In its second form, the variable of interest X_1 is the tax factor. It is a puzzle because the results do not consistently provide support for the importance of X_1. The variability of results is not a puzzle; rather, the opposite would be true. As for why firms do not maximize debt, plenty of intuitive and formal explanations can be found in the literature. The capital structure puzzle is not a puzzle at all.

4.2   THE PRESIDENTIAL PUZZLE

The presidential puzzle can be traced back to the work of Santa-Clara and Valkanov (2003), who write the following:

> The excess return in the stock market is higher under Democratic than Republican presidencies ... The difference in returns is not explained by business-cycle variables related to expected returns, and is not concentrated around election dates. There is no difference in the riskiness of the stock market across presidencies that could justify a risk premium. The difference in returns through the political cycle is therefore a puzzle.

This observation is regarded as a puzzle because Republicans are viewed as being more business-friendly than Democrats. Republicans tend to be free marketeers who typically call for lower taxes and less stringent regulation.

The results of Santa-Clara and Valkanov (2003) that give rise to the puzzle are based on a straight number-crunching exercise without a valid theory. They are derived from a process of trial and error by running regressions containing 'control variables' defined in a particular way, including inflation, the annualized log dividend-price ratio, the term spread between the yield to maturity of a ten-year Treasury note and the three-month Treasury bill, the default spread between yields of BAA- and AAA-rated bonds, and the relative interest rate computed as the deviation of the three-month Treasury bill rate from its one-year moving average. They also try several definitions of the presidential party variable. Santa-Clara and Valkanov admit that 'a clear possibility is that our findings might be the product of data mining' and that their empirical model is 'inspired by the literature, rather than by a clearly formulated theoretical model'. They admit that their empirical investigation is not preceded by a clear theoretical model, and that it is only motivated by a conjecture. Yet, we are told that the results constitute a puzzle rather than the outcome of a 'stir-fry regression'.

Apparently Santa-Clara and Valkanov 'tried to correlate political variables with stock market returns', even though they acknowledge that the possibility of data mining is 'certainly a concern in the case of the presidential party variable'. Yet, they 'tried other political variables, related to the party in control of Congress, without success' ('success' here means finding results that confirm prior belief or tell a good story that makes the paper publishable in the *Journal of Finance*). They make the point that they were inspired by 'researchers (and investors)' who 'over the years, have tried countless variables to forecast stock market returns', which means that they might have 'stumbled upon a variable that tests significantly even when there is actually no underlying relation between the presidency and the stock market'. Sullivan et al. (2001) suggest that 'if one correlates enough variables with market returns, some spurious relations are likely to be found'.

This kind of work is typically based on an asset pricing equation whereby stock return is determined by a small or large number of variables with various definitions and measurements, in addition to two dummy variables, one for Republicans and the other for Democrats. Subrahmanyam (2010) surveys the literature on cross-sectional predictors of stock returns and identifies 50 variables that have been suggested to extend the capital asset pricing model (CAPM). These variables are classified under four categories: (1) informal Wall Street wisdom (such as value investing); (2) theoretical motivations based on risk–return model variants; (3) behavioural biases or mis-reaction by cognitively challenged investors; and (4) frictions, such as illiquidity or arbitrage constraints. With all of these possibilities at the researcher's disposal, it is not that difficult to get a puzzle by finding that the coefficient on the Democrats dummy is significantly positive; or no puzzle by finding that the coefficient on the Republican dummy is significantly positive. This is data mining at its best, making true the attitude of 'tell me what you want, and I will prove it'. Naturally, finding a puzzle is better for the publishability of a paper than not finding a puzzle, even though the two outcomes are equally likely.

Yet, the puzzle has been taken seriously, and attempts have been made to explain it. Cocquemas and Whaley (2016) suggest that 'the presidential puzzle remains a popular and recurring subject of discussion' and that 'any conclusion on this topic will undoubtedly bring out a flurry of passionate political reactions'. Kräussl et al. (2014) argue that the presidential cycle effect in US financial markets remains a 'puzzle that cannot be easily explained by politicians employing their economic influence to remain in power, as is often believed'. Thus, a set of results derived from a particular model has become a puzzle.

Possible explanations for the alleged puzzle have been suggested in terms of higher inflation, a higher degree of risk and increased government spending under Democratic presidents. In terms of inflation, Leblang and Mukherjee (2005) construct a model of speculative trading predicting that rational expectations of higher inflation under 'left-wing' administrations reduces trading volume, consequently leading to a decline in the mean and volatility of stock prices. It is not obvious, however, how this translates into higher returns under 'left-wing' administrations.

In terms of a higher level of risk under Democrats, Sy and Al-Zaman (2011) use a conditional version of the Fama–French model that allows risk to vary across political cycles (which has a different set of explanatory variables to those used by Santa-Clara and Valkanov) to find out whether the return differential is explained by risk. Accordingly, they suggest that 'the presidential puzzle can be explained when risk is properly taken into account', and that 'much of the return differential can be attributed to the fact that Democratic presidencies are associated with higher market and default risk premiums than their Republican counterparts'. On this point, Santa-Clara and Valkanov argue that the difference in riskiness might arise from differences in economic policies pursued by each party, or from varying levels of uncertainty among investors about these policies. While they admit that a difference in the riskiness of the stock market should command a risk premium, they find that market volatility is actually higher under Republican presidents. Hence, a puzzle arises as to the presence in an efficient market of persistent difference in returns that is not compensation for risk.

In terms of increased government spending under Democratic presidents, Beloa et al. (2013) find that firms with a high level of government exposure experience stronger cash flows and higher stock returns during Democratic presidencies, while the opposite pattern holds true during Republican presidencies. They suggest that business cycles, firm characteristics and standard risk factors do not account for the pattern in returns across presidencies, and point out that their results indicate market underreaction to predictable variation in the effect of government spending policies.

Let us look at the facts and figures. Figure 4.1 shows, on a year-by-year basis, stock market return under each president since 1929. The highest return (52.6 per cent) was recorded in 1954 under a Republican president, Eisenhower, who also recorded the fourth-largest gain of 43.7 per cent. The two lowest returns of −43.8 per cent and −36.6 per cent were recorded under a Republican, Hoover, but the third-lowest return of −35.3 per cent was recorded under a Democrat, Roosevelt, in 1937, still reeling under the effect of the Great Depression. The pattern is simply not there.

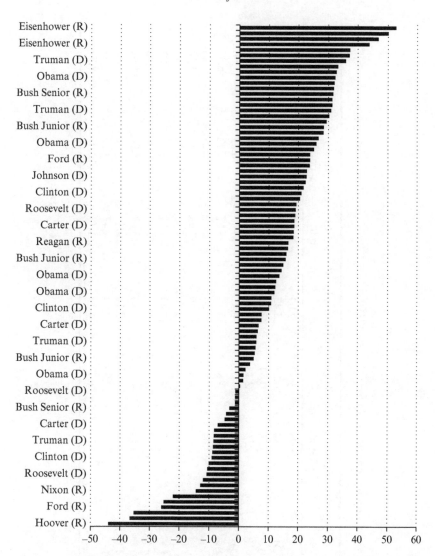

Figure 4.1   Return on the S&P 500 under Republicans and Democrats (1929–2019)

Table 4.1 reports return on the S&P 500 (including dividends), three-month Treasury bill rate, yield on Treasury bonds, as well as the equity premia with respect to Treasury bills, Treasury bonds and Baa corporate bonds. The data are annual, covering the period 1929–2019 when 15 presidents were in office, including eight Republicans and seven Democrats. The

Table 4.1 Returns and premia during presidential terms (1929–2019)

Period	President	Return on S&P 500	T-bill	T-bond	Stocks: bills	Stocks: bonds	Stocks: Baa bonds
1929–32	Hoover (R)	−25.73	3.37	2.03	−29.13	−27.83	−21.73
1933–44	Roosevelt (D)	12.83	0.27	3.42	12.57	9.42	4.09
1945–52	Truman (D)	16.26	0.84	2.15	15.45	14.13	12.65
1953–60	Eisenhower (R)	19.36	2.15	1.01	17.20	18.33	16.98
1961–62	Kennedy (D)	13.45	2.65	6.85	10.85	6.65	7.60
1963–68	Johnson (D)	9.40	3.80	2.18	5.67	7.22	6.47
1969–73	Nixon (R)	7.84	5.36	5.54	2.48	2.28	1.06
1974–76	Ford (R)	−1.07	6.87	3.10	−7.93	−4.17	−4.70
1977–80	Carter (D)	10.45	6.90	4.30	3.60	6.20	2.78
1981–88	Reagan (R)	16.43	9.18	12.49	7.25	3.93	2.23
1989–92	Bush Senior (R)	18.78	6.93	11.78	11.90	7.00	5.08
1993–99	Clinton (D)	20.13	4.46	7.13	15.69	13.00	11.01
2001–08	Bush Junior (R)	2.76	3.19	7.18	−0.41	−4.36	−5.71
2009–16	Obama (D)	8.65	0.26	4.94	8.43	3.75	1.41
2017–19	Trump (R)	16.20	1.47	4.13	14.73	12.07	8.77

Table 4.2   Testing for difference between two means

	Return on S&P 500	T-bill	T-bond	Stocks: bills	Stocks: bonds	Stocks: Baa bonds
Republican (mean)	8.26	4.82	6.06	3.45	2.20	1.18
Republican (SD)	14.90	2.70	4.21	14.54	13.86	11.33
Democrat (mean)	11.38	2.74	4.25	8.67	7.14	5.50
Democrat (SD)	6.75	2.48	2.09	8.16	6.16	5.91
t-statistic	−0.53	1.55	1.07	−0.87	−0.91	−0.94
Variance ratio	4.88*	1.19	4.06	3.17	5.06*	3.67

Note: * Significant at the 5% level.

Hoover years of 1929–32 witnessed the biggest losses under one president, but those were the years of the big crash and Great Depression. The performance of the stock market was dismal under another Republican president (Gerald Ford) in 1974–76, the years of the first oil crisis that witnessed a quadrupling of oil prices. It was dismal under another Republican president, Bush Junior, during a period that witnessed the global financial crisis and the crash of the early 2000s. We can blame the three Republican presidents for the dismal performance under their watch, but only if we blame Hoover for the 1929 crash and the Great Depression, Gerald Ford for the quadrupling of oil prices and Bush Junior for the global financial crisis. By 7 April 2020, the S&P 500 was down 17.5 per cent compared to the beginning of the year, mainly due to Covid-19. Are you supposed to blame another Republican president, Donald Trump, for the coronavirus outbreak?

In Table 4.2, we observe the means and standard deviations of returns and risk premia under Republicans and Democrats. The t statistics show the absence of significant differences in means for any of the variables, returns as well as risk premia. On average, therefore, Democrats have not produced higher returns. However, the variance ratio test (of the equality of variances) shows a statistically significant difference in volatility, indicating that returns have been more volatile under Republicans, which means that the risk-adjusted return explanation is not valid.

In the literature on the presidential puzzle, Republicans are described as 'right-wing', while Democrats are described as 'left-wing'. The fact of the matter is that both of them implement right-wing free market policies, at least since the days of Franklin Delano Roosevelt (FDR) where left-wing policies were implemented as part of the New Deal. These days both parties are pro-business and pro-military adventurism, which are good for the stock market and campaign donations. Amadeo (2019) argues that

Democrats and Republicans have widely different views on the economy, but once in power, candidates' actions do not always coincide with their party's views. That makes it difficult to determine whether Democratic presidents or Republican presidents are better for the economy.

Take the case of public debt and deficit spending. Republicans advocate fiscal responsibility, but their contribution to the mushrooming public debt is conspicuous. Obama added $8.6 trillion to public debt, the biggest dollar amount ever added by one president. Bush Junior comes in second place as he added $5.8 trillion. On the other hand, the Clinton era witnessed a $63 billion budget surplus. Amadeo (2019) mentions that every Republican president since Calvin Coolidge has added to public debt. The fact of the matter is that Republicans do not mind spending beyond their means if spending is directed at the military or used to salvage failed financial institutions. They just do not want to spend if spending is needed for health and education.

Both parties are as eager as the other when it comes to channelling money to the military–industrial complex even though Republicans accuse Democrats of being 'soft' on defence (meaning that Democrats do not drop as many bombs as Republicans on defenceless countries). Obama, a Democrat, received the Nobel Peace Prize, but his military spending was between $700 billion and $800 billion a year, much more than the war hawk Bush Junior. While the two parties disagree on minor issues, they do not differ at all when it comes to militarism, military adventurism and regime change, which are very expensive endeavours. In the State of the Union speech given by Trump in February 2020, Nancy Pelosi, who ripped Trump's speech for refusing to shake her hand, was as enthusiastic as Mike Pence in applauding the self-declared, US-backed, Central Intelligence Agency (CIA)-appointed president of Venezuela, Juan Guaido, a symbol of US interventionism and regime change policies.

The presidential puzzle can be confirmed easily by playing around with the data and model specification. However, it can also be rejected by doing the same thing. A puzzle cannot be a puzzle if it is based on pure number crunching without solid theoretical or at least intuitive explanation – an explanation that makes sense.

4.3   THE EQUITY PREMIUM PUZZLE

The equity premium puzzle is the observation that over the last 100 years or so, the average real return on US stocks has been substantially higher than the return on bonds. My immediate reaction is that this is not a puzzle; rather, the opposite should be a puzzle. We teach our students the risk–return trade-off that investors seeking a higher return must bear more risk, and that if they want to reduce the risk they are exposed to, they should accept a lower return. We tell them that bonds are less risky than stocks because the coupon payments received by bondholders are contractual, unlike the dividends that may or may not be received by stockholders. Even in terms of capital gains, bonds are less risky because if the price of a bond goes down, the investor can hold it until maturity when the contractual face value will be received by bondholders. In terms of the risk of default, some bonds (such as Treasury bonds) are virtually risk-free because governments have the power to tax people and print money. The equity premium, which is the excess of return on equity over bond yield, arises because more risk is associated with more return.

As usual, this is a puzzle because a number of different theories have been put forward to explain the observation but no definitive agreement exists on the explanation. However, it is not clear what is puzzling about this puzzle: it is not a puzzle that returns on stocks are higher than returns on bonds, and no rule of God or law of physics defines the limits on excess equity return. Mehra and Prescott (1985) suggest that 'restrictions that a class of general equilibrium models place upon the average returns of equity and Treasury bills are found to be strongly violated by the US data in the 1889–1978 period'. They conclude that 'an equilibrium model which is not an Arrow–Debreu economy will be the one that simultaneously rationalizes both historically observed large average equity return and the small average risk-free return'. Thus, it seems that Mehra and Prescott claim the existence of a law of physics that defines limits on equity premium. However, the term 'risk-free' says it all: if Treasury bills are risk-free then investors would be willing to hold them even if they offer a lower return than the riskier stocks.

The puzzle can be stated differently, as follows: returns on equities have been on average so much higher than returns on US Treasury bonds that it is hard to explain why investors buy bonds, even after allowing for a reasonable amount of risk aversion. Well, perhaps the degree of risk aversion is higher than what it is thought to be. If this argument is valid, then why do people even in the age of ultra-low interest rates keep their savings in fixed deposits with banks? Is this the bond premium puzzle, or can it be explained easily in terms of risk aversion and perhaps financial illiteracy? The other version is that the difference between equity and fixed-income yields is so huge that it cannot be rationalized in terms of a reasonable degree of risk aversion. As Mehra (2003) puts it, 'the historical US equity premium (the return earned by a risky security in excess of that earned by a relatively risk free US T-bill) is an order of magnitude greater than can be rationalized in the context of the standard neoclassical paradigm of financial economics'. Again, perhaps the degree of risk aversion is higher than what it is thought to be, and perhaps the explanation lies in the concept of loss aversion. If a high degree of risk aversion is incompatible with standard economic models, which typically simplify the real world, then perhaps these models can benefit from an injection of a dose of reality.

Mehra (2003) describes as 'intuitive' the proposition that stocks are 'riskier' than bonds and that investors require a premium for bearing this additional risk. He actually puts the word 'riskier' in quotation marks to imply that this is debatable, yet he mentions historical figures on the standard deviation of returns as 20 per cent a year for stocks and 4 per cent a year for Treasury bills. For Mehra, assets are priced in such a way that, *ex ante*, the loss in marginal utility incurred by sacrificing current consumption and buying an asset at a certain price is equal to the expected gain in marginal utility contingent on the anticipated increase in consumption when the asset pays off in the future. If this is the case, the risk premium should be lower. Mehra contends that 'stocks and bonds pay off in approximately the same states of nature or economic scenarios', implying that they should generate approximately the same rate of return. In fact, using standard theory to estimate risk-adjusted returns, he asserts that stocks, on average, should command at most a 1 per cent return premium over bills. This line of reasoning is based on a model that assumes a frictionless economy with a single, representative, 'stand-in' household that orders its preferences over random consumption paths by some hypothetical condition.

A possible explanation is that the puzzle is based on a model of neoclassical economics and finance: these are the same models that tell us that bubbles do not form (which is convenient when they cannot explain bubbles) and the same models that cannot explain a common characteristic of financial markets, bubbles followed by crashes. These are also the same models that cannot explain dozens of anomalies in financial markets. Neoclassical finance is based on two key assumptions: (1) market participants are rational; and (2) financial markets generate 'fair prices' that are close to the intrinsic values of the underlying assets. These two assumptions are embodied in two major pillars of neoclassical finance: the efficient market hypothesis (EMH) and the capital asset pricing model (CAPM). The fall of neoclassical finance was triggered by the loss of faith in its basic pillars as a result of observations that are inconsistent with the predictions of the underlying principles, most notably unexplainable excessive volatility. Obsession with the principles of neoclassical finance and the belief that these principles are capable of describing the behaviour of market participants brought about the global financial crisis.

For Shiller (2003), the most important factor casting doubt on the validity of neoclassical finance models is excess volatility, as he argues that 'excess volatility seems to be much more troubling for efficiency markets theory than some other financial anomalies, such as the January effect or the day-of-the-week effect'. Volatility, according to Shiller, implies that 'changes in prices occur for no fundamental reason at all, that they occur because of such things as "sunspots" or "animal spirits" or just mass psychology'. He further argues that 'theoretical models of efficient financial markets that represent everyone as rational optimizers can be no more than metaphors for the world around us'. Nothing could be more absurd than suggesting that everyone knows how to solve complex stochastic optimization models, which is implicit in the rational expectations hypothesis.

In the 1990s a shift took place away from the analysis of prices, dividends and earnings (for the purpose of demonstrating market anomalies) to the development of psychology-based models used to explain behaviour in financial markets, which is the essence of behavioural finance. Shiller (2003) contends that 'in further research, it is important to bear in mind the demonstrated weaknesses of efficient markets theory and maintain an eclectic approach'. Models of neoclassical finance that embody the assumption of market efficiency may be appropriate for the characterization of an imaginary ideal world, but they are far away from providing a valid description of behaviour in financial markets. Recent developments followed the emergence of behavioural finance (including ecological finance, neurofinance, experimental finance and emotional finance) in an effort to find more eclectic and realistic alternatives to neoclassical finance. Unfortunately, the die-hard supporters of neoclassical finance are still in business as usual. And it is neoclassical finance that has produced the equity premium puzzle.

Unlike neoclassical finance, behavioural finance discards the assumption of rationality by introducing and allowing a role for emotion and other psychological factors, seeking to combine finance theory with behavioural and cognitive psychology to explain why people make irrational financial decisions. It also discards the assumption of fair pricing, allowing for the possibilities of overvaluation and undervaluation. While neoclassical finance seeks to explain the actions of the theoretical rational person, behavioural finance seeks to explain observed behaviour, which is significantly different from the behaviour of the rational decision-maker envisaged by neoclassical thinking.

Benartzi and Thaler (1995) offer an explanation for the equity premium puzzle based on the prospect theory of Kahneman and Tversky. If investors are loss-averse (as opposed to risk-averse), they are distinctly more sensitive to losses than gains. If, in addition, these investors evaluate their portfolios frequently (even if they have long-term investment goals such as saving for retirement or managing a pension plan), this would create myopic loss aversion. By using simulations, they find the size of the equity premium to be consistent with the previously estimated parameters of prospect theory if investors evaluate their portfolios annually. In other words, a close monitoring of portfolios allows investors to detect small losses more frequently, and if these investors are exposed to loss aversion bias, they would reduce their investment in risky assets. By using survey data, Lee and Veld-Merkoulova (2016) confirm the proposition that myopic loss aversion curbs the tendency to invest in the stock market.

A related concept that can be used to explain the puzzle is that of 'ambiguity aversion'. Ellsberg (1961) found that people place higher values on bets with known probabilities (risk) than bets with unknown probabilities (uncertainty). This reaction, which is called 'ambiguity aversion', has been used to rationalize the equity premium puzzle and to explain why people act differently in complex situations (Seo, 2009). Hansen (2005, 2007) establishes conditions under which the prices of risky and uncertain choices depend separately on risk aversion and ambiguity aversion. Rieger and Wang (2012) test the hypothesis that ambiguity aversion can explain the equity premium puzzle by measuring the amount of ambiguity aversion in a large-scale international survey. By relating the extent of ambiguity aversion to the average equity premia in these countries, they find that ambiguity aversion has a significant influence on the size of the equity risk premium, even when controlling for macroeconomic parameters.

Kocherlakota (1996) puts forward two possible explanations for what he calls 'the wedge in average returns between stocks and bonds'. The first is the large differential in the cost of trading between the stock and bond markets. The second explanation is that, contrary to Mehra and Prescott's (1985) original parametric restrictions, the coefficients of relative risk aversion of individual investors are larger than ten (with respect either to their own consumption or to per capita consumption). It is perhaps a puzzle why economists do not believe that individuals are that risk-averse. According to Kocherlakota (1996), one way to support the 'high risk aversion' view is to demonstrate that this apparently strange assumption about human behaviour is consistent with data. It seems that Kocherlakota puts the burden of proof on those believing that people are typically risk-averse; hence, we are all gamblers until proven otherwise.

Barro (2005) builds on the argument put forward by Rietz (1988) that the equity premium puzzle could be explained by infrequent but very large falls in consumption (as a result of wars, depressions and disasters), if the intertemporal elasticity of substitution of consumption is low or when the return distribution has a long, fat lower tail. To preserve the myth of a puzzle, Mehra and Prescott (1988) dismiss Rietz's arguments by wondering whether his disaster scenarios are reasonable, suggesting that the need for such extreme assumptions to account for the average returns on debt and equity provides support for their contention that standard theory still faces an unsolved puzzle. Barro (2006) responds by arguing that the allowance for low-probability disasters, as suggested by Rietz (1988), explains a number of puzzles pertaining to asset returns. Moreover, he argues, this approach achieves these explanations while maintaining the tractable framework of a representative agent, time-additive and isoelastic preferences and complete markets, as well as independently and identically distributed shocks to productivity growth.

Jobert et al. (2005) present a Bayesian solution to the puzzle that standard intertemporal economic models cannot account for the magnitude of the observed excess return earned by a risky security over the return on T-bills. While they follow convention and assume a single representative agent, this agent is not certain about the parameters of the dividend process, in which case uncertainty is modelled by a prior distribution, so that inferences can be made in a Bayesian fashion. The price of the stock is still the net present value of future dividends, but the agent is now averaging not only over the possible future paths of the dividend process, but also over the parameters that govern its dynamics. They use 'particle filtering' to work out the posterior distribution of the parameters of the problem, and reach the striking conclusion that coefficients of relative risk aversion lie in the interval 1–2 with high probability. In other words, they dismiss the equity premium puzzle.

Figure 4.2 displays annual rates of return on the S&P 500, Treasury bills and bonds over the period 1929–2019. In Table 4.3 we can see measures of risk, calculated from the raw return data, including the standard deviation (SD), downside semi-standard deviation (DSSSD), and value at risk (1 per cent VAR and 5 per cent VAR). All measures of risk are much higher for the S&P 500 than for bills and bonds. As a matter of fact, value at risk is positive in the case of Treasury bills because no negative returns were recorded during the period. What is more significant is risk-adjusted return, or return per unit of risk, measured by the ratios of the mean to standard deviation or DSSSD. Bills and bonds produce higher ratios (hence higher levels of risk-adjusted return) than the S&P 500.

Ordinary people shy away from the stock market for several reasons despite the availability of a high equity premium. These people know of the events of 1929 when those who lost their savings in the crash jumped to their deaths from the top of tall buildings in New York City. They hear stories about companies going bankrupt because the chief executive officer (CEO) embezzles and runs away, leaving shareholders to lick their wounds. They hear about the directors of shareholding companies diverting money from shareholders to incompetent and corrupt CEOs and their

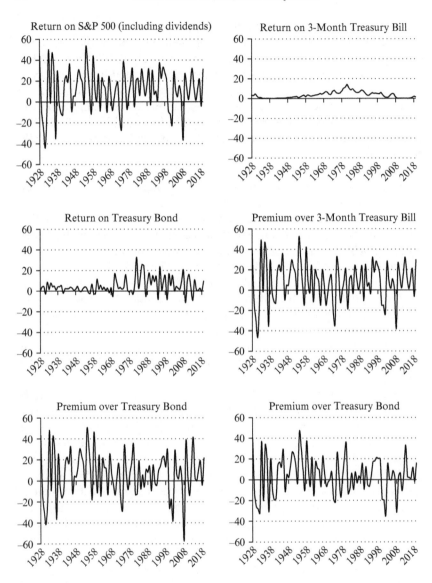

Figure 4.2   Annual return and equity premium

cronies in the form of huge salaries, lavish bonuses and extravagant golden parachutes.

Plentiful serious reasons are available to explain why ordinary people do not participate in the stock market and solve the stock market

Table 4.3   Measures of return and risk (1929–2019)

	S&P 500	Treasury bill	Treasury bond
Mean return	11.57	3.40	5.15
Standard deviation	19.58	3.03	7.67
Downside semi-standard deviation	14.57	1.82	3.35
1% value at risk	−37.21	0.04	−9.28
5% value at risk	−23.39	0.06	−4.98
Ratio of mean to SD	0.59	1.12	0.67
Ratio of mean to DSSD	0.79	1.87	1.54

participation puzzle or the shareholding puzzle. These reasons (hence explanations) include lack of financial awareness (Guiso and Jappelli, 2005); lack of trust in the stock market (Guiso et al., 2008); financial illiteracy (Van Rooij et al. 2011); narrow framing – that is, overlooking the full range of investment outlets (Barberis et al., 2006); lack of financial sophistication (Calvet et al., 2007, 2009); hyperbolic discounting – that is, the tendency to choose smaller, immediate rewards rather than larger, later rewards (Love and Phelan, 2015); high interest rates on personal debt, including mortgage debt (Becker and Shabani, 2010); and frictions, such as information and transaction costs (Bogan, 2008). Further evidence on limited participation in the stock market and suggested explanations can be found in Guo (2001), Naudon et al. (2004) and Mauricas et al. (2017).

Brown et al. (2017) present the results of a survey in which the participants stated the reasons for not participating in the stock market (in order of importance) as: too risky, lack of knowledge, efforts, transaction costs, lack of money, priority to paying off mortgage, partner objections, priority to paying off other debt, and priority to pay off credit card debt. It is interesting to note that 90 per cent of the participants said that they did not participate in the stock market because it was too risky. It is therefore a puzzle that the equity premium puzzle and the market participation puzzle are perceived to be puzzles.

4.4   THE DIVIDEND PUZZLE

The dividend puzzle, which can be traced back to the work of Fischer Black (1976), is the observation that companies pay dividends to shareholders even though better tax advantages can be obtained through stock repurchase. Black raises two questions, as to: (1) what the investor should do about dividends; and (2) what the corporation should do about dividend policy. He gives one answer to both questions: 'We don't know'. Fourteen years later, Black (1990) wondered why firms pay dividends and predicted that 'dividends that remain taxable will gradually vanish', but this is yet to be seen. Bernstein (1996) notes that 'dividend yields have no particular significance as a stock market forecasting device', and that 'the harder we look at the dividend picture, the more it seems like a puzzle, with pieces that just don't fit together'. Frankfurter (1999) admits to failure in the pursuit of a solution to the puzzle and wonders whether the puzzle is solvable, concluding that 'it is either not possible, or extremely difficult, to find an economically rational solution to the dividend puzzle'.

It makes no sense for shareholders to receive dividends when they are taxed at a higher rate than capital gains. Dividends are actually taxed twice, because they are paid from after-tax profits and yet investors still have to pay income tax on dividends unless they receive franking credits, which represent a tax rebate for the payment of company tax. Shareholders lose immediately because of the higher income tax rate and also because of the lost compounding of taxes over time. Furthermore, a dividend distribution is effectively a partial liquidation of the company, because a payment of x million in dividends will be accompanied by a corresponding x million decline in the market value of the company, which means that paying dividends is not good for the company either. In reality, however, shareholders complain when dividends are cut or are not paid at all. It follows that four questions constitute the dividend puzzle: (1) why do investors need dividends as an incentive to buy shares in a company? (2) why do firms pay dividends? (3) why do investors like dividends? and (4) why do investment advisors recommend buying dividend-paying stock?

While writing an article on the dividend puzzle for *Business Insider* (2012) Cameron Hight wrote the following:

> I was sitting beside an economist on a flight to New York City while writing this article and I asked the question, 'How much money do you have if a $10 stock pays you $1 dividend?' He said, '$11, the $10 stock plus the $1 in dividend.' In actuality, you still have $10 because the price of stock declines by the value of the dividend to create a net neutral transaction. That is, until you get your tax bill and that $1 dividend turns into $0.85. So in reality, the dividend payment turned your $10 into $9.85. That doesn't sound like smart financial strategy to me.

A number of no-nonsense explanations for the puzzle have been suggested. For example, in a bearish stock market, dividends provide a 'glimmer of hope'. According to *The Economist* (2003), when stock markets are down, 'investors notice the minimal amounts of cash they were earning from their shares'. Another reason for the love affair with dividends is that investors have become increasingly sceptical about accounting profits in the wake of Enron, WorldCom, and other accounting scandals. As a result, investors seek evidence of profitability in the form of cash dividends. Corporate fraud is so rampant that shareholders find reassurance of financial soundness in dividends.

Behavioural finance provides an explanation for the puzzle, based on the concept of mental accounting whereby individuals classify funds differently, which makes them prone to irrational decision-making in their spending and investment behaviour. In this case, money received from dividends is different from money received from capital gains. By putting capital gains and cash dividends into separate mental accounts, the investor keeps control of spending. Shefrin and Statman (1985) argue that investors strive to prevent themselves from consuming too much at present, particularly elderly investors, as they may be retired and rely more heavily on investment income. They therefore purchase dividend-paying stocks to meet liquidity requirements. They could alternatively sell an amount of non-dividend-paying stock equivalent to the income needed and have the same cash flow impact as long as dividend and capital gains tax rates are equal. However, by doing so, they will dip into capital, which they do not like to do. As Shefrin (2002) puts it: 'Don't dip into capital' is akin to 'don't kill the goose that lays the golden eggs'. Statman (1999) explains the situation as follows:

> 'Not one drop' is a good rule for people whose self-control problems center on alcohol. 'Consume from dividends but don't dip into capital' is a good rule for investors whose self-control problems center on spending.

Another behavioural finance explanation is based on the concepts of loss aversion, mental accounting and framing. When stock prices fall, dividends serve as a silver lining and when they rise, the investor likes dividends because they are regarded as a separate gain. Shefrin and Statman (1985) argue that cash dividends are not equal to the capital gains realized by selling stocks because each investor has a different choice for high-dividend and low-dividend stocks. For example, retirees like high-dividend stocks, because they can be used to alleviate the pressure of lacking cash and also because they enable retirees to avoid selling their own stocks. One dollar dividend and one dollar capital gains are different because they belong to two completely independent mental accounts.

Other explanations have been put forward to explain preference for dividends. When companies choose to retain earnings, they effectively replace dividends with capital gains that may or may not be realized in the future. This is the 'bird in the hand' motto. It follows that if two companies are exactly the same, the one that pays higher dividends will have its stock valued higher because some investors prefer value now to uncertain capital gains in the future. A related explanation pertains to liquidity concerns. If liquidity is low, high transaction costs make investors more inclined to receive dividends rather than acquire the same amount by selling stocks. Since rational investors prefer liquid stocks, firms with low liquidity pay dividends as a compensation for illiquidity.

Yet another explanation rests on the proposition that an increase in dividends represents a signal of unexpected and persistently higher future earnings. In this sense, dividends convey information on how managers view the future prospects of the underlying firm. An increase in dividends is likely to be interpreted as implying that the directors predict high profitability potential, which is why the board of directors think twice before taking a decision to suspend dividends. On the other hand, dividend cuts can be interpreted as a signal of impending financial problems. Furthermore, a dividend increase may be interpreted as indicating that the company has entered a mature life-cycle stage of lower profitability and diminished risk. If reaction to news about risk reduction dominates the reaction about lower future profits, the stock price response to a dividend increase announcement may be positive. Conversely, the decision to reduce dividends is likely to signal the transitioning from maturity to the zone of higher systematic risk and diminished profitability.

Last, but not least, a dividend increase is conducive to the reduction of the agency problems between shareholders and senior management in public companies where ownership and control are separated. The managers of companies with sizeable cash reserves tend to overinvest for the sake of empire-building. If this is the case, then an increase in dividends reduces the free cash available to managers, which curtails their ability to overindulge in acquisitions.

Frankfurter (1999) argues that the love of dividends is something that investors have been conditioned to feel for centuries, and that only education will change their attitudes. However, if there is a dividend puzzle, there must also be a 'rent puzzle', as to why property owners go through the trouble of dealing with tenants when they can relax and realize capital gains in due course. And what about a 'coupon puzzle' for bondholders? It may be true that people invest in stocks mainly for the sake of capital gains, in which case a dividend may represent a welcome windfall gain. No evidence indicates that dividend-paying stocks do not provide as much capital gains as stocks that do not pay dividends. Why not enjoy both dividends and capital gains?

4.5 OTHER PUZZLES IN FINANCE

An empirical finding that is very specific to the sample, definitions and testing techniques becomes a law of physics. Research in academic finance is aimed at publishing papers, so once a puzzle has been established, a finding that the puzzle does not exist is destined for the bin, and the belief that we have a puzzle on our hands persists. Otherwise, a proposition that makes sense and is not supported unanimously by empirical evidence is also regraded as a puzzle. In this section, two puzzles that belong to one of the two categories are examined: the idiosyncratic volatility puzzle and the stock return–inflation puzzle.

Idiosyncratic (firm-specific) risk refers to the inherent factors that can have a negative impact on individual assets or groups of assets. The opposite of idiosyncratic risk is systematic risk, which refers to broader trends that impact upon the overall market. Neoclassical asset pricing models, in which investors hold well-diversified portfolios without exposure to unsystematic risk, imply that disconnection between idiosyncratic volatility and expected return. Ang et al. (2006) kick-started the puzzle by finding a negative relation between estimated idiosyncratic volatility and subsequent realized returns. So, it is a puzzle only because Ang et al. (2006) found negative correlation by using a specific set of data covering a specific period of time, using specific definitions of the variables as well as specific estimation method and model specification.

The puzzle has persisted even though some economists have found completely different results. Fu (2009) documents a significant positive relation between idiosyncratic volatility and returns. Cao and Han (2016) find a positive (negative) relation between the two variables among relatively undervalued (overvalued) stocks. Bali and Cakici (2008) and Han and Lesmond (2011) found no connection whatsoever. The contrasting results, however, did nothing to undermine the 'law of nature' revealed by Ang et al. (2006), as their set of empirical results has become an undisputed fact of life. Contrasting results, if they see the light at all, are questioned, scrutinized, perhaps even ridiculed to preserve the puzzle and the glory that comes with it.

Houa and Loh (2016) suggest that the debate about the puzzle is complicated by 'the fact that existing studies typically differ in terms of empirical methodology and sample construction, thus making direct comparisons of their results difficult'. This is not a complication but rather an indication that any set of results can be obtained by using the con art of econometrics. The real puzzle is that the Ang et al. (2006) results have become the standard, and the burden of the proof falls on others who should justify the contrasting results by providing logical explanations that are dismissed swiftly. For the sake of fairness and justice, Ang et al. should demonstrate the validity and universality of their 'discovery' by betting their superannuations on a trading rule based on the puzzle. Instead, it seems that puzzles are granted on a first come, first served basis. Puzzles have become like patents.

Numerous attempts have been made to uncover 'this mystery', as Houa and Loh (2016) put it. Proposed explanations include those based on idiosyncratic skewness (Boyer et al., 2010), coskewness (Chabi-Yo and Yang, 2009), maximum daily return (Bali et al., 2011), retail trading proportion (Han and Kumar, 2013), one-month return reversal (Fu, 2009), illiquidity (Bali and Cakici, 2008; Han and Lesmond, 2011), uncertainty (Johnson, 2004), average variance beta (Chen and Petkova, 2012) and earnings surprises (Jiang et al., 2009; Wong, 2011). One good thing about puzzles is that they encourage the churning out of papers, except that the contribution of these papers to human knowledge is typically zero.

Cannon (2015) claims that despite these 'gigantic efforts' to solve the puzzle, 'the observed relationship remains largely debated and unexplained'. He goes on to propose an alternative explanation for the puzzle by postulating that the negative relation observed between idiosyncratic volatility and future returns is driven by investor sentiment. In periods of high investor sentiment, investors are so optimistic that they are attracted to assets with high idiosyncratic volatility, creating the negative correlation observed by Ang et al. (2006). When investor sentiment is low, the results indicate a positive relation between idiosyncratic volatility and future returns, supporting the notion of risk–return trade-off. Cannon concludes that the results imply that sentiment plays a significant role in the process of picking volatile stocks. In times of high sentiment, investors may inappropriately assign higher probabilities of favourable outcomes because of their emotional state. Overconfidence and inflated probability induce frequent acquisition of riskier stocks, sustaining the idiosyncratic volatility puzzle. This is yet another plausible explanation that is bound to be dismissed by the supporters of the idiosyncratic volatility puzzle.

Let us now turn to the stock return–inflation puzzle. Fisher (1930) envisaged a positive relation between the nominal rate of return and (expected) inflation, on the grounds that investors demand and obtain higher nominal returns when they expect inflation to pick up. The original proposition was put in terms of interest rate as the nominal return, but this proposition was extended subsequently to stock returns where the rationale is that because stocks are claims on real assets, stock returns are expected to vary positively with inflation, which makes stocks a viable inflation hedge. This sounds plausible, and it is why the observation of negative correlation between inflation and stock returns represents the stock return–inflation puzzle.

Fama (1981) argues that stocks represent ownership of the income generated by real assets, which would not be the case if stock returns are affected negatively by inflation. To explain the puzzle, he puts forward the proxy hypothesis according to which negative correlation between stock returns and inflation is spurious, induced by positive correlation between stock returns and real activity, and negative correlation between inflation and real activity. Geske and Roll (1983) extend Fama's work to come up with the reverse causality hypothesis (also called the debt monetization hypothesis), whereby negative correlation between stock returns and inflation is attributed to fiscal and monetary linkages. The main underlying argument is that negative correlation between inflation and income growth arises because of countercyclical monetary growth. If, for example, the economy is expected to slide into recession, government revenue will be expected to fall, and if a portion of the budget deficit is monetized, the economy will experience inflation. It follows that lower income growth is associated with higher inflation.

The empirical evidence on the relation between stock returns and inflation has been a mixed bag, which is not surprising, given that a large number of possible model specifications are used to test the underlying hypothesis (see, for example, Hoque et al., 2007). The specifications include stock prices as a function of the general price level, stock prices as a function of inflation, nominal return as a function of inflation, and real return as a function of inflation. Furthermore, some models distinguish between expected and unexpected inflation, between symmetric and asymmetric responses, and between short-run and long-run effects. The fact of the matter is that the empirical evidence on this issue could be anything, and that it should be taken with a big grain of salt. The proposition that stock returns should be positively correlated with inflation makes a lot of sense, in which case finding mixed evidence should not be taken to imply a puzzle. This is economics, not physics: we cannot isolate the effect of inflation on stock prices and measure it, just like physicists can isolate the effect of pressure on the volume of gas and measure it by using a laboratory experiment.

4.6 CONCLUDING REMARKS

Finance is a field where puzzles arise because of firm (perhaps dogmatic) belief in theories and models depicting how financial markets should behave or how things should be. They also arise because a set of empirical results that someone stumbles on becomes a finding that is as powerful as saying that an object falling under gravity accelerates at the rate of 32 feet per second per second. This is the field where the majority of economists think that the market efficiency hypothesis is the law of the land, even though casual empiricism tells us otherwise; for example, calendar anomalies and bubbles followed by crashes are not supposed to be observed in an efficient market. It is also the field where the so-called 'asset pricing models', such as the full menu of the Fama–French models, are perceived to provide exact figures on what the return on a particular asset should be. Claims of puzzles persist even if 100 plausible explanations are put forward.

The capital structure puzzle is a puzzle because no unified theory explains how the capital structure is determined. The presidential puzzle is a puzzle because in 1983 two researchers found that returns are higher under Democrats than Republicans. The equity premium puzzle is a puzzle because the difference between the return on equity and fixed income securities is higher than it should be in a theoretical Arrow–Debreu economy that does not exist in reality. The dividend puzzle is a puzzle because no one knows why shareholders like dividends. The idiosyncratic volatility puzzle is a puzzle because in 2006 four researchers found that volatility in one period is negatively correlated with return in the following period. This result has become a law of physics that has withstood the test of time despite the 'gigantic efforts' aimed at solving the puzzle, as one puzzle enthusiast puts it. The stock return–inflation puzzle is a puzzle because they should be negatively correlated when it appears that they are positively correlated. The fact of the matter is that it is possible to find negative, positive or no correlation.

Mehra (2003) asks the question why the equity premium puzzle is still a puzzle. I suppose that the answer would be 'because it is my puzzle', and because 'subsequent results defy my model'. Neither the equity premium puzzle, nor any of the puzzles examined in this chapter, is a puzzle. However, talking about puzzles and why they cannot be solved sounds sophisticated and 'sciency', which is probably why they persist.

5. The myths of econometrics

5.1 RELIABILITY OF ECONOMETRIC FORECASTING

When I was exposed to econometrics as an undergraduate student for the first time in the early 1970s, I thought that it was the best human endeavour. I thought I would be able to use econometric models to forecast interest rates, exchange rates, stock prices and the state of the economy, making a fortune in the process. Apparently I thought wrong, which became clear in my days in investment banking during the 1980s. It is a myth that econometric forecasting is reliable and that econometric sophistication is conducive to forecasting accuracy. Economists observed long ago that simple univariate models that involve trend extrapolation produce better forecasts than those generated from complex econometric models (see, for example, Christ, 1951, 1956).

In its issue of 1 August 1998, *The Economist* published an article entitled 'The Perils of Prediction', which casts significant doubt on the ability of forecasters to predict crises like the Asian crisis of the late 1990s. The article concludes by saying that 'it seems near impossible to create models that neither miss too many crises that have occurred nor predict too many that never happen'. The same article cites Richard Portes, an academic economist, who describes these models as 'one of the most egregious examples of data mining in all of empirical economics'. In a comment posted as a letter to the editor published in the 15 August 1998 issue, a reader described forecasting models as 'financial tools which the world is better off without', because they can 'attract enough believers to become self-fulfilling'. In the more recent issue of 26 November 2015, *The Economist* highlights the 'perils of planning on the basis of economic forecasts', arguing that 'governments plan years ahead on the basis of economic forecasts that must be wrong'.

In reality, successful forecasters do not use econometrics. George Soros made a killing in 1992 by taking short positions on the pound and Italian lira, based on his forecast that the two currencies would come under pressure within the European Monetary System (and he was right). He made a killing again during the Asian financial crisis of the late 1990s when he took a massive short position on the Thai baht. Warren Buffett has made his wealth by betting on the appreciation of undervalued assets, where values are calculated from the analysis of financial statements (without the use of econometrics). Michael Burry, who is a physician and not an econometrician, correctly predicted that the real estate bubble would burst as early as 2007, reaching this conclusion by conducting research on the values of residential real estate and mortgage-backed securities. He took a short position on the market by persuading Goldman Sachs to sell him credit default swaps against the subprime deals he saw as vulnerable. He was right, and he did it without econometrics. On the other hand, those who put their faith in econometric forecasting caused the collapse of a big hedge fund (Long-Term Capital Management) with massive losses (and this is not the only story). The copula model used by American International Group (AIG) predicted the impossibility of United States (US) house prices declining nationwide, which actually happened. As a result, taxpayers were called to the rescue, bailing out the company by footing a massive bill of $160 billion.

Econometric forecasting is criticized by insiders and outsiders. In fact the criticism goes as far as making jokes about the inaccuracy of forecasting. For example, some cynics would say that 'economists were invented to make weather forecasters and astrologers look good', that 'an economist is a trained professional paid to guess wrong about the economy', that 'economic forecasting is like driving a car blindfolded and getting instruction from a person looking out the rear window', that 'an economist will know tomorrow why the things she or he predicted yesterday didn't happen', and that 'economists have predicted six of the last two recessions'. Some people would tell the story of three economists who went target shooting: the first missed by a metre to the right, the second missed by a metre to the left, and the third exclaimed: 'we got it'. These jokes reflect the track record of econometric forecasting, which has been nothing short of dismal, appalling and egregious.

Observers note that forecasters tend to overestimate cyclical upturns and underestimate cyclical downturns. When the forecasts turn out to be way off the mark, forecasters put the blame on extraneous variables or unreliable data, effectively saying that if everything had followed their assumptions, the forecasts would have turned out to be accurate. This kind of argument is never put forward by a physicist. Economic forecasters try to think of some other variables that they could add to the model, variables with increasingly tenuous links to the outcome that becomes increasingly difficult to explain. Forecasters do a horrendous job, although forecasts may generate a self-fulfilling prophecy. For example, when a forecast is announced saying that the economy will grow at 5 per cent next year, this may encourage those who believe the announcement to spend more, thus lifting the economy, perhaps to the vicinity of 5 per cent. The same reasoning is valid for an announcement of a predicted recession, which discourages consumption.

Evidence against the reliability of economic forecasting is provided by economists themselves. For example, Frankel (2011) examines the forecasts of real growth rates and budget balances provided by official government agencies in 33 countries to find out that these forecasts have a positive average bias, that they are more biased in booms, and that they are even more biased at the three-year horizon than at shorter horizons. He suggests that overoptimism in official forecasts explains excessive budget deficits and the failure to run surpluses during periods of high output. Frankel's results show that the average upward bias in the official forecast of the budget balance, relative to the realized balance, is '0.2 percent of GDP [gross domestic product] at the one-year horizon, 0.8 percent at the two-year horizon, and 1.5 percent at the three-year horizon'. He concludes as follows: 'evidently official forecasters . . . over-estimate the permanence of the booms and the transitoriness of the busts'.

Commenting on Frankel's results, de Rugy (2011) argues that forecasting errors are rampant not only in government, as 'private-sector forecasters aren't that much better'. She cites Cardiff Garcia of the *Financial Times* as saying that 'economists who tend to predict near the consensus are, by definition, unlikely to anticipate extreme events, while those who correctly predict the occasional Black Swan tend to get everything else wrong (or most everything else)'. She makes it clear that she is not optimistic about the profession getting better at forecasting the future, arguing that 'it's not the forecast per se that matters, but how these forecasts are used to achieve policy/political goals', and that 'it's always a good idea for forecasters to remind readers that they should be highly skeptical of their forecasts'. This is good advice that is almost never followed.

Practitioners criticize econometric forecasting. For example, Oliver (2017) warns of the hazard of relying too much on precise forecasts when making investment decisions regarding asset allocation. He makes the sarcastic comments that 'if forecasting was easy I wouldn't be writing this . . . and you wouldn't be reading it' and that 'we would be very rich and sipping champagne in the south of France'. Inaccurate forecasting, he argues, is not limited to macroeconomic variables, but extends to the forecasting of company profits and other corporate financial indicators. He refers to 'numerous examples of gurus using grand economic, demographic or financial theories – usually resulting in forecasts of "new eras" or "great depressions" – who may get their time in the sun but who also usually spend years either before, or after, losing money'.

As an example, Oliver talks about the 'gurus who foresaw a "new era" in the late 1990s – with books like *Dow 36000*' before the advent of the collapse of the early 2000s. Oliver warns that forecasts of economic and investment indicators should be treated with care, stating the following specific points: (1) forecasters suffer from psychological biases, including the tendency to assume that the current state of the world will continue; (2) quantitative point forecasts convey no information on the risks surrounding the forecasts, when in fact they are conditional upon the information available when the forecast was made; (3) what counts in investment management is the relative direction of one asset price relative to others; and (4) forecasting financial variables is made harder by the need to work out what is already factored in. Yet, gurus like the ones Oliver talks about claim that they can forecast financial volatility. Naturally they are so humble and altruistic that they do not use their forecasts of volatility to make money by betting on options; rather, they publish the forecasts and how they are generated for the benefit of society. Remember that those who know do not tell, and those who tell do not know.

Academic economists also criticize econometric forecasting. Weber (2011) surveyed the opinions of academic economists participating in the 2011 Davos meeting, which witnessed a session on the perils of economic prediction. Carmen Reinhart, of the University of Maryland, argues that economists can see where the problems are, and sense who is vulnerable to a crisis, but she wishes good luck to anyone trying to get the timing of a crisis right. Looking back at his days as director of research at the International Monetary Fund (IMF), Raghuram Rajan admits that they were 'always wrong on Africa', in the sense that they would issue a forecast for the continent, then conflict would break out somewhere, making the local economy plummet 20 per cent (like everything else, it seems, the failure of forecasting models is blamed on Africans, as if the IMF economists are good at forecasting Europe or Antarctica). Robert Shiller compares weather forecasting with model-based economic forecasting, suggesting that the weather follows certain immutable rules, in which case the underlying models can be based on experience. The models used by economists, he argues, are based on what used to happen, although the ingredients of the economy change over time. Still, Shiller adds that 'the economic profession got too much in love with its models'. Simon Johnson, a former IMF chief economist, talks about 'group think' whereby 'everybody is unwilling to stick their nose out and challenge the consensus'. He warns economists as follows: 'If you step outside the comfort band of the consensus forecast, you get beaten up, you can risk your career'.

Economists are sceptical of the usefulness of forecasting for specific applications. Smith and Aaronson (2003) criticize forecasting in health economics by referring to a 1996 widely circulated forecast for the

Philadelphia Metropolitan Area. The forecasters warned that a decline in hospital and healthcare employment in the region would occur over the following five years, suggesting that the anticipated decline would exacerbate the problem of an oversupply of nurses seeking hospital employment. By the end of 2001, regional hospitals were experiencing problems in recruiting sufficient numbers of nurses, pharmacists and technicians. The forecasters failed to anticipate the impact of a strong regional economy on supply, and underestimated the resilience of the underlying forces that had driven long-term growth in the demand for healthcare personnel.

Likewise, Smil (2000) warns of the perils of long-range energy forecasting by detecting a 'remarkable extent of individual and collective failure in predicting actual developments in major energy conversions, primary energy requirements, sectoral needs, exhaustion of energy resources, and energy substitutions'. As a result, he recommends the abandonment of detailed quantitative point forecasts in favour of decision analysis or contingency planning under a range of alternative scenarios. Whitmore (2008) highlights the perils and pitfalls of oil price forecasting, referring to analysts who at one time thought that $10 a barrel was the new normal, and those who forecast $200 a barrel when the price was just below $150. Faulty forecasts of oil prices are blamed on a 'whole host of unknown factors that are independent of classic supply-and-demand calculations – from the weather, to unexpected fluctuations on the financial markets, to civil wars and major geopolitical crises'. Forecasters rarely, if at all, present their forecasts with such caveats; they only use them *ex post* to justify why they got it all wrong. If there is an element of correctness in the forecasts, it is sheer brilliance, but when they get it horrendously wrong, they pick and choose from a menu of excuses.

Meng (2019) suggests that the global financial crisis destroyed the illusion of econometricians that their models can be used to predict the future. Econometricians, he argues, are unwilling to admit the failure of their statistical tests and econometric models; instead, they come up with an amazing explanation: 'the underlying distribution of the shock changed during a recession'. This explanation is tantamount to admission that even a correct econometric model with robust statistical tests cannot be used to predict the future. He observes the claim made by those practising 'fortune-teller style of forecasting' that it is hard to forecast a rare event like the global financial crisis (GFC), because these rare events are not in the data, and suggests that 'the purpose of forecasting is to prevent or to be prepared for a disastrous rare event'. Econometric forecasting is useless because some people, with minimal or no knowledge of econometrics, predicted the crisis and made money on the basis of their predictions. They did that without using autoregressive conditional heteroscedasticity (ARCH), generalized autoregressive conditional heteroscedasticity (GARCH) or XYZ-ARCH (I made up the last one but I would not be surprised if it turns out to be real, one of the 50+ disciples of the original ARCH).

I must at this stage tell this story about the time I spent with a major econometric forecasting firm to be trained on exchange rate forecasting. That was in the 1980s when I was a young professional economist and a forecasting enthusiast. The economists working for that firm generated forecasts from a sophisticated econometric model estimated by full information maximum likelihood. The output distributed to subscribers, including the investment bank I worked for at that time, was a set of monthly forecasts for the following three years of the exchange rates of the dollar against major currencies. It took me time to realize that forecasting ten exchange rates at the end of each of the coming 36 months is a formidable task, even for a model involving partial differential equations. Even the forecasters themselves realized that, but they had a job to do and subscribers to please. They would generate the forecasts and look at them only to realize that they did not make sense (for example, forecasting the dollar to depreciate when it was in a bubble in the 1980s). They would then change the forecasts manually by putting in values that made sense and seemed plausible. While this may be called 'judgemental forecasting', I wondered then what was the point of using the model to start with. Those forecasts were simply useless at best and hazardous to use at worst. I benefited much more from a qualitative narrative about where exchange rates are likely to go, written by a brilliant economist who did not do econometrics.

The fact of the matter is that econometric forecasting is not really forecasting. In-sample forecasting is simply a curve-fitting exercise. Out-of-sample *ex post* forecasting cannot be used for decision-making but it is good for writing academic papers, perhaps to confirm the Meese–Rogoff puzzle. Forecasts are generated out-of-sample by using the actual realized values of the explanatory variables, yet these forecasts turn out to be dreadful. *Ex ante* forecasting, which is useful for decision-making, must involve the forecasting of the explanatory variables to be able to forecast the dependent variable, which augments the forecasting error. This is why simple trend extrapolation produces less bad forecasts than those produced by 'structural' econometric models with all of the trimmings.

5.2   COINTEGRATION AS A TEST FOR SPURIOUS CORRELATION

Burns (1997) defines a spurious relation as a 'situation in which measures of two or more variables are statistically related but are not in fact causally linked'. Hence a spurious relation, which is 'generally unnoticed', is meaningless, although this is 'not widely recognized by most people' and it is a 'common and serious interpretation fallacy'. Spurious relations are false indicators of causality, typically arising when an extraneous variable that affects two other variables is omitted (time can be such an extraneous variable). Yule (1926) referred to 'nonsense correlations', which undermine the 'serious arguments that are sometimes put forward on the basis of correlations between time-series'. Granger and Newbold (1974) used the term 'spurious regression' to describe the same phenomenon.

One of the proclaimed contributions of the so-called 'cointegration revolution', in which I believed firmly at one time, is that cointegration testing can be used to reveal spurious correlation: that is, cointegration allows us to distinguish between spurious relations and genuine ones. This is a myth, because only common sense tells us whether an observed relation is genuine or spurious. Common sense tells us not to accept as logical such spurious relations as the following, even though correlation is very high: (1) iPhones lead to more people killed by falling downstairs; (2) the consumption of ice cream leads to murder; (3) a pirate shortage caused global warming; (4) eating organic food causes autism; and (5) obesity caused the debt bubble. Meng (2019) refers to the impossibility of overcoming spurious regression within a statistical framework because statistical theory says nothing about whether or not correlation in a particular case makes sense. He argues correctly that 'there is no need, and no means, to test a spurious correlation in the statistic framework'.

Spurious correlation is believed to have been a reason for the development of cointegration analysis. The underlying proposition is that if two integrated variables are highly correlated, this correlation is spurious unless the two variables are cointegrated. However, one would tend to think that the only way to distinguish between a spurious relation and a genuine one is to use common sense, intuition and theory, rather than by looking at a test statistic (such as the Dickey–Fuller statistic). Kennedy (2002) presents ten rules (or commandments, as he calls them) that, if followed, lead to sound empirical work. The first of these rules is to use common sense and economic theory, arguing (as Voltaire did in 1764) that 'common sense is not all that common'. Likewise, Preece (1987) notes that 'the procedures of good statistical practice are founded on experience and common sense', suggesting that 'it is good practice to stop and think before running a regression'.

If common sense tells us that a relation between two variables is obviously spurious but the two variables turn out to be cointegrated, do we believe common sense or econometrics? If cointegration testing is as good in detecting spurious correlation as it is portrayed to be, it should be consistent with common sense. For example, spurious correlation is observed between the number of PhDs in mathematics awarded by US universities and the number of suicides by hanging, strangulation and suffocation. If the results of cointegration testing are to be trusted, these two variables must not be cointegrated. If the results confirm cointegration, it is either that the particular cointegration test is wrong, in which case it should be abandoned, or that the very idea of using cointegration to detect spurious correlation is bizarre. It follows that if cointegration can reveal spurious correlation, then there must be some highly correlated variables that are not cointegrated and others that are not highly correlated but cointegrated. If that was not the case, no value added would be provided by cointegration over correlation, in which case cointegration is no more than glorified correlation.

The ability of cointegration to reveal spurious relations seems to be accepted without scrutiny. For example, Stroe-Kunold and Werner (2009) suggest that 'cointegration tests are instruments to detect spurious correlations between integrated time series'. They demonstrate that the Dickey–Fuller and Johansen tests provide a 'much more accurate alternative for the identification of spurious relations compared to the rather imprecise method of utilizing the R^2 and DW [Durbin–Watson] statistics'. They go further to argue that cointegration provides 'precise methods of distinguishing between spurious and meaningful relations even if the dependency between the processes [that is, correlation] is very low'. It is ludicrous to use the adjectives 'accurate' and 'precise' to describe the Johansen test: this is a travesty.

Lin and Brannigan (2003) suggest that 'cointegration models can be regarded as remedies to the problems of "spurious regression" arising from nonstationary time series'. Granger (1986) considered cointegration as a 'pre-test to avoid spurious regression'. Stroe-Kunold and Werner (2009) go as far as arguing that spurious regression and cointegration are opposite concepts, as cointegration implies a meaningful relation between integrated time series. This belief, which is based on flawed reasoning, is sustained by massive groupthink.

One of the few economists who challenged the cointegration orthodoxy is Guisan (2001), as she argues that 'cointegration tests fail very often to recognize causal relations and, on the other hand, that approach does not always avoid the peril of accepting as causal relations those that really are spurious'. She demonstrates the inadequacy and limitations of cointegration by examining the relation between private consumption expenditure and gross domestic product in 25 Organisation for Economic Co-operation and Development (OECD) countries over the period 1961–97. Her results confirm the limitations of cointegration tests, showing that United

Kingdom (UK) consumption is not related to its GDP, but rather to the GDPs of 23 other OECD countries. Cointegration, therefore, can lead to a rejection of genuine relations and the acceptance of spurious ones.

In a paper entitled 'Blaming Suicide on NASA and Divorce on Margarine: The Hazard of Using Cointegration to Derive Inference on Spurious Correlation', Moosa (2017b) demonstrates that highly correlated series appear as cointegrated, even though common sense tells us that the underlying relation does not make sense. Empirical testing based on simulated data, data from daily life and historical data on interest rates shows that cointegration may fail not only to detect spurious correlation but also to capture cointegration in a genuine relation.

For example, it is suggested that if cointegration, as it is claimed, is a reliable test for spurious correlation, then a finding of cointegration tells us the following: (1) margarine is bad for marital life; (2) ski resorts must design their beds in such a way as to make it easier for guests to die by becoming entangled in bed sheets, because that will boost their revenue; (3) to boost revenue, arcades must campaign so that Australia does not reduce the price of uranium exported to the US; (4) motorcycle riders must, for their own safety, refrain from eating sour cream and encourage other people to do so; (5) to reduce suicide, US universities must encourage graduate students studying for a PhD in mathematics to convert to marketing or something else; and (6) another way to reduce suicide is for the US government to close down the National Aeronautics and Space Administration (NASA). On the other hand, it is demonstrated that cointegration may not pick up a genuine relation as implied by theory. For example, one would expect, based on theories of the term structure of interest rates, to find that the Treasury bill rate is cointegrated with the Treasury bond yield, but the bounds test shows otherwise.

In days gone by, students were told that a cointegrating relation must make sense in terms of economic theory. But no more, as econometrics, which is supposed to be the means to an end, has become the end itself. These days we are supposed to believe that margarine is good for marital life because a cointegration test says so; at least, we can call it a puzzle. However, it is wise to trust common sense and economics rather than econometrics when it comes to distinguishing between spurious relations and genuine ones.

5.3 DERIVING MEANINGFUL INFERENCE FROM MULTIPLE REGRESSION

Imagine a physicist wanting to test Boyle's law of the relation between the volume of gas and the pressure exerted on it. This physicist does not run a multiple regression equation relating volume to pressure while controlling for other factors that affect volume, such as temperature, by including control variables. In physics, controlling for the effects of the other factors is not part of the statistical analysis but part of the experiment. The experiment is conducted in a laboratory, where temperature is kept constant, by increasing pressure and recording volume at each level of pressure. This physicist will end up with a sample of data containing observations on volume and pressure.

The statistical analysis starts with a scatter plot of volume as a function of pressure to determine the shape of the functional relation, which can then be estimated by ordinary least squares (OLS). The physicist will get a perfect fit without having to test for serial correlation, functional form, heteroscedasticity, normality and ARCH effect. The physicist, unlike an economist, does not have to worry about choosing an appropriate estimation method from a diversified menu, including (among others) maximum likelihood, instrumental variables, jackknife instrumental variables, Bayesian estimation of dynamic discrete models, superparametric estimation of bivariate Tobit models, quantile regression, non-parametric instrumental regression, and local generalized method of moments (GMM). And the physicist does not have to worry about how to define and measure his variables, volume (in litres) and pressure (in atm).

Compare the physicists with an economist trying to test the catch-up hypothesis, that poor countries tend to grow faster than rich countries; or the effect of government size on growth. These two relations are tested by estimating regression equations in which the economic growth rate (r) is a function of per capita income (y) for the first hypothesis and a function of government expenditure as a percentage of GDP (g) for the second hypothesis. Since growth is affected by numerous other factors (some 65 of them), these variables must be controlled for. Thus the economist must estimate functional relations of the form $r = f(y, x_1, x_2, \ldots x_n)$ or $r = f(g, x_1, x_2, \ldots x_n)$. The economist will then face the formidable task of determining the control variables to be included as $x_1, x_2, \cdots x_n$, how they should be measured, and the form of the functional relation (for example, linear versus non-linear). The results will depend on these choices, and this is why empirical studies invariably produce a mixed bag of results. Klees (2016), who describes the use of multiple regression for empirical testing as 'empirical fishing expeditions', describes the situation as follows:

> The conditions necessary for regression analysis to yield valid causal inferences are so far from ever being met or approximated that such inferences are never valid. Despite being common, in many fields such empirical fishing expeditions

are frowned upon because the result of particular interest (the coefficient on the key independent variable under examination) will depend on which covariates are selected as 'controls'.

Klees identifies the components of the formidable task facing the economist, or what he calls 'three necessary conditions for the proper specification of a causal model' as: (1) including all relevant variables in the model; (2) measuring all variables properly; and (3) choosing the correct functional form. Young and Holsteen (2017) make the same point by suggesting that theory rarely says which variables should be in the model, how to define the variables and what the functional form should be. As a result, they argue, 'theory can be tested in many different ways and modest differences in methods may have large influence on the results'.

As far as the first task is concerned, Klees believes that 'all relevant variables that may affect the dependent variable can never be included'. Likewise, Meng (2019) refers to 'an unknown number of relevant factors', some of which may be unknown, making it impossible for the economist to claim that all important variables are included in the model. He adds that 'an unknown number of known and unknown variables' may be relevant, but it is impossible to obtain a complete list of significant variables, which means that the omission of significant variables is a most likely outcome. In practice, he argues, 'neither econometric testing, or economic theory, or common sense is able to select all significant variables', which makes the task of including all relevant variables valid in theory but impossible to put into practice. Klees (2016) suggests that 'with just one omitted variable, all regression coefficients may be biased to an unknown extent and in an unknown direction'.

While the physicist controls the effects of other variables in the experiment itself, the economist does that in the regression equation, which is rather dubious. Meng (2019) suggests that the inclusion of control variables in the regression equation does not exclude the impact of these variables in the same way as do the controlled conditions in scientific experiments; otherwise, 'scientists working in their laboratories should give up scientific experiments and join the econometricians to conduct controlled modelling at a much lower cost'. Likewise, Young and Holsteen (2017) are sceptical about the use of control variables because they are a 'common source of uncertainty and ambivalence'. When the 'true model' is unknown, which is invariably the case, 'control variables can have unpredictable consequences'. A misspecified model with ten control variables is not superior to or less biased than a misspecified model with only five of them. Extra controls can leverage correlations with other omitted variables, amplifying omitted variable bias (Clarke, 2005).

The measurement problem has two effects: (1) errors of measurement produce biased results; and (2) the availability of more than one definition, measure or proxy make the results sensitive to the choice of the definition. As far as the first problem is concerned, economic variables invariably contain measurement errors, and this is why statistical agencies keep revising their estimates of growth, inflation, and so on. Meng (2019) refers to the 'dubious status of economic data', which makes it necessary 'to improve the data quality in order to make any economic study reliable'. Econometricians use econometric procedures to deal with faulty data, which Meng dismisses as 'effort in vain' because 'these procedures do not address the sources of errors in measurement'. He argues that econometric techniques 'introduce additional measurement errors and/or magnify the existing errors and thus worsen the quality of the data'. As for the second problem, the results vary, depending on which measure is used for the dependent and explanatory variables. For example, Moosa (2017a) examines the determinants of capital structure, defining the leverage ratio in six different ways. He shows that only when the first and third definitions of leverage are used do we find significantly positive correlation between the leverage ratio and growth opportunities and significantly negative correlation with profitability.

As far as functional form is concerned, the process typically involves the use of log-transformation. For example, studies of the environmental Kuznets curve use various model specifications, including the quadratic specification, $y = a + bx + cx^2$, the cubic specification, $y = a + bx + cx^2 + dx^3$, the quadratic log specification, $log(y) = a + b\ log(x) + c[log(x)]^2$, the cubic log specification, $log(y) = a + b\ log(x) + c[log(x)]^2 + d[log(x)]^3$, and so on (see, for example, Moosa, 2017d). The functional form may be any one of these with another five or so control variables. Studies in corporate finance in particular use a functional form where one or more explanatory variables are measured in logs without saying why, such that the functional relation appears like $y = f[x_1, x_2, log(x_3), x_4, log(x_6), \cdots]$. Interestingly, the variables to which the log transformation is applied typically have large values (when measured in dollars rather than millions of dollars): examples are sales, GDP and assets. In effect, the log transformation is used as a scaling factor when scaling can be done by making the unit of measurement million or billion dollars or by converting the variables into indices. Economists using the log transformation in this way do not seem to realize that the log transformation introduces non-linearity of a specific kind. In the environmental Kuznets curve, using a polynomial of $log(x)$ means the introduction of double non-linearity, which is rather awkward and unjustifiable.

Meng (2019) highlights the apparent failure of economists to understand that 'there is only one true mechanism for one reality which their models have failed to uncover'. Instead, he argues, 'they continue to harbour their statistical illusions and explain vaguely that the shift of underlying distribution of shocks causes the breakdown of their model during a recession'. Young and Holsteen (2017) make the same point by noting that 'the true causal model is assumed to be known and only one model is ever applied to a sample of data'. In common practice, they argue, 'the true model is not known and there are many possible variants on one's core analytic strategy'. Meng (2019) refers to Donohue and Levitt (2001) who found that abortion in the 1970s, explains as much as 50 per cent of the decline in crime in the 1990s, using the reasoning that abortion reduces the number of unwanted children who are at the risk of committing crimes when they grow up. Foote and Goetz (2008) and Joyce (2009) argue that it is inappropriate that Donohue and Levitt regressed the log of crime counts on the log of abortion rates. When the log of crime rate is regressed on the log of abortion rate, they found that the results changed greatly. Of course, none of them says why they use the log-log functional form without theoretical justification.

Klees (2016) suggests that proper model specification requires a 'very well elaborated theory that allows one to fulfill these [three] conditions', which is problematical for regression analysis because of the absence of 'sufficiently complete theories' that allow the specification of proper causal models. Typically, a regression equation containing *n* explanatory variables is a representation of several theories or hypotheses. Even worse, sometimes a specification is suggested by lumping together in one equation the variables recognized in the literature as being important. This is how the presidential puzzle arose (Chapter 4). Klees concludes that the empirical literature is effectively 'discussions about the degree of misspecification and its consequences'. He sums up the miserable state of affairs as follows:

> More to the point, we are never talking about the simple case of a single omitted variable. We are faced with multiple failures of all three assumptions: many variables are always omitted[;] we have little idea of how to best measure the variables we are able to include; and we have hardly any idea of their functional form.

He goes on to say:

> The result of this state of affairs is endless misspecification – by necessity. Each researcher has an almost infinite array of choices in how they specify the earnings function they estimate. Each regression study is never a replication but always different from others in many respects. The upshot is each regression study is idiosyncratic. Since it is relatively easy to get significant coefficients,

especially with large data sets, everyone finds their particular variable of interest to be significant. When there is controversy, everyone finds empirical evidence to support their side of the debate.

To support the proposition that anyone can produce evidence for a controversial view, consider two studies of the impact of socio-economic policies as highlighted by Goertzel (2002). Using US data, the results of multiple regression analysis tell us that: (1) every time a prisoner is executed, eight future murders are deterred; and (2) a 1 per cent increase in a state's citizens carrying concealed guns causes a 3.3 per cent decline in the murder rate. These counterintuitive results are designed to please the proponents of capital punishment and the gun lobby. The fact of the matter is that out of every nine executed prisoners, one turns out to be innocent (the ultimate form of miscarriage of justice), and that more guns lead to more crime by making killing easier and more efficient (ask the survivors of mass shootings). Even more bizarre is the finding of Beard et al. (2011) that reducing the total budget of all US federal regulatory agencies by 5 per cent produces 1.2 million more private sector jobs each year. They also predict that firing one regulatory agency staff member creates 98 jobs in the private sector. These results sound ridiculous and look too precise to be true; most likely the product of extensive data mining motivated by an ideological anti-regulation stance. Naturally, Beard et al. do not tell us anything about the mechanism whereby the firing of a regulator boosts demand for burger flippers. What matters for them are the numbers coming out of a computer, particularly if those numbers support prior beliefs.

The availability of 'infinite array of choices', which makes it possible to obtain desirable results, arises from the possibility of mixing and matching a set of explanatory variables measured in various ways with all possible functional forms. It is convenient to overlook the warning of Heckman (2005) that empirical findings are a joint product of both the data and the model, and that of Ho et al. (2007) that data do not 'speak', because different methods and models applied to the same set of data often allow different conclusions. Hence, Ho et al. suggest that choosing which model to report in a paper is difficult, fraught with ethical and methodological dilemmas, and not covered in any serious way in classical statistical texts. Combined with ideology, prior beliefs or motives, any result can be obtained: hence more guns lead to less crime, executions reduce crime, slavery is justifiable, greed and corruption are good for business, firing regulators is conducive to growth, and so on.

The results obtained from multiple regression analysis are useless at best and dangerous at worst. Consider the functional relations $y = f(x_1)$

and $y = f(x_1, x_2, \cdots x_n)$. In the first one, the coefficient on x_1 is a measure of the response of y to changes in x_1 when all other variables that affect y change at the same time. In the second one, the coefficient on x_1 is a measure of the response of y to changes in x_1 when all other variables that affect y are held constant. In an economy, other variables cannot be held constant, in which case measuring the response of y to changes in x_1 under an unrealistic assumption does not make sense. It is more realistic to use a regression with one explanatory variable to measure the response of y to x_1 when everything else changes, which is what happens in reality. If a stable relation is found between y and x_1, it can be used for policy analysis and other purposes; this is the essence of the Phillips curve and Okun's law. If not, the alternative is not to use multiple regression, because the results tell us either nothing or what the audience want to hear. It is a myth that multiple regression provides useful results.

5.4 ECONOMETRICS AS A SCIENCE

One of the myths of econometrics is that it is a science or that it is as 'sciency' as physics. This myth is one reason why puzzles arise in economics: when the results of empirical testing fail to support a theory, this is considered a puzzle because of firm belief in the theory and uncompromised confidence that econometric testing reveals the truth. After all, deriving inference from a regression equation is as valid as deriving inference from a laboratory experiment. This is because econometrics is a science, or so we are told by the true believers.

Econometrics, we are told, provides as a quantitatively rigorous treatment of economic issues as physics provides in dealing with natural phenomena. If this is the case, then econometrics must be a science that is no different from physics. Econometrics is allegedly a science because, as the name implies, it is about measurement. Scientists measure with precision the speed of light, the speed of sound, acceleration under gravity and the thrust of a jet engine. Econometricians, on the other hand, measure (imprecisely, to say the least) the response of unemployment to changes in economic growth, and some bizarre items such as the rise in productivity as a result of the closure of a regulatory agency, or the drop in the number of murders as a result of gun ownership. Ehrbar (2000) contends that 'one cannot expect econometrics to automatically become a science just because it deals with data' and that 'such an expectation commits the ontic fallacy, i.e., it assumes that the ontological makeup of the world necessarily generates correct scientific methods'.

A number of distinguished economists are sceptical about power of econometrics to yield sharp predictions. In his presidential address to the American Economic Association, Wassily Leontief (1971) characterized econometric work as follows:

> An attempt to compensate for the glaring weakness of the data base available to us by the widest possible use of more and more sophisticated techniques. Alongside the mounting pile of elaborate theoretical models we see a fast growing stock of equally intricate statistical tools. These are intended to stretch to the limit the meagre supply of facts.

Expressing ideas in exact mathematical form is a strict requirement of science. Tinbergen (1951) described econometrics as a 'name for a field of science in which mathematical-economic and mathematical-statistical research are applied in combination'. He went on to say the following:

> Econometrics forms a borderland between two branches of science, with the advantages and disadvantages thereof; advantages, because new combinations are introduced which often open up new perspectives; disadvantages, because the work in this field requires skill in two domains, which either takes up too much time or leads to insufficient training of its students in one of the two respects.

However, Mitchell (1937) suggested that 'there is slight prospect that quantitative analysis will ever be able to solve the problems that qualitative analysis has framed, in their present form'. Econometrics, it seems, was created by the desire to make economics as scientific as physics, which is neither necessary nor realistic. The problem is that while there are laws in physics, there are no laws in economics; at best, econometrics provides empirical regularities or stylized facts.

The claim that econometric work constitutes scientific endeavour follows from the writing of economic theories in mathematical form and subsequently estimating and testing them by using statistical methods, which sounds like the representation and testing of Boyle's law. A theory is rejected if a model estimated from observed data is found to be incompatible with the predictions of the theory, and vice versa. This is indeed a scientific procedure, but its application in econometrics is not straightforward. It is typically the case that insufficient or poor-quality data are available, which means that the theory cannot be tested in the first place or that testing gives flawed results which have little or no value. Testing may not be possible because of the problem of multicollinearity, which is dealt with by using principal component analysis. This procedure, however, amounts to testing by using artificially generated data, which even some econometricians do not agree with (for example, Pagan, 1984). Then a large number of problems are encountered, including specification errors and measurement errors as well as the problems of identification and aggregation. More importantly, however, testing an economic theory can produce any set of results; hence the expression 'mixed bag', which cannot be found in science.

Even representation is different in econometrics from what it is in science. For example, while Boyle's law is written as an exact relation between the volume of gas and the pressure exerted on it, Okun's law is written as a stochastic equation with an error term. Econometrics is primarily concerned with the properties and behaviour of the error term in a regression equation, and this is why econometricians are generous in providing a menu of estimation methods. In science, the error term is not encountered and simple curve fitting by OLS is adequate. The problem of multicollinearity does not arise in science as a two-variable relation (for example, the volume of gas and the pressure exerted on it) can be isolated from the effects of other variables (for example, temperature). This is a better solution for multicollinearity than what is provided by econometricians.

In view of the remarks made so far, Falk (1995) concludes that 'econometrics has not contributed to the scientific status of economics'. While scientists do not claim to be able to test all their theories empirically, they are generally able to acquire more consistent and accurate results than those acquired from the work of econometricians. Economics is a social science where the behaviour of decision-makers is governed not only by economic considerations but also by social and psychological factors, which are not amenable to econometric testing. This is why no economic theory holds everywhere all the time. And this is why the results of empirical testing of economic theories can be a mixed bag. And this is why econometricians use time-varying parametric estimation to account for changes in the values of estimated parameters over time. And this is why so many estimation methods can be used to produce the desired results. In physics, on the other hand, a body falling under the force of gravity accelerates at the rate of 32 feet per second per second; this is true anywhere, at any time. In physics too, the boiling point of water under any level of atmospheric pressure can be predicted with accuracy.

Unlike physicists, economists are blessed with econometrics, which puts them in a position to obtain the results they want and aspire for, armed with the arsenal of tools produced by econometric theory. When an economist fails to obtain the desired results, they may try different functional forms, lag structures and estimation methods, and indulge in data mining until the desired results are obtained. Mukherjee et al. (1998) describe data mining as 'the greatest sin any researcher could commit'. If the empirical work is conducted for the purpose of writing an academic paper, the researcher will seek results that are 'interesting' enough to warrant publication, or results that confirm the view of the orthodoxy or the findings of a potential referee. And it is typically the case that the results cannot be replicated. Physicists do not have this luxury: it is unthinkable and easily verifiable that a physicist manipulates data (by using principal components or various transformations) to obtain readings that refute Boyle's law. Economists study the behaviour of consumers, firms and governments where expectations, uncertainties and emotions play key roles in the translation of economic theory into real-world economics. These uncertainties mean that econometric modelling cannot produce accurate representation of the working of the economy.

An econometrics enthusiast, Kearns (1995), goes on the defensive and disagrees with the propositions put forward by Falk (1995). He starts by defining science as 'any mode of investigation by which impartial and systematic knowledge is acquired'. This definition is adequate for rejecting the proposition that empirical work in economics is a scientific endeavour because the knowledge acquired from empirical results is neither impartial nor systematic (let alone being useful). In science, the motivation is a quest for the truth; but in econometrics, the motivation is to prove a prior belief, which means that any evidence that does not support the prior belief will be hidden away or declared as a puzzle.

Two of the characteristics of a scientific discipline are identified by von Mises (1978) and Schumpeter (1978). For von Mises, a scientific method requires the verification of a proposition by numerous sets of data pertaining to sufficiently comparable situations. For Schumpeter (1978) correct prediction is the best or only test of whether a science has achieved its purposes, which means that correct prediction, within the bounds of what one can reasonably expect of an uncertain future, is a requisite for scientific status. Kearns (1995) argues that the two characteristics of a scientific discipline noted by von Mises and Schumpeter are found in econometrics. Well, they are not. While it is possible that a proposition can be verified, the same proposition can be rejected by using a different set of data, econometric technique or model specification. I have yet to see a hypothesis in economics or finance that has been supported or rejected universally. As for forecasting, a look at the literature on exchange rate economics gives us an idea of how bad econometric forecasting is. We can predict precisely when a falling object will hit the ground and where a projectile will land, but we cannot predict with a reasonable level of confidence whether a currency will appreciate or depreciate on the announcement of unemployment data; that is, we cannot even predict the direction, let alone the magnitude, of change.

An argument that can be put forward in favour of the proposition that econometric work represents a scientific endeavour is based on the desirable properties of econometric models as identified by Koutsoyiannis (1977). The desirable properties are: (1) theoretical plausibility, in the sense that the model must describe adequately the underlying economic phenomena; (2) explanatory ability, in the sense that the model should be able to explain the observations of the real world; (3) accuracy of the estimates of the model parameters, which should converge as far as possible on the true parameters of the model (that is, they should be efficient, consistent and unbiased); (4) forecasting ability, as the model should provide satisfactory predictions of future values of the dependent variable; and (5) simplicity, as the model should represent economic relations with maximum simplicity. I doubt very much whether anyone is capable of coming up with such an econometric model, at a time when all of these desirable properties are met by the models describing the laws of physics.

Unlike the models of science, econometric models typically fail to explain what happens in the real world, let alone predict what may or can happen. Blommestein (2009) refers to the 'common situation where the empirical results of different studies of a similar topic have often a very wide range of outcomes and values for structural parameters' (and without a convincing or clear explanation of why this is the case), arguing that 'such a situation would be unthinkable and unacceptable in the physical sciences'. If a physicist obtained different outcomes when addressing a similar problem, this would be a key reason for an urgent scientific debate until the discrepancy in results had been resolved. Unlike scientists, Blommestein argues, 'economists are prone to an attitude where they stick to their favourite theories and models come hell or high water and where no mountain of evidence can move them'. It seems, however, that Ritholtz (2009) emphasizes this point by arguing that 'economics has had a justifiable inferiority complex versus real sciences the past century'.

Econometrics is not a science because economics is not a science, at least not in the same sense as physics is a science. The science-like quantification of economics has created barriers to entry into the economics profession, impeded endeavours to integrate economics with other social sciences and learn from them, forced some good non-quantitative economists to leave the profession, led to a brain drain by attracting people from science and engineering, and encouraged 'scientific economists' to follow empirical results blindly, sometime with serious adverse consequences. Yet, the excessive 'scientification' of economics has not contributed anything to our knowledge of the economy and financial markets. It is a myth that econometrics (or economics) is a science.

5.5   CAUSALITY IN ECONOMICS

Causality, as defined by Hicks (1980), is the relation between cause and effect. As in any other field, the concept of causality is as important in economics as it is in other fields. The full title of Adam Smith's (1776) great foundational work, *An Inquiry into the Nature and Causes of the Wealth of Nations*, illustrates the centrality of causality to economics. The concept is evident in the works of David Hume (1739, 1742, 1777) and John Stuart Mill (1848), both offering important contributions and philosophical discussions. Causality is central to economics because it is concerned with the making of decisions and the consequences that follow from the decisions.

Hicks (1980) argues that the concept of causality is common to economics and history. Historians study the past to find out not only what happened, but also why it happened: this is causality. If historians find that A caused B, A is likely to be a decision that someone made, whereas B is the consequences of the decision. Hicks points out that one cause may have many effects and that one effect may have many causes. This is why he thinks that the statement that A caused B is 'to some extent ambiguous' because it may mean that A was one of the causes of B ('weak' causation) or that A was the sole cause of B ('strong' causation).

The myth is not about the use of the concept of causality in economics, but that causality can be detected by using econometric methods, which was pioneered by Clive Granger (1969). Hoover (2006) suggests that Granger causality is 'an inferential approach, in that it is databased without direct reference to background economic theory' and that 'it is a process approach, in that it was developed to apply to dynamic time-series models'. Detecting causality by using a regression equation is not the same as detecting causality from a laboratory experiment. The causal link between pressure and the volume of gas can be detected from a laboratory experiment, which is also true for detecting the causal link between atmospheric pressure and the boiling point of water. No one can dispute the proposition that force causes motion: pushing a trolley makes it move forwards; pulling the trolley makes it move backwards. However, it would take suspension of common sense, reason and disbelief to accept the proposition that more guns cause crime to fall, just because a regression equation says so.

Morck and Yeung (2011) try to reconcile causality in economics and history by suggesting that in economics, causality is detected by using instrumental variables; while in history it is detected by 'weighing the plausibility of alternative narratives'. However, they point out that instrumental variables can lose value with repeated use because of what they call 'an econometric tragedy of the commons': that is, each successful use of an instrument creates an additional latent variable problem for all other uses of that instrument. Hence, they make the recommendation that economists should 'consider historians' approach to inferring causality from detailed context, the plausibility of alternative narratives and external consistency'. On the other hand, Meng (2019) does not compromise in his criticism of causality in economics, arguing effectively that Granger's causality is temporal ordering. This is because the logic behind the Granger causality test is that if an earlier change in time series A is correlated (positively or negatively) with a subsequent change in time series B, A must cause B. It is a necessary but not a sufficient condition that a cause must occur earlier than the consequence, but economists seem to believe that temporal order-ing is both a necessary and a sufficient condition for causality.

Heckman (2000) reviews causality and policy analysis in economics and concludes that 'the information in any body of data is usually too weak to eliminate competing causal explanations of the same phenomenon'. Meng (2019) makes a very good point: Granger himself differentiated Granger causality from causality, in the sense that 'A Granger causes B' does not mean that 'A causes B'. One can only wonder that, if Granger causality is not causality, the Granger causality test has no ability to solve the spurious regression issue, thus the test itself is pointless. And if Granger causality is not causality, why is it called 'causality' and used as such to derive causal inference from useless results?

Here I am going to demonstrate the might of the Australian economy, which apparently determines what happens in Japan, the UK and the US. Five variables are examined: the bilateral exchange rate against the US dollar, industrial production, interest rate, consumer prices and the money supply. This exercise is based on quarterly data covering the period 1992:2 to 2017:2 (obtained from *International Financial Statistics*).

By testing for causality from the Australian variables to the variables of other countries, we find significant effects, as shown in Table 5.1. The economies of Japan, the UK and US seem to be at the mercy of Australian policy-makers and what happens in the Australian economy. The Australian exchange rate 'causes' industrial production in Japan and the US. The Australian interest rate 'causes' Japanese industrial produc-tion and consumer prices. Australian monetary policy is so important for the rest of the world that the Australian money supply 'causes' Japanese industrial production and consumer prices as well as UK consumer prices, US money supply and US consumer prices. What happens to the Australian consumer price index is vital for the rest of the world because it 'causes' Japanese industrial production and consumer prices in Japan, the UK and US. You do not need to be an economist to realize that this

Table 5.1   Results of causality testing

From	To	$\chi^2(2)$*	F(2, 159)*
Australian exchange rate	Japanese industrial production	15.37	8.22
Australian exchange rate	US industrial production	7.49	3.81
Australian interest rate	Japanese industrial production	7.01	3.55
Australian interest rate	Japanese consumer prices	9.16	4.70
Australian money supply	Japanese industrial production	13.85	7.33
Australian money supply	Japanese consumer prices	27.87	16.28
Australian money supply	UK consumer prices	22.06	12.36
Australian money supply	US money supply	7.08	3.58
Australian money supply	US consumer prices	19.61	10.80
Australian consumer prices	Japanese industrial production	6.74	3.41
Australian consumer prices	Japanese consumer prices	11.99	6.27
Australian consumer prices	UK consumer prices	14.73	7.84
Australian consumer prices	US consumer prices	13.67	7.23

Note: The 5% critical values of $\chi^2(2)$ and F(2, 159) are 5.99 and 3.05, respectively.

is utter nonsense, which is typically what we get by believing the results of causality testing. This is not causality, it is mumbo jumbo.

5.6   OTHER MYTHS IN ECONOMETRICS

So far in this chapter five myths of econometrics have been discussed. But there is more where these came from. This section deals briefly with two more myths, presenting them as concluding remarks. These are the myth of the success of econometrics, and the myth that econometrics is (or still is) about measurement in economics. We start with a discussion of the alleged success of econometrics.

Econometricians typically hail the evolution of econometrics as a 'big success'. For example, Geweke et al. (2006) argue that 'econometrics has come a long way over a relatively short period'. As indicators of the success of econometrics, they list the following: (1) applications of econometric methods can be found in almost every field of economics; (2) econometric models have been used extensively by government agencies, international organizations and commercial enterprises; (3) macroeconometric models of differing complexity and size have been constructed for almost every country in the world; and (4) both in theory and in practice, econometrics has already gone well beyond what its founders envisaged. Other measures of the success of econometrics include the observation that there is now scarcely a field of applied economics into which mathematical and statistical theory has not penetrated, including economic history. Pagan (1987) declares econometrics as an 'outstanding success' because the work of econometric theorists has become 'part of the process of economic investigation and the training of economists'. Yet another indicator of the success of econometrics is the observation of excess demand for well-trained econometricians.

These claims represent no more than self-glorifying rhetoric. The widespread use of econometrics is not indicative of success, just as the widespread use of drugs does not represent social success. Application of econometric methods in almost every field of economics is not the same as saying that econometrics has enhanced our understanding of the underlying issues in every field of economics. The use of econometric models by government agencies has not led to improvement in policy-making, as we move from one crisis to another. Constructing models for almost every country in the world has not helped to alleviate poverty or solve recurring economic problems. The observations that econometric theory has become part of the training of economists, and of excess demand for well-trained econometricians, are far from being measures of success. The alleged success of econometrics has led to the production of economics graduates who may be good at number-crunching but do not know much about various economic problems faced by humanity. It has been a setback for economics that econometrics has gone beyond what its founders envisaged, perhaps because the founders were wise enough to realize that econometrics should not go too far.

As for the myth that econometrics is about measurement: well, perhaps in days gone by, but no longer. These days the word 'econometrics' is stretched to cover mathematical economics, and the word 'econometrician' refers to an economist, or otherwise, who is skilled and interested in the application of mathematics, be it mathematical statistics, game theory, topology or measure theory. Baltagi (2002) argues that research in economics and econometrics has been growing more and more abstract and highly mathematical without an application in sight or a motivation for practical use. Heckman (2001) suggests that econometrics is useful only if it helps economists to conduct and interpret empirical research on economic data. Like Baltagi, Heckman warns that the gap between econometric theory and empirical practice has grown over the past two decades. This is why a joke goes as follows: during the rule of Nicolai Ceausescu in Romania, the government banned all 'Western' economics journals; the exception was *Econometrica* because it had nothing to do with economics.

As a concluding note, I refer to the work of McAleer et al. (1985), who start their paper by telling a story about a new typist for Carl Christ (a famous econometrician). He gave her something to type, in which the word 'econometrics' appeared repeatedly. Not knowing what econometrics was, she typed the word as 'economic tricks'. For the sceptics, the typist must have been observant and foresighted.

6. The myths of laissez-faire

6.1 INTRODUCTION

In this chapter, three myths are examined, all of which pertain to the concept of laissez-faire, a French term that means 'leave us [the oligarchs] alone'; that is, the oligarchs telling the government not to interfere with their striving to accumulate wealth, for which they have an insatiable appetite. The term can be traced back to an answer that Jean-Baptiste Colbert, comptroller general of finance under King Louis XIV, received when he asked the oligarchs what the government could do to help them. The doctrine of laissez-faire is associated with the economists known as Physiocrats, who flourished in France during the period 1756–78. In 1776 Adam Smith published his influential work, *The Wealth of Nations*, in which he advocated the doctrine of laissez-faire.

As the industrial revolution gained momentum in the 19th century, the doctrine of laissez-faire became increasingly popular, justified in terms of the principles of classical economics. In his *Principles of Political Economy*, John Stuart Mill (1848) put forward arguments for and against the role of the government in economic activity. The popularity of laissez-faire reached its peak around 1870, but by the late 19th century the fundamental changes caused by industrial growth and the adoption of mass production techniques cast some doubt on the soundness of the laissez-faire doctrine as a guiding philosophy. In the wake of the great depression in the 1930s, laissez-faire yielded to Keynesian economics, which advocated a role for the government in the economy, on the grounds that the economy does not have the tendency to return automatically to full employment. In the 1970s, the notion of laissez-faire was revived by right-wing economists such as Milton Friedman and Friedrich von Hayek. The principles were accepted by political leaders on both sides of the Atlantic as those principles provided the intellectual rationale for the waves of privatization and deregulation that took place consequently.

The term 'laissez-faire' has the same meaning as an extreme form of market economy and unfettered capitalism. The underlying issues are controversial, and with controversy come myths: propositions that are accepted by some and perceived as illusion by others. In this chapter, I will argue against three propositions that are put forward by free marketeers as undisputed facts of life: (1) superiority of the free market system over other alternatives, and superiority of the extreme form of the free market system relative to the mild form; (2) the efficiency of the private sector relative to the public sector, which provides justification for privatization; and (3) privatization is conducive to economic growth. These propositions represent the myths of laissez-faire.

6.2   SUPERIORITY OF THE FREE MARKET SYSTEM

It is a puzzle that the destruction inflicted by the global financial crisis has not quelled the enthusiasm of the true believers for free markets. Even in the aftermath of the crisis and great recession, free marketeers still insist that economic salvation can only be found in the free market system. The crisis, which led to the recession, was caused by financial institutions operating in line with the free market doctrine, aided and abetted by senior government officials who have a love affair with (let alone are the beneficiaries of) the almighty market. Free marketeers claim that the global financial crisis was not caused by the free market system even though the financial oligarchs wreaked havoc on humanity in their pursuit of self-interest. For example, Brook (2016) argues that 'free markets would never cause the 2008 crisis because they have correcting mechanisms that would never allow it to get that bad'. He puts the blame on the government, suggesting that when 'the government is involved, it lets bad things accumulate'. This is strange, given that the free market system would not have flourished in 19th century Britain if it were not for action by the government to allocate private property. Governments, which are invariably captured by corporate interests, work hard to support free-market entrepreneurs via tax brackets, subsidies, bailouts and bail-ins. It seems that the free market system operates on the principle of privatizing profits and socializing losses.

The superiority of the free market system is a myth, and so is the absence of a viable alternative. A free market economy, as envisaged by free marketeers, does not exist in reality because any sort of intervention or regulatory action taken by the government, no matter how insignificant it may be, violates the conditions required for the establishment of a free market system in its extreme form. Accordingly, the myth may be stated as follows: moving towards the 'ideal' market economy will enhance our welfare as we become increasingly happy and thriving. A champion free marketeer, who later changed his mind, was Alan Greenspan who once said that 'unfettered markets create a degree of wealth that fosters a more civilised existence' (Romer, 2020). The fact of the matter is that even the degree of market freedom that we have today is producing considerable misery and suffering. People die unnecessarily because they cannot afford the cost of healthcare and the exorbitant prices of prescription drugs. People live in poverty even in rich countries like the United States (US). On this point, Akerlof and Shiller (2015) note:

> Even in the US, as rich as we are by all historical standards, most of us go to bed at night worried about how to pay our bills. We are continually tempted, and have a very hard time sticking to a budget. Thus, the median American family has on average less than one month's expenditure in its bank account; half of all US respondents in a 2011 survey said they would have a very hard time raising US$2000 in a month's time if an emergency occurred.

Homelessness is rampant, rising at an accelerating pace and becoming visible even in countries such as Australia where at one time it was unobservable, even unthinkable. Students can obtain higher education only by drowning themselves in debt and ending up working as hamburger flippers, spending the rest of their lives paying off the loans they used to finance their studies. More importantly, this system is largely responsible for war and military aggression for the benefits of a few war profiteers acting, in the free market tradition, in pursuit of their own interest. The solution to a very unsatisfactory state of affairs is not to move further to the right by giving more freedom to big businesses to do what they like, but to keep them on a short leash. This is not a choice between capitalism and communism; rather, it is a choice between unfettered capitalism and tamed capitalism.

Economic systems have evolved from bad to better, from slavery to feudalism to capitalism. During the industrial revolution, capitalism proved to be a brutal system with a fundamental and inherent contradiction stemming from the fact that households are both consumers and providers of labour. To maximize profit, workers must be paid the minimum possible, but this means that they will not have enough to buy the goods they produce, which would have a negative effect on corporate profit. It is for this reason that imperialism thrived during the industrial revolution as governments, acting on behalf of corporate entities, used their navies and armies to find new markets and cheap raw materials to fuel industrial growth. Workers were exploited to the maximum, as children were forced to work long hours in mines for a subsistence wage and had no rights whatsoever.

In the 20th century things started to change by moving away from unfettered capitalism. To start with, the 1917 Bolshevik Revolution in Russia made European monarchies so worried about enduring the same fate as the Tsars that their governments started implementing reforms aimed at improving working conditions and protecting workers' rights (Al-Nakeeb,

2016). In the US, the New Deal was put in place by President Franklin Roosevelt between 1933 and 1939, which was a series of programmes, public work projects, financial reforms and regulations. The New Deal came as a response to the realization that unfettered capitalism produced boom–bust cycles, the worst bust being the great depression. There was also the political fear of workers' revolt, particularly with the strengthening of trade unions.

In the 1970s things started to change in the opposite direction. The notion of the free market resurged with a vengeance as a result of the influential writings of Milton Friedman and Fredrich von Hayek (both of them were, naturally, awarded the Nobel Prize in economics). In the 1980s the path towards unfettered capitalism resumed with wholesale deregulation and privatization. The financial tranquillity that followed the implementation of the Glass–Steagall Act, which was a component of the New Deal, came to an end as financial crises and bank failures took on a new dimension, culminating in the global financial crisis of 2008 and the great recession of 2009. Yet, free marketeers still tell us that salvation is not to go back to a New Deal type of environment, and that crises occur because of government intervention. The myth is that moving further towards the ideal free market will be the solution to our current problems.

A free market is a type of economic system that is operated by the market forces of supply and demand, as opposed to government controls and directives. Brook (2016) defines a free market as follows:

> A free market is a market free of government control, regulations, coercion and force. A free market means freedom to act without coercion in the pursuit of the values we need in order to live and to thrive and to flourish and to prosper. In a free market, people can act without force in order to produce economic values, create and produce wealth. In a free market, the only job of government is to catch crooks, to protect people from fraud, to help arbitrate disputes using a justice system. Government has to define property rights, to make them clear: intellectual property rights, physical property rights. But other than that, the government has no role, no economic policy – it leaves the market alone.

He adds:

> The only job of government in a free market should be to protect individuals: our freedoms, our ability to go out into the world and do what we want to do in pursuit of the values that we need in order to live and to thrive. So the government is there to protect individual rights. That is the ideal government, the government that only protects individual rights and does not regulate, does not control, does not tell us what to do in our bedroom, does not tell us what to do in business. A system like that is to protect people who are rational and who want to use their minds in order to live the best. The free market idea says that the more constraints society or government places on you, the more limited scientific

research is, the more limited entrepreneurship is, the more limited human beings' ability to pursue the things that they think are necessary for their lives is.

Brook keeps repeating the principles of reason, individualism, individual rights and freedom, and argues that 'the idea of free markets can really exist' but it needs a different culture, new ideas and a different attitude about morality, ethics, right and wrong. Focus, according to him, should be placed on the individual instead of the group and the collective, on what it takes to achieve individual flourishing, rather than 'how can I sacrifice?' and 'how can I be selfless?'.

This extreme right-wing rhetoric should not go without a response, even though I am inclined to think that it should not be dignified with a response. We have already seen that the move towards the target of the free market since the 1980s has brought crises, poverty, inequality and misery, in which case I am not sure how moving further towards that goal will make us thrive, flourish and prosper, unless Brook is talking about the prosperity of the oligarchy. It is true that value and wealth can be created under capitalism, but the created wealth, and the power that goes with it, is highly concentrated. Governments do define property rights by giving privileged individuals and the companies they own the right to dig out natural resources and sell them for private profit without paying any taxes. The freedom that Brook talks about is the freedom of the oligarchs to generate profit by any means, not the freedom of people from poverty and illness. The freedom that free marketeers are after is corporate freedom from regulation which, according to Romer (2020), provides leeway for companies to 'generate a profit even if they did pervasive harm in the process'. The governments of the so-called 'Western' countries harness the freedom of corporate entities to go out into the world, by providing the services of the army, navy and air force to make it possible for the oligarchs to create wealth for themselves by exploiting the riches of other countries.

Brook wants governments to stop regulating so that the oligarchs can make profit without bounds by abusing human rights and destroying the environment. He also defends greed and selfishness as human virtues, because they are conducive to efficiency, and condemns altruism, morality and ethics. He calls on the government to catch crooks, choosing to ignore the fact that crooks thrive in a free market. He condemns a government that tells us what to do in our bedrooms, which everyone agrees with, but he implies that this is as unjustifiable as when the government orders the people running a factory not to get rid of toxic waste by dumping it in rivers. I imagine that he would also condemn a government that orders people to stay at home while closing bars, restaurants and casinos to fight the coronavirus.

We must salute free marketeers for their willingness to die for the economy, the ultimate sacrifice for the noble cause of saving business. In an interview with Tucker Carlson of Foxtel (aired on Monday, 23 March 2020) the lieutenant governor of Texas, Dan Patrick, suggested that the US should go back to work, saying that grandparents like him do not want to sacrifice the country's economy during the coronavirus crisis. That came following the declaration of Donald Trump that he wanted to reopen the country for business in weeks, not months. Speaking on behalf of all American grandpas and grandmas, Patrick said that grandparents 'wouldn't want to sacrifice their grandchildren's economic future'. He also said that grandparents do not want to 'lose our whole country' over the current public health crisis and face an economic collapse. In solidarity with his 'lieutenant', and for the sake of business, the Republican governor of Texas, Greg Abbott, resisted a state-wide stay-at-home order (Rodriguez, 2020). It seems that the 'lieutenant', his bosses and their corporate handlers choose to overlook the fact that the coronavirus can kill mums, dads, uncles, aunties, sons and daughters. Free market thinking is all about short-termism: grab what you can while you can.

Brook (2016) condemns regulation because it interferes with the working of the 'law' of supply and demand, which (he argues) always holds, just like the law of gravity. This must be a joke, because there are no laws in economics, certainly nothing like the law of gravity. He recommends that 'in order to achieve individual human flourishing we must extract force from society'; just like any faithful free marketeer, he hates anything called 'society'. He recommends that 'we must build governments in order to protect us, but otherwise leave us free – that is, to protect us from criminals, terrorists, invaders, and to arbitrate disputes'.

What about protecting us from the criminals who, in the name of the free market, caused the global financial crisis and continue to commit fraud with impunity? They were not punished, but rather rewarded with lavish bonuses and golden parachutes. On this issue, Akerlof and Shiller (2015) argue that 'the economic system works as well as it does not just because of individual incentives, but also because a whole raft of individual heroes, social agencies and government regulation puts limits on this downside of markets to phish us for phools'. It is not the greed of the chief executive officers (CEOs) and entrepreneurs that will take us through the Covid-19 crisis, but rather the bravery and altruism of health workers and those maintaining essential services.

Free marketeers like Brook tell us that a free market offers a range of benefits, so let us take a look at these benefits. The first benefit is the freedom to innovate, as if innovation is a monopoly of the private sector that is motivated by one factor and one factor only: profit. The Soviet

Union sent the first satellite and the first cosmonaut into orbit long before the US did it. And when the US sent a man to the moon in 1969, that giant leap for humankind was achieved by a government agency, not a private enterprise. When the Russian mathematician Grigori Perelmen solved the Poincaré Conjecture, a major breakthrough in mathematics, he was not motivated by greed; on the contrary, he refused $1 million in prize money for his achievement.

Another alleged advantage of the free market is that customers drive choices: the customer is king, as they say. In a free market, the argument goes, consumers decide which products become a success and which ones fail. No one responds to this point better than Akerlof and Shiller (2015), who argue that 'free markets, as bountiful as they may be, will not only provide us with what we want, as long as we can pay for it; they will also tempt us into buying things that are bad for us, whatever the costs'. They suggest that as long as profit can be made, markets (or the entrepreneurs working according to the free market principles in pursuit of self-interest) will deceive us, manipulate us and prey on our weaknesses, tempting us into purchases that are bad for us. This is why we celebrate Father's Day, Mother's Day, Uncle's Day, Auntie's Day, Grandma's Day, Grandpa's Day, and so on; this is when we buy presents for people who do not need them.

In terms of financial products, Akerlof and Shiller (2015) note that people should not have bought overrated mortgage-backed securities, which they did only because they were told that those products provided fantastic risk–return combinations. Likewise, banks operating on the principles of the free market should not have created the insecure loans that backed those products. Apart from the finance industry, the consumer is deceived by the free market that gives us tobacco, which is responsible for almost 20 per cent of deaths in the US. In a free market, the pharmaceuticals industry sells us drugs with unknown long-term effects, which can be severe, and fast food companies serve sugar and fat. They also mention casinos as 'another example of how free markets tempt us into doing things we should not do'. They conclude that 'markets are not benign forces working for the greater good but instead are filled with businesses that "phish" by exploiting our weaknesses to get us to buy their products'. The consumer is not king, the consumer is a fool.

Yet another alleged advantage is that a free market economy benefits society through competition, which leads to lower prices for goods and services and a wider selection of products. As a result, consumers enjoy low prices for high-quality goods and services. In reality, however, competition leads to the 'survival of the fittest', turning a competitive industry into oligopoly or monopolistic completion where a huge amount of resources goes into wasteful advertising and manipulation of consumers. Go no further than the healthcare industry and higher education, where exorbitant prices are set for mediocre services. Higher education in particular has been delivering products of rapidly declining quality while fees are skyrocketing. At one time in the United Kingdom (UK), high-quality higher education was delivered free of charge, without the blessing of the free market; but the corporatization of universities has produced low-quality products commanding ever-rising prices, the name of the game (from the corporate perspective) being less for more.

I must not forget to say that soon there will be a competitive market in euthanasia where, through advertising, private sector firms attempt to convince people to commit suicide and pay for it. It will not be long before we see advertisements saying 'we will kill you in a better way for a lower price'. I must also mention the price hikes of items such as toilet paper and hand sanitizers, resulting from competition among scammers and profiteers acting in the spirit of the free market to maximize profit under the extraordinary conditions created by the coronavirus outbreak.

Competition, it is argued, pushes individuals and businesses to use resources in an efficient manner in order to maximize profits, and this is why free market economies are generally less wasteful. Again, look at the wasteful expenditure on advertising and lobbying. Rent-seeking, which involves the manipulation of the social and political environments in which economic activities occur, is a symptom of the free market economy. From a societal perspective, this activity involves waste of resources that can otherwise be used to create new wealth. The profit maximization motive leads to malpractice and the tendency to cut corners.

Moosa and Ramiah (2014) give examples of what happens when regulation is lax, let alone absent. These include the widespread production and distribution of fake medicines, marketed as genuine ones; the marketing of beef that is infected with the mad cow disease virus; the marketing of food products containing horse meat but labelled as 'beef'; trade in fake aircraft parts marketed as genuine ones; faulty materials or less-than-adequate construction standards that eventually lead to the collapse of buildings; compromising safety standards in dealing with hazardous chemicals, which often causes disasters involving multiple deaths and horrific injuries; compromising the safety standards of the disposal of toxic waste, particularly by multinationals operating in developing countries; unscrupulous financiers, such as Bernie Madoff, running Ponzi schemes and ripping off clients; and the reporting of false financial statements to cover losses (Enron is one notorious example). These are not trivial matters, because they invariably involve injury, health deterioration, financial losses and even death. Yet, Brook (2016) glorifies the free market system by saying the following:

It is hard to imagine the world with a completely free market. People would be much richer. We would have such advanced technology. We would live to be a hundred and fifty or older, because biotechnology has the capacity, if freed up from regulations and freed up from state control, to really extend human life dramatically. We might have rocket ships going to Mars, we might be colonizing Mars. More importantly than that, there would be no poor people in the world.

Yes, indeed, it is hard to imagine the world with a completely free market; he is saying something that makes sense, for a change. Some people would be much richer, but the majority of people would be struggling to survive. Poor people would become richer, or less poor, if we moved in the opposite direction and tackled massive inequality. Instead of giving one person or a company the right to dig out minerals and sell them for private profit without paying taxes, it would be better for the average person if the government took over the mining sector and used the proceeds to finance a scheme of universal basic income, as well as health and education; this would kill poverty and inequality. It is because of the free market system that we find poverty and homelessness in a mineral-rich country with a small population such as Australia. As for living longer under a free market system, Brook seems to be unaware of the horrific death toll produced by the move towards a free market economy in Russia in the 1990s. Private sector companies will never produce a cure for diabetes, even if that is feasible, because it would be like killing the goose that lays golden eggs. As for going to Mars, I am sure that Brook knows that a man landed on the moon not as a result of the endeavours of a private enterprise, but rather the endeavours of the taxpayer-funded National Aeronautics and Space Administration (NASA).

Neoclassical economics provides the theoretical rationale for why the free market system will take us to Mars. However, Semion (2011) brings attention to the 'significant flaws to the theory underpinning the market', which depends on the concept of 'perfect competition', the ideal state in neoclassical economics that requires certain restrictive assumptions to hold. One of these conditions is the free flow of and access to information, which does not suit financial institutions wishing to sell junky and toxic assets such as mortgage-backed securities. The assumption of rational consumers does not hold, because people have emotions, biases and prejudices. The assumption of free entry and exit does not hold, because oligopolistic firms strive to erect barriers to entry. The assumption of a large number of firms within a given industry, each selling a homogenous product, does not hold simply because this is not what we observe in the real world. The assumption that the actions of individual firms have little to no effect on market prices does not hold, because large firms have the market power that enables them to affect market prices.

The free market system can be dangerous. The profit maximization objective is prioritized over the needs of ordinary people, leading firms to compromise the safety of workers and disregard environmental standards and ethical conduct. Recall the WorldCom and Enron scandals of the early 2000s, and the 2010 *Deepwater Horizon* oil spill. Recall also the Bhopal disaster of central India in 1984, when (for the sake of cost minimization and profit maximization) a highly unstable chemical leaked into the night sky, killing thousands of people while they were asleep. On that occasion the profit-maximizing oligarch, who ran the company according to the free market doctrine, got away with murder as he was smuggled to the US under the cover of chaos. A free market economy can spin out of control, producing dire consequences such as the 'two greats': depression and recession. The free market system creates a grotesque level of inequality and leads to the rise of monopolies and boom–bust cycles.

Yet, Dorfman (2016) tells us that we should be thankful to the free market system, describing it as 'the most powerful, nonreligious force for good in the history of the world'; for that he gives ten reasons. One reason is that median income is rising; but median income means nothing to the poor, unemployed and homeless. Another reason is that free markets know what we want; but in a free market consumers are deceived into buying things that they do not need (or want). Yet another one of Dorfman's reasons is that failed businesses are punished and economic growth accelerates. I am sure that Mr Dorfman is old enough to have witnessed the 2008 bailout of failed financial institutions and the rewarding of oligarchs with taxpayers' money. On that occasion, growth came to a standstill rather than accelerating. He claims that competition keeps prices low, blaming government involvement for higher prices in healthcare and education. And of course we should thank the free market system for 'freedom': the freedom of oligarchs to rip us off by charging $10 000 for one pill and $50 000 a year for a university degree that is more or less no different from toilet paper.

This section comes to an end with two quotes from Semion (2011) and Akerlof and Shiller (2015). Semion (2011) brings in the 'invisible hand' (of the oligarchs), which slaps all of us, by saying:

> At their core, the invisible hand and free market economy are romantic notions, born from a romantic time. The conditions necessary for the free market economy to function simply do not exist in today's world, if they ever did. A pure free market does not provide for the greatest social good, only the greatest good to those with the means to exploit weaknesses in a free market system.

I am not sure what is 'romantic' about the invisible hand (when it is invisible) and the free market (which is visibly brutal). While romance and brutality do not typically go together, every rule has exceptions, the exception in this case being the romance and brutality of Eva Braun and Adolf Hitler.

Akerlof and Shiller (2015) warn of the hazard of overlooking the dark side of the free market by saying:

> Free markets may lead to prosperity, but unwillingness to acknowledge their dark side undergirds the basic fundamental thinking of economists and leads to bad government policies. A grownup's view of the economy that incorporates the downsides of capitalism is a prerequisite for sane policy.

The superiority of the free market system is a myth that should be relegated to the dustbin of history. It is a puzzle why free market enthusiasts, despite warnings like that of Akerlof and Shiller, refuse to acknowledge the dark side, or admit to the adverse consequences, of the free market. Even worse, they think that the free market is 'romantic'.

6.3 EFFICIENCY OF THE PRIVATE SECTOR

Free marketeers tell us that privatization is useful because it boosts efficiency; for them, it is axiomatic that the private sector is more efficient than the public sector. Free marketeers believe that this is an undisputed fact of life, but it is a myth that is used to justify the concentration of wealth and power. For free marketeers, what matters is the size of the pie, not how it is distributed.

Let us start by defining efficiency, and for this purpose I quote Banton (2020) who suggests the following definition:

> Efficiency signifies a peak level of performance that uses the least amount of inputs to achieve the highest amount of output. Efficiency requires reducing the number of unnecessary resources used to produce a given output including personal time and energy. It is a measurable concept that can be determined using the ratio of useful output to total input. It minimizes the waste of resources such as physical materials, energy, and time while accomplishing the desired output.

Efficiency, therefore, is 'the fundamental reduction in the amount of wasted resources that are used to produce a given number of goods or services (output)'. A question that arises here is why (allegedly) more waste is found in the public sector than the private sector. Free marketeers would tell us that this is the case because the private sector is motivated by profit maximization, which calls for reduction in waste and the production of a given amount of output using the smallest possible amount of input. Even if we assume, for the sake of argument, that this is true, the alleged increase in efficiency is bound to be achieved at a massive social cost.

Consider an example of a recently privatized firm, taken away from public ownership and given to an oligarch in a good deal for the oligarch and a bad deal for the public at large. The new CEO will fire 20 000 workers in the name of efficiency, while taking a $30 million annual salary in addition to all of the perks that go with it, including a bonus that is independent of performance and a promised golden parachute. Members of the CEO's inner circle (the CEO's cronies) will also be paid high salaries and enjoy perks, to the extent that the saving on the wage bill obtained by firing 20 000 workers will be offset by lavish executive pay. Workers who are fortunate enough to keep their jobs will have to accept pay cuts (again in the name of efficiency). They will be paid less than the minimum wage, to the extent that they will be qualified for food stamps and other handouts, meaning that taxpayers will subsidize the new private sector firm.

In the name of efficiency, the firm starts cutting corners to reduce costs. The waste produced by operations can go into the atmosphere, rivers and lakes instead of being treated, because waste treatment is costly. Efficiency is enhanced through tax evasion. The firm has a monopoly power which enables it to charge higher prices than otherwise. If the firm produces goods the demand for which is inelastic, then God help consumers (look no further than the pharmaceutical companies and utilities). The increase in efficiency is achieved at massive social costs, including unemployment, poverty, inequality and environmental degradation. If efficiency is calculated by considering not only private costs, but also social costs, the private firm will not be as efficient as it is portrayed to be. I forgot to say that if or when this firm collapses, it will claim 'too big to fail' status and demand a taxpayers' bailout so that the CEO and his cronies get their bonuses and golden parachutes.

In a public hospital, where someone bitten by the neighbour's dog is treated immediately for free, patients might have to wait for some time to receive treatment for non-urgent matters. In a private hospital, on the other hand, patients will not be treated at all if they cannot pay, irrespective of the urgency of their conditions, but the minority who can pay will get super service. As a result, people will die, because only a minority can afford a $200 000 operation, whereas the rest have to sell their homes and become homeless. Millions of people died during the Russian massive privatization programme of the 1990s because of unemployment and the loss of healthcare, when the oligarchs blessed by Boris Yeltsin got bargains for the acquisitions of public assets. While ordinary Russians could not afford to bury their dead (a blessing of the free market, since burying the dead is a market transaction), a wave of Russian billionaires emerged, most of them ended up residing in London or in tax havens (not that London is not a tax haven for the Russian oligarchs).

The proposition that the private sector is more efficient than the public sector is taken for granted. Stone (2013) quotes two Australian (Liberal)

MPs repeating this idea like parrots, without any evidence. Paul Fletcher, member for Bradfield, says the following: 'the reality is that government employees around the world are known not to be as efficient as the private sector'. Likewise, Peter Lindsay, member for Herbert, says that 'the efficiency of the public system is about half of that of the private system'. Can you see the precision and generalization here? Apparently Lindsay has done some calculations to find out that the efficiency of the public sector is half that of the private sector, not half plus or minus one standard deviation. Fletcher says that it is a worldwide phenomenon that only those with low intelligence quotients (IQs) work for the public sector, which explains why it is inefficient. It seems to me that Fletcher and Lindsay had forgotten that they were public sector employees, receiving salaries and perks from taxpayers in return for providing public services. Unfortunately for taxpayers, Fletcher was not as efficient as a private sector employee, and Lindsay was only half efficient (their words, not mine).

A common misconception is that the private sector is inherently more efficient than the public sector, which means that public enterprises should be privatized, or at least that some of the activities should be outsourced to the private sector. This proposition is not supported by casual empiricism or formal empirical evidence. For example, Hodge (1996) reviews 129 reports and case studies and finds that outsourcing works well in some cases and badly in others. Stone (2013) suggests that many studies claiming the benefits of outsourcing do not take into account the broader economic and social cost of outsourcing. For example, outsourcing frequently results in significant job cuts, such that the welfare costs of a higher level of unemployment may exceed any savings. Stone refers to evidence indicating that public and private hospitals show similar efficiency levels once their different roles are taken into account. Likewise, public and private schools show similar levels of attainment once the demographic profile of the students is factored in. The fact of the matter is that no civilized society should have private schools or private hospitals.

Simms (2013) dismisses the superiority of the private sector by writing the following:

> Private sector dynamism versus public sector inefficiency has been a dominant political narrative of the last few decades. It has supplied the excuse for upheaval in many of the public services that we rely on. Yet from healthcare costs to train company subsidies, evidence of private sector superiority is thin. The public sphere in its broadest sense – including voluntary, mutual, cooperative and social enterprise models – can be more efficient and more effective.

As an example, he uses the privatization of British Rail in 1996 when John Major's government divided British Rail into more than 100 different businesses and sold them off. According to the *Financial Times* (2001), this operation 'introduced hard-nosed commercial tensions into relationships that often needed to be co-operative' and 'broke traditional bonds and practices of passing on skills and experience'. The complexity of contracts, targets and blurred lines of responsibility introduced numerous inefficiencies. For example, the *Financial Times* notes that the post-privatized industry employed hundreds of people just to fight over who is to blame for every minute of delay to trains.

A variety of studies dismiss the superiority doctrine; it is even called a 'myth'. Godrej (2015) refers to 'Myth 5', which is that the private sector is more efficient than the public sector, describing it as 'the abiding myth of mainstream economics'. This is how he describes the myth:

> It's an ideological position that suits governing elites and has led, among other things, to a fire sale of public assets and the increasing privatization of what were once public goods and services. The magic of the market and the vigour of private enterprise will make the cream of cost-effectiveness and efficiency rise to the top. At least, that's how it's spun.

A major review of the international literature and experience, covering a number of different sectors and services, reaches the conclusion that 'the evidence shows no significant difference in efficiency between public and privately owned companies in public services' (PSIRU, 2014). The Public Services International Research Unit (PSIRU) study examines the international experience with the privatization of various sectors. For example, it has been found that privatized sectors perform significantly worse than telecom companies remaining in state hands. For the healthcare sector, the report refers to international evidence and evidence from individual countries, strongly suggesting that 'public providers have higher levels of technical efficiency than the private sector in healthcare'. This is probably why basic health outcomes are worse in the US than in Cuba, even though Cuba, which has a totally public healthcare system, spends a fraction of the US per capita healthcare expenditure. The Institute of Medicine (2012) says the following about the private healthcare system in the US:

> 30 cents of every medical dollar goes to unnecessary healthcare, deceitful paperwork, fraud and other waste. The $750 billion in annual waste is more than the Pentagon budget and more than enough to care for every American who lacks health insurance ... Most of the waste came from unnecessary services ($210 billion annually), excess administrative costs ($190 billion) and inefficient delivery of care ($130 billion).

In a study for the United Nations Development Programme (UNDP), prepared by the Global Centre for Public Service Excellence (2015), it is stated that no conclusive evidence is found to indicate that one model of ownership (public, private or mixed) is intrinsically more efficient than the others, irrespective of how efficiency is defined. Instead, the efficiency of service provision depends on the type of service (health, education, and so on) and other specific contextual factors (such as regulation and market competition).

Simms and Reid (2013) describe as 'old dogma' the proposition that the private sector is superior to the public sector and refer to the myth of private sector superiority, arguing that there is no evidence for private sector efficiency. They use British Rail as an example, pointing out that public subsidy to Britain's railways rose dramatically following privatization. They also refer to two facts on the ground: (1) the failure of Metronet Rail's contract to work on the infrastructure of London Underground, to which taxpayers contributed more than £400 million; and (2) the single remaining state-run mainline rail service requires less public subsidy than any of the 15 privately run rail franchises in Britain.

An industry that has not been dealt with in these studies is funeral services. In the 'West', it is a private sector activity involving a small number of operators in a market characterized by oligopolistic competition where competing oilgopolists advertise their services in the spirit of the free market. These services can be expensive, costing up to $20000, perhaps more (and rising by far ahead of the inflation rate). For a family that cannot afford a $1000 emergency, it would be problematical if a member of the family died without a contingency plan to cover the cost of the funeral. In a compassionate society, a concept that is vehemently rejected by free marketeers, the funeral may be paid for through donations. Otherwise, I would imagine that the Russian syndrome of the 1990s would be relevant; that is, the bodies will be disposed of somehow. This 'efficiency' of the private sector is to be compared with the inefficiency of the public sector in providing funeral services. In Kuwait, where mineral resources are owned by the public sector, the Ministry of Health is responsible for the provision of funeral services free of charge. The less efficient public sector treats the dead with dignity, whereas the efficient private sector treats with dignity only the dead who can pay for the funeral, such that the degree of dignity in death is a positive function of the ability of the dead person to pay.

You can pick and choose studies that, based on evidence, reject the superiority of the private sector. Petersen et al. (2011) note that 'it is not possible to conclude unambiguously that there is any systematic difference in terms of the economic effects of contracting out technical areas and social services'. Bel et al. (2010) do not find a 'genuine empirical effect of cost savings resulting from private production'. Knyazeva et al. (2013) find that 'the privatisation group underperforms the group of sectors remaining public', adding that this finding is consistent with the Russian experience, when in the 1990s gross domestic product (GDP) declined with privatization as faster privatization did not lead to improved performance. Muhlenkamp (2015) notes that 'research does not support the conclusion that privately owned firms are more efficient than otherwise-comparable state-owned firms'.

Perhaps the best way to close this section is to quote Chris Hedges on private prisons and the 'corporate coup'. In a magnificent speech, Hedges (2017) said the following about private prisons:

> Our [US] system of mass incarceration is not broken – it works exactly the way it is designed to work. The bodies of poor people of color do not generate money for corporations on the streets of our deindustrialised cities but they generate 40 or 50 thousand dollars a year if we lock them in cages and that is why they are there . . . One million prisoners now work for corporations inside prisons as modern day slaves, paid pennies on the dollar without any rights or protection. They are the corporate state's ideal workers.

In the same speech, he said the following about the 'corporate coup':

> Corporations are legally empowered to exploit and loot. It is impossible to vote against Goldman Sachs and Exxon Mobile. The pharmaceutical and insurance industries are legally empowered to hold sick children hostage while their parents frantically bankrupt themselves trying to save their sons or daughters. Banks are legally empowered to burden people with student loans that cannot be forgiven by declaring bankruptcy. The animal agricultural industry is legally empowered to charge those who attempt to publicize the conditions in the vast factory farms where diseased animals are warehoused for slaughter, with a criminal offence. Corporations are legally empowered to carry out tax boycotts.

Naturally, free marketeers would respond to Hedges by using the terms 'freedom', 'democracy', 'efficiency' and so on, none of which has anything to do with the free market. They would also accuse Hedges as being 'lefty', even 'communist' and a 'Putin apologist'. Yes, the private sector is definitely superior to the public sector, but only with respect to exploitation, looting and total disregard for human life.

6.4   THE EFFECT OF PRIVATIZATION ON ECONOMIC GROWTH

In the early 1990s the Russian President Boris Yeltsin, the darling of the 'West', launched an aggressive privatization programme that was a bonanza for the oligarchs and an act of aggression against ordinary

Russians. In what was the largest sell-off of state-owned assets in history, enterprises were sold at a rate of about 800 a month. Rigged auctions allowed the oligarchs to acquire public assets for a fraction of what they were worth. Naturally, free marketeers described the sell-off as reform, which is why we should always be careful of the word 'reform'. Some of the 'reformers' profited most from what the Russians often refer to as the 'great grab'. The exercise was a massive portrayal of corruption and *quid pro quo* deals where the oligarchs helped Yeltsin to stay in power while he helped them steal the wealth of the Russian people.

Jeffrey Sachs, a Harvard economist with extensive experience in Eastern Europe, once wrote the following (Hays, 2016):

> Russia's resources provided unparalleled opportunities for theft by officials. Oil, gas, diamonds and metal ore deposits were nominally owned by the state and thus by nobody. They were ripe for stealing . . . the system was often skirted or compromised by ad hoc decrees and hidden arrangements.

As a result, the wealth of the Russian oligarchs has become conspicuous. They have their own private jets and huge mansions, and they travel around in armoured Mercedes sedans led and followed by vehicles with bodyguards carrying customized assault rifles. One of the oligarchs reportedly ordered a new Boeing 767 equipped with its own anti-missile system. Under Yeltsin, they became so powerful that one of his aides told the *New York Times* that 'the oligarchs regarded themselves as the real government of Russia and to some degree they were the real government', to the extent that 'they could easily dismiss ministers and nominate people who would be loyal to them in ministerial positions' (Hays, 2016). More importantly, and unfortunately for the Russian people, the wealth was smuggled, as most of them settled abroad; the richest of them chose London.

The privatization programme had dire consequences for the Russian economy. The seizure of assets at bargain prices deprived the government of the financial resources that could have been used to jump-start the economy. The oligarchs refrained from putting money into the companies they acquired to help them grow, prosper and become more efficient, in the process stimulating the economy and creating jobs. Instead, they were more inclined to sell off anything of value, converting assets into dollars that were smuggled out of the country, depriving the Russian economy of growth-spurring financial resources. Crime became rampant as a result of poverty. The death toll was enormous as people lost their jobs and access to free healthcare.

The dire consequences listed above could not have been conducive to economic growth. Neither could those identified by Joseph Stiglitz, as quoted by Hays (2016): (1) the economic incentives encouraged asset

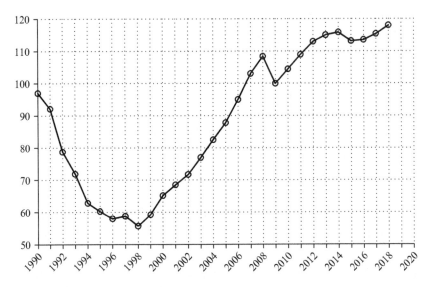

Figure 6.1   Russia's economic size measured by GDP (1989 = 100)

stripping rather than wealth creation; (2) Russia's human capital in technical and scientific areas was wasted; and (3) the large, relatively equal middle
class had its livelihood taken away. The result can be seen in Figure 6.1: by
1998, the Russian economy (measured by GDP) had shrunk by 44 per
cent. Naturally, free marketeers would argue that this dramatic fall in GDP
cannot be attributed to privatization and that this observation should not
be generalized. Well, just look at the economic performance of the countries accepting the International Monetary Fund's (IMF) 'stabilization
programmes', which has privatization as a major component. Almost all
of those countries go from bad to worse, as the primary objective changes
from boosting the economy to paying off debt (Moosa and Moosa, 2019).

Free marketeers present a variety of weak arguments for the proposition
that privatization is conducive to growth. The first is that privatization
enhances the system of property rights, which contributes to growth
because property rights encourage the owners to invest and make it easier
for them to obtain credit. The second is that the private sector is effective
in solving the problem of externalities through costless bargaining, driven
by individual incentives. This is questionable because one of the justifica-
tions for government intervention in economic activity is externalities that
cannot be dealt with by the private sector. The third is that privatization
reduces the size of the government, which must be good for growth, since
a big government is bad for growth. Another reason is that privatization

enables countries to pay a portion of their existing debt, thus reducing interest rates and raising the level of investment. This sounds as ludicrous as paying off debt by selling one's own furniture. In any case, investment is not interest-sensitive, which is why the policy of ultra-low and negative interest rates will never work. The last reason they put forward is that privatization gives ownership to a larger percentage of the population, which encourages them to work harder and invest in their property. This is not true, because the benefits of privatization are realized by a very small minority of well-connected people. After all, privatization is a reverse Robin Hood transfer of wealth from the poor to the rich.

The empirical evidence on the effect of privatization on economic growth is typically based on a multiple regression containing a large number of control variables. As we saw in Chapter 5, deriving inference from multiple regression is hazardous, even meaningless, and this is why we have not learned anything from the empirical studies of the determinants of economic growth. As usual, the empirical evidence on this issue is mixed: the effect of privatization has been found to be positive, negative and neither, depending on the mode of privatization and the underlying country or region. Those finding a positive effect include Plane (1997), Barnett (2000), Boubakri et al. (2009) and Koyuncu (2016). Those finding a negative effect include Cook and Uchida (2003) and Naguib (2012). Moshiri and Abdou (2010) find that privatization has no statistically significant impact on growth in most regions, except for East Asia and the Pacific, and in South Asia where a positive impact is observed. Rahbar et al. (2012) conclude that whether privatization has an effect or no effect on growth depends on where in the world it takes place. Bennett et al. (2007) note that only voucher privatization has a positive effect, whereas Cieslik and Tarsalewska (2013) reached the conclusion that only small-scale privatization is positively associated with growth.

I am not saying here that we should believe the results showing a negative effect and discard those showing a positive effect. For all we know, both sets of results were produced by extensive data mining to confirm prior beliefs or to please potential editors and referees. The fact of the matter is that we do not need shaky empirical evidence to argue that privatization can be detrimental to growth. While the explanations put forward by free marketeers for the positive effect of privatization on growth are weak, rhetorical and counterfactual, more plausible explanations (guided by actual experience) can be put forward to argue that privatization has negative consequences for growth. To start with, privatization causes unemployment, which cannot be good for growth. Privatization involves corruption, which is also bad for growth. Privatization is corrosive for human capital, which cannot be good for growth. It leads to concentration of wealth, which is not good for growth. Privatization deprives the government of sources of revenue, particularly if public assets are sold significantly below value, which reduces the funds available for investment in infrastructure and human capital; this cannot be good for growth. Privatization intensifies the financialization of the economy, which is bad for growth. Last, but not least, when the oligarchs smuggle funds abroad, they divert away financial resources that can otherwise be used to finance capital formation.

Claiming that privatization boosts economic growth is ideological rhetoric that is counterfactual and implausible. Explaining why and how privatization hurts growth is not such a difficult task: just recall the case of Russia in the 1990s. If this is not adequate, refer to the experience of so many countries that have been forced to privatize by the IMF for the benefit of big multinationals. It is a myth that privatization boosts growth.

6.5   WHERE DOES DEMOCRACY COME IN?

Free marketeers claim that democracy and the free market system are intertwined; they go together. You would then expect free marketeers to cherish a move towards a free market and condemn fascism. On 11 September 1973, General Augusto Pinochet seized power in Chile in a violent *coup d'état*, sometimes referred to as 'the other 9/11' or 'Chile's 9/11'. Pinochet overthrew the democratically elected government of Salvadore Allende, in the process committing massive crimes against humanity. Allende was accused of introducing 'socialist' policies, which were reversed by the Pinochet regime, opting instead for extreme free market policies. As Meadowcroft (2019) puts it: 'Practically from day one the Pinochet regime replaced the interventionist policies of the previous government with policies designed to introduce market forces into the Chilean economy'. This is how Frank (1976) described the policy change:

> At the same time, the state divests itself of state sector enterprises at bargain basement prices to Chilean and particularly to foreign big capital, doing so not only with enterprises that became state-owned or controlled under the Allende government, but also with enterprises that had been financed through state investment for over a generation.

On that occasion, the free market system went hand in hand with fascism (which was also the case in Nazi Germany and Fascist Italy in the 1930s). Free marketeers applauded the Pinochet regime for adopting free market policies and overlooked the atrocities they committed. According to Meadowcroft (2019), Milton Friedman, Friedrich von Hayek and James Buchanan are 'alleged to have given explicit, tacit or covert support to the regime', meaning that they did give explicit, tacit or covert support to the regime.

Enthusiastic support for the Pinochet regime came from von Hayek, who (in the name of freedom) supported other authoritarian governments of the time. For Hayek, democracy does not have any intrinsic value; rather, it is valuable because of its consequences. For him, democracy is important as a peaceful means of removing an unpopular or ineffective government (meaning a government that does not pursue free market policies), but no special value should be attributed to a decision because it happened to reflect the will of a numerical majority of the voting population. According to Meadowcroft (2019), Hayek believed in 'transitional dictatorship' that could use authoritarian methods to set a country on the path towards economic liberalism and limited government, and that short-lived dictatorship might be justified to curb the excesses of majoritarian rule that threatened economic freedom. For Hayek, if democracy does not bring about good outcomes (meaning a market economy), then it is desirable to dispense with it temporarily (where 'temporarily' could mean ten years, and half a million lives lost).

An essential feature of a democratic system is the notion of choice. Since free markets allow choice, the argument goes, they must inevitably lead to a democratic form of government. This claim is easy to refute, as many authoritarian countries allow free markets to exist. Take a look at Figure 6.2, which is a scatter plot of measures of democracy (provided by the Economist Intelligence Unit) and economic freedom (provided by the Heritage Foundation). Although we can see positive correlation, the dispersion around the best fit line should be smaller if we are to believe that free markets and democracy go hand in hand. More important, however, is that the measure of democracy does not reflect the true state of affairs.

Democracy means much more than the process of free and fair elections: it is a system for accomplishing what can only be achieved by citizens joining together to further the common good. On a scale of 0–10, Australia, Canada, the UK and US register 9.09, 9.22, 8.52 and 8.38, respectively. In these countries, no one from outside the two major parties can win a general or presidential election; this is quite a choice. Nominees of other parties cannot participate in televised debates. This is why Jesse Ventura calls the system in America a 'two-party dictatorship' where no difference can be observed between the policies of the two parties, particularly when it comes to militarism and regulatory capture. And it is why Chris Hedges refers to the only party in America, the 'corporate party'. Once in power, governments do whatever they like, including taking part in wars of aggression. In Australia, the prime minister can, on their own wish, declare war on a country that lies 10000 miles away without consulting

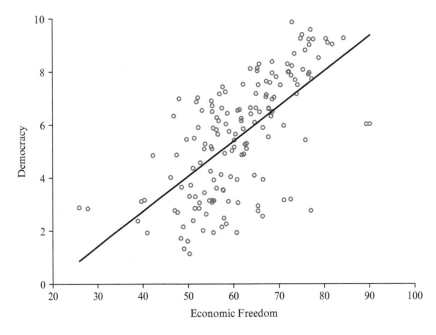

Figure 6.2   Democracy versus economic freedom

with Parliament. This is bound to happen after the prime minister receives a phone call from the White House.

In all of these countries, particularly the US, corporate interests run the show. A major contradiction between the free market system and democracy is that the free market gives political power to corporate interests and a minority of oligarchs. This cannot be compatible with democracy as the 'rule of people'. Contradiction between the free market system and democracy was recognized a long time ago by Rothschild (1947), who wrote the following:

> When we enter the field of rivalry between [corporate] giants, the traditional separation of the political from the economic can no longer be maintained ... Fascism ... has been largely brought into power by this very struggle in an attempt of the most powerful oligopolists to strengthen, through political action, their position in the labour market and vis-à-vis their smaller competitors, and finally to strike out in order to change the world market situation in their favour.

If free market policies are associated with democracy, how do we explain the observation that governments pursuing free market policies are becoming increasingly autocratic, using 'national security' as a pretext to infringe on people's democratic rights and civil liberties? Signs of fascism are crystal clear in the US and other 'Western' countries, including nationalism, disregard for human rights, identification of 'enemies' as a unifying cause, supremacy of the military, controlled mass media, obsession with national security, religion becoming intertwined with the government, protection of corporate power, suppression of labour power, obsession with crime and punishment, rampant cronyism and corruption, and fraudulent elections (recall Florida 2000, and the Democratic primaries of 2016 and 2020).

At least two of these signs – protection of corporate power and suppression of labour power – indicate that the free market goes hand in hand with fascism, not with democracy. Reich (2009) argues that while free markets are supposed to lead to free societies, 'today's supercharged global economy is eroding the power of the people in democracies around the globe'. He describes the current state of affairs as a 'world where the bottom line trumps the common good and government takes a back seat to big business'. Democracy has been weakened by unfettered capitalism because corporate interests invest ever greater sums in lobbying, public relations, and even bribes and kickbacks, seeking and extracting favourable laws, in the process drowning out the voices of average citizens. Let us not forget that the Nazis indulged in pro-business privatization in Germany during the period 1933–37, when the government sold off public ownership in several state-owned firms in a wide range of sectors, including steel, mining, banking, public utilities, shipyards, ship-lines and railways. The delivery of some public services produced by public enterprises prior to the 1930s was transferred to the private sector, mainly to several organizations within the Nazi Party.

Another point is that propaganda has no place in a democratic society. Meyssan (2020) argues that 'democracy presupposes the ability to hold honest public debates', which means that 'propaganda would be the prerogative of non-democratic regimes'. Yet, he notes, 'history teaches us that modern propaganda was conceived in the United Kingdom and the United States during the First World War, and that the USSR [Union of Soviet Socialist Republics] and Nazi Germany were pale copycats'. Remember that the United Kingdom and the United States are the custodians of the free market system.

6.6   CONCLUDING REMARKS

It is a myth that the free market system enhances democracy; it is even a myth that free markets are associated with democracy. In fact, the opposite is true. This myth goes hand in hand with the other myths of laissez-faire:

the myth of the superiority of the free market system, the myth of the efficiency of the private sector relative to the public sector, and the myth that privatization boots growth.

Those having a sanguine view of the free market system refer to competition between small producers and sellers, such as those selling fruit and vegetables in a local market. This, however, does not represent the dark side of the free market. The free market system is where people who cannot afford healthcare are allowed to die. It is where public health is put at risk by charging for the coronavirus test. The free market system is about big companies lobbying for war so that they can sell arms to the government, paid for with taxpayers' money. The free market system is about big firms paying workers less than the minimum wage, in which case they are subsidized by taxpayers who foot the bill for food stamps and similar welfare payments. The free market system is about the atrocities committed by the East India Company, which had its own army and prisons. The free market system is about the atrocities committed by imperialism in India, China and the whole of Africa. Free marketeers celebrate selfishness, condemn altruism and dismiss poverty, homelessness and extreme inequality as non-issues. This is the ugly face of the free market system.

It is unimaginable that the current coronavirus outbreak can be dealt with by the private sector acting on the free market principles. Profit maximization by 'efficient' private sector firms means that people will be charged thousands of dollars for the test, and those needing intensive care will have to spend their lifetime savings. To preserve corporate profit, no concert, sporting event or any profit-generating event will be cancelled. The coronavirus is good for the profit of the healthcare industry and funeral agencies, as more people require testing and more die. When a vaccine becomes a reality, God help us all if pharmaceutical companies have their way in pricing the product while demanding patent protection. This is efficiency at its best.

7. The myths of financial economics

7.1 THE ACCURACY OF CREDIT RATINGS

In the run up to the global financial crisis, institutional and individual investors rushed to accumulate mortgaged-backed securities and collateralized debt obligations because they were perceived as providing excellent risk–return combinations: high return and low risk. Investors were impressed by the verdict of the credit rating agencies (Standard & Poor's, Moody's and Fitch Risk) that these securities commanded top rating (AAA or equivalent), meaning that the holder would have little exposure to risk. When the United States (US) housing market slowed down, the incidence of default on mortgage payments started to rise, leading to declining prices of these instruments. We know the rest of the story, as we recall the collapse of Bear Stearns, Merrill Lynch and Lehman Brothers.

In hindsight we know that the credit rating agencies were wrong. However, there is no agreement on whether they were wrong because they tried their best and got it wrong, or because they knew that those securities were risky but gave them top ratings in exchange for lucrative financial rewards from the issuers. In a television interview with the Australian Broadcasting Corporation (ABC), I said some years ago that the credit rating agencies were either corrupt or incompetent, or both. I even said that the world will be a better place without them. Unfortunately, they are back in business as usual, which can be explained in two ways: either that investors do believe in the usefulness of ratings as indicators of the degree of default risk, or because the agencies are oligopolists whose services are required by law. I think that it is the latter, because it is a myth that the credit rating agencies provide accurate or useful information on the level of risk embodied in the financial instruments they rate.

Credit rating agencies (CRAs) perform the function of assigning credit ratings to the issuers of debt securities, where a rating represents the creditworthiness of the issuer (borrower) as well as the quality of the issued security in terms of credit risk (the risk of default). Utzig (2010) argues that 'the growth of the international financial markets over the last 20 years would have been unthinkable without CRAs'. He goes on to say the following:

Only because of the availability of clear, internationally accepted indicators of the risk of default were investors willing to invest in international securities – whether corporate or government bonds – whose credit quality they would have been virtually unable to assess on their own. The CRAs worked for decades on designing a simple and readily understandable system that would allow any investor to invest in international securities with which they were not directly familiar.

This is a rather sanguine view of the CRAs. We will never know whether financial markets would have grown the way they did in the absence of the CRAs. And we have to remember that the use of the services of the CRAs is typically required by regulators, rather than emanating from the desire of investors to be guided by the ratings. Contrary to Utzig's sanguine view, the ratings provided by the CRAs are far away from being 'clear, internationally accepted indicators of the risk of default', and their work is rather sloppy.

The CRAs have been under scrutiny since the advent of the global financial crisis, as they are accused of contributing massively to the turmoil. Despite his favourable view of CRAs, Utzig (2010) contends that they 'bear some responsibility for the financial crisis', which is 'acknowledged by policymakers, market participants, and by the agencies themselves'. According to him, the CRAs 'underestimated the credit risk associated with structured credit products and failed to adjust their ratings quickly enough to deteriorating market conditions'. He admits that 'their work involves both methodological errors and unresolved conflicts of interests, with the result that market participants' confidence in the reliability of ratings was seriously shaken'.

Hundreds of thousands of securities that had been previously given the highest ratings were downgraded to junk status during the crisis, causing the downfall of big names in the finance industry, most notably Lehman Brothers. The Financial Crisis Inquiry Commission puts a big chunk of the blame for the global financial crisis on the agencies (FCIC, 2011). European Union officials blame the agencies for contributing to the advent of the European sovereign debt crisis. While the agencies are meant to provide investors with reliable information on the riskiness of debt securities, they have instead been accused of defrauding investors by offering overly favourable evaluations of insolvent financial institutions and giving their seal of approval to extremely risky mortgage-backed securities.

The performance of the CRAs, in the sense of providing investors with useful information, has been dismal, to say the least. They are accused of supplying inaccurate ratings; and that was not only during the global financial crisis. Critics refer to the near-defaults, defaults and financial disasters that escaped detection by the rating agencies as well as failure to downgrade troubled firms until just before (or even after) the declaration of bankruptcy. For example, critics complain that 'not a single analyst at either Moody's or S&P lost his job as a result of missing the Enron fraud' and that 'management [of the agencies] stayed the same' (McLean and Nocera, 2010). Enron was exposed by the activities of short sellers who got it right by analysing the situation thoroughly while the rating agencies gave the impression that there was nothing to worry about. And despite rising mortgage delinquencies, Moody's continued to give the AAA designation to Freddie Mac's preferred stock until mid-2008, when it was downgraded to one tick above junk bonds. *The Economist* (2005) casts doubt on the ability of the rating agencies to provide reliable estimates of the probability of default, arguing that they missed the crises of Enron, WorldCom and Parmalat.

It has been found that the CRAs follow the market; that is, the market alerts the CRAs of trouble, and not vice versa (Kliger and Sarig, 2002). Hawkins and Turner (2000) warn that 'many would be wary of putting too much emphasis on the assessment of credit-rating agencies'. To support their argument, they refer to the performance of the agencies during the Asian crisis. While the agencies did not downgrade most Asian countries before the crisis (when imbalances were developing), their downgrades in the midst of the crisis made it even worse. They conclude that 'rating agencies were backward-looking rather than forward-looking in their assessments'. Likewise, Rodriguez (2002) argues that the ratings tend to follow market trends rather than anticipate them.

In response to the claim that their performance has been less than satisfactory, defenders of CRAs complain about the market's 'lack of appreciation'. According to Robert Clow, 'when a company or sovereign nation pays its debt on time, the market barely takes momentary notice . . . but let a country or corporation unexpectedly miss a payment or threaten default, and bondholders, lawyers and even regulators are quick to rush the field to protest the credit analyst's lapse' (Sinclair, 2005). Other advocates of CRAs point out that bonds assigned low credit ratings by rating agencies have been shown to default more frequently than bonds that receive high credit ratings, suggesting that ratings still serve as a useful indicator of credit risk (Madura, 2011). It is not clear what the appreciation is for, because CRAs are paid well to do their job (it sounds as if the CRAs should receive tips or bonuses on top of the regular fees paid for their services).

The proposition that CRAs get it right most of the time is not consistent with the record. During the global financial crisis, hundreds of billions of dollars' worth of AAA-rated mortgage-backed securities were abruptly downgraded to junk status within two years of the issue of the original ratings. About 73 per cent (over $800 billion worth) of all mortgage-backed securities that Moody's had rated AAA in 2006 were downgraded to junk status two years later. It is inconceivable that a vast number of mortgage-backed securities turn rotten so quickly and decline from the top to the bottom of the quality ladder. One would tend to think that those securities were not top quality to start with, which means that they did not deserve the AAA designation. Critics, therefore, are justified in characterizing the work of the agencies as 'catastrophically misleading' and in believing that they 'provided little or no value' (Casey, 2009; Lippert, 2010).

McLean and Nocera (2010) attribute the failure of the CRAs partly to staff shortage, pointing out that they may have been significantly under-staffed during the subprime boom, which made them unable to assess properly every debt instrument. A related human resources issue is that the analysts working for the CRAs may be underpaid relative to those holding similar positions in financial institutions, resulting in a migration of credit rating analysts to higher-paying jobs with the issuers of securities. Brian Clarkson, who oversaw the structured finance group before becoming the president of Moody's, told the Financial Crisis Inquiry Commission (FCIC) (2011) that retaining employees was always a challenge, for the simple reason that banks paid more. Such a state of affairs: (1) aggravated the understaffing problem at the CRAs; and (2) made it possible for the issuers to manipulate the ratings by acquiring insider information on the mechanics of ratings (Lewis, 2010).

The FCIC (2011) discusses this problem with respect to Moody's. The increase in the collateralized debt obligation (CDO) group's workload and revenue was not paralleled by a staffing increase. In his testimony, Gary Witt (formerly of Moody's CDO unit) said the following:

> Moody's penny-pinching and stingy management was reluctant to pay up for experienced employees. The problem of recruiting and retaining good staff was insoluble. Investment banks often hired away our best people. As far as I can remember, we were never allocated funds to make counter offers. We had almost no ability to do meaningful research.

Eric Kolchinsky, a former team managing director at Moody's, told the FCIC that 'from 2004 to 2006, the increase in the number of deals rated was huge . . . but our personnel did not go up accordingly'. By 2006, Kolchinsky recalled, 'my role as a team leader was crisis management' because 'each deal was a crisis'.

The CRAs did not do a good job, in the spirit of 'why bother about product quality if customers are willing to buy it'; even worse if they are forced to buy it. Rating agencies have come under fire for sacrificing quality ratings to win a bigger share of the booming structured products business. By 2006, Moody's had earned more revenue from structured finance ($881 million) than all of its 2001 revenues combined (Council on Foreign Relations, 2015). The Financial Crisis Inquiry Commission points out in its report on the global financial crisis that from 2000 to 2007, Moody's rated nearly 45000 mortgage-related securities as AAA. This compares with six private-sector companies in the US that held this rating in early 2010. In 2006, Moody's put its AAA seal of approval on 30 mortgage-related securities every working day (FCIC, 2011). How on earth did they have time to do that, given the complexity of the underlying products and the understaffing problem?

Incompetence as a reason for the failure of CRAs implies that the agencies did not have the expertise to do the job they were entrusted to do, particularly when it came to the evaluation of risk embodied in structured products. Hill (2010) notes that search on Google for 'rating agency incompetence' yields 2010 hits and that the same search performed without the quotation marks yields approximately 180000 hits. In his testimony in front of the FCIC, Gary Witt (formerly of Moody's CDO unit) said that 'Moody's didn't have a good model on which to estimate correlations between mortgage-backed securities – so they made them up'. He added: 'they went to the analyst in each of the groups and they said, "Well, you know, how related do you think these types of [mortgage-backed securities] are?"'

The Economist (2013) notes that 'it is beyond argument that ratings agencies did a horrendous job evaluating mortgage-tied securities before the financial crisis hit', but 'whether that failure was a crime has long been a matter of debate'. In this sense, fraud means that the CRAs sold an inferior product knowing that it was inferior, that they deliberately and knowingly rated securities above where they should have been, and that they put their AAA stamp on securities without doing the necessary work to determine the rating. In a confidential memorandum tendered in evidence to the US House of Representatives Committee on Oversight and Government Reform, Moody's CEO indicated that the agencies may have suffered from an overconfidence syndrome, and that they often acted under considerable pressure from institutional investors not to downgrade the ratings. His comments are particularly significant as they indicate awareness, in the sense that the CRAs persisted in doing something although they knew it was wrong, just to boost the bottom line.

Hill (2010) refers to evidence indicating that rating agencies indulged in cutting corners, even in the absence of a huge deal volume. In effect, Hill argues that the agencies deliberately overlooked the possibility that their ratings may have been unwarrantedly high. A. Jones (2009) tells a story about one analyst at Moody's who recalled rating a consignment of $1 billion worth of structured products in 90 minutes. Waxman (2008) tells a story about the rating of a CDO called Pinstripe, which Moody's was asked to rate. When Mr Raiter, who was in charge of the task, asked for the 'collateral tapes' so that he could assess the creditworthiness of the home loans backing the CDO, he got a shocking response from the managing director:

> Any request for loan level tapes is TOTALLY UNREASONABLE!!! Most investors don't have it and can't provide it. Nevertheless we MUST produce a credit estimate . . . It is your responsibility to provide those credit estimates and your responsibility to devise some method for doing so.

I should note that words written in upper-case letters represent shouting. Mr Raiter was ordered by his boss to rate Pinstripe (as AAA, of course) without access to essential credit data. The malpractices of the CRAs did not escape the attention of Transparency International, which commented on the fiasco as follows (Herman, 2009):

> The ratings agencies, in particular, had a conflict of interest and turned a blind eye towards high levels of risk. They were paid and trusted to give honest advice on financial products and we now have sufficient evidence to see that many did not. This is a form of corruption.

It is indeed corporate corruption at the highest level. According to Herman (2009), Mr Poortman (global programmes director at Transparency International) accepts that some rating errors were the result of oversight or misunderstanding, but insisted that others were deliberate, saying that he knows of 'at least one instance where incorrect ratings were given for financial gain'.

Negligence, incompetence, greed and corruption represent a lethal combination that is bound to produce faulty products. The CRAs should not be in this privileged position where their services are mandatory by law, which provides inelastic demand for their services. Experience shows that their products are faulty. Now that they are back in business as usual, beware the rubber stamps of the rating agencies. It is a myth that credit rating agencies provide useful information.

7.2   THE MYTH OF TOO BIG TO FAIL

A government that believes in and follows the too big to fail (TBTF) doctrine does not allow big firms to fail for the very reason that they are big. With respect to financial institutions, this doctrine is justified on the basis of the adverse consequences of the failure of one institution for the whole financial system (and the economy at large). Too big to fail is a myth that is used primarily by the financial oligarchs for the purpose of fear mongering aimed at maintaining their privileges and lavish lifestyles.

The global financial crisis has brought the TBTF debate back to centre stage. The crisis has made it clear that the TBTF doctrine amounts to saving financial institutions from their own mistakes by using taxpayers' money; hence, the debate has a moral dimension. Government bailout of failed financial institutions amounts to funnelling funds into parasitic operations at the cost of starving the real economy of financial resources. It also makes one wonder why free marketeers hate big governments when a big government is so generous when it comes to saving failed financial institutions belonging to the allegedly efficient private sector.

The only argument that can be put forward to justify TBTF actions pertains to systemic risk and failure. However, supportive evidence can hardly be found for the proposition that the failure of one institution could bring about the failure of the financial system and the economy at large. Financial institutions have been allowed to fail without significant systemic problems as the resulting losses can be shared by a large number of investors and creditors, who would have been making good returns in previous years. On the other hand, numerous arguments can be put forward against government bailout and the TBTF doctrine. There is no objective way of determining which financial institution is worthy of the TBTF status and therefore government bailout, both pre- and post-failure. The outcome is that the money spent on bailouts can be otherwise spent on the creation of jobs in the productive sectors of the economy.

On the other hand, TBTF protection boosts rent-seeking unproductive activities and the lobbying of government officials. TBTF creates moral hazard of a significant magnitude. Bailouts financed by taxpayers' money impose a financial burden on future generations, whereas financing by printing money may bring about the menace of hyperinflation. Bailouts amount to saving a reckless minority (the financial oligarchs) at the expense of the prudent majority (mums and dads). Rescuing an institution experiencing difficulties sends out the worst possible signal, as it leads others to think that they will be rescued when they experience difficulties. TBTF makes institutions even bigger (hence a vicious circle is unleashed). Last, but not least, the 'too big to fail' problem has been central to the degeneration of and rampant corruption in the financial system.

Even though the oligarchs and their supporters would argue otherwise, a sound course of action is to let them fail if they must fail. Ironically, the oligarchs reject this free market prescription although they typically shout 'laissez-faire'. In every case of government bailout, a typical argument is put forward that allowing a big institution to fail wreaks havoc on the financial system and the economy as a whole. A doomsday scenario would be used by the management of a failed institution and regulators alike to 'bail out or else'. Some would argue that finance is deeply interconnected, so that even a moderately large institution can take down the system if it implodes. Those who argue along these lines would say that it was the failure of Lehman Brothers that 'brought the world to the brink'. This claim is far-fetched, because the world came to the brink as a result of the collective malpractice of the oligarchs. Saving Lehman in any shape or form could not have changed the course of the global financial crisis.

Take, for example, American International Group (AIG) whose management claimed that failure by the government to bail out the company would have 'catastrophic' consequences. I do not believe that it would have been catastrophic to let AIG's partners in derivative transactions (which are mainly buyers of the credit default swaps issued by AIG) to take substantial losses: this is business as usual. The alternative to bailout would have been to put AIG into Chapter 11 bankruptcy, in which case the creditors (including derivative counterparties) would have obtained a certain recovery ratio on their claims (say 20 per cent), bearing the losses themselves. Likewise, Dowd (1999) argues that financial markets could have absorbed the shock arising from the failure of Long-Term Capital Management (LTCM) in 1998 without going into the financial meltdown that Federal Reserve officials feared.

History does not provide even circumstantial evidence for the proposition that the failure of one institution can cause the failure of the whole system. Such a proposition cannot be substantiated by intuition or theoretical reasoning, neither can it be supported by empirical evidence. Good economics tells us that if a firm must fail, we should let it fail. This means that 'too big to fail' is a myth that policy-makers should stop believing or (more likely) pretending to believe. What is not a myth is that they are too big to jail and too politically connected to fail. Unfortunately, policy-makers have gone out of their way to support zombie financial institutions, and enrich the financial oligarchs running these institutions, by inventing bail-ins (confiscating depositors' money) and by declaring war on cash in the name of financial national security and to accomplish the noble goal of defeating the coronavirus.

7.3   GENDER AND RISK AVERSION

The literature on gender and risk-aversion reveals that women are more risk-averse than men. Those reaching this conclusion are, *inter alia*, Arano et al. (2010), Bernasek and Shwiff (2001), Booth and Nolen (2012) and

Borghans et al. (2009). This conclusion follows from the observation of statistically significant differences between men's and women's behaviour, on average, in experimental lotteries and retirement investments, or in responses to survey questions. By reviewing the literature, Croson and Gneezy (2009) conclude that there is a 'fundamental' difference between men and women with respect to risk aversion. The underlying myth is that men are more inclined to bear risk than women, a proposition that is described by Nelson (2014) as confirming 'popularly held stereotypes of men as the braver and more adventurous sex'.

Nelson (2014) attributes this finding in part to 'stereotypes affecting economics research', whereby researchers tend to find results that confirm 'socially held prior beliefs'. This is confirmation bias, the tendency to confirm the dominant view or own belief. An element of publication bias is also apparent, as a finding that is inconsistent with the dominant view may make the paper reporting the results less likely to be published. We have already seen that empirical work in economics and finance can produce any set of desired results, and if the desired results are influenced by confirmation and publication biases, they will only be reported if they confirm prior beliefs.

Nelson (2014) surveys the empirical literature on gender and risk-aversion and demonstrates that the degree of overlap between women's and men's distributions is considerable (that is, a large percentage of women have the same attitude towards risk as a large percentage of men). Furthermore, she points out that earlier studies are cited or interpreted inaccurately in a stereotype-confirming way; that the results confirming the stereotype are emphasized, while results that do not are downplayed; that stereotype-confirming results are more likely to be published (hence, publication bias); that the effect of confounding variables is neglected; and that the examined areas of risk are chosen selectively. She notes that the claims made in the literature about differences in risk-aversion are exaggerated and overgeneralized far beyond what the data actually support. The results, she argues, demonstrate that the supposedly robust claim that women are more risk-averse than men is far less empirically supported than what is claimed. Moosa (2019) suggests that this is one of many areas where the results are driven by a combination of publication and confirmation biases.

Nelson also suggests that a methodological issue is involved, pertaining to the distinction between 'empirical' and 'essentialist' statements. With respect to the issue under consideration here, an empirical statement goes as follows: 'In our sample, we found a statistically significant difference in mean risk aversion between men and women'. The corresponding essentialist statement is that: 'Women are more risk averse than men'.

In the literature, the two statements are typically taken to have the same meaning, when in fact they convey different information. According to Nelson, the empirical statement is narrow, in the sense that it can be factually correct within the confines of a particular study. The essentialist statement, on the other hand, implies stable characteristics of individual people according to gender. It implies that women are more risk-averse than men because of their 'womanly nature'. This is a statistical issue pertaining to the interpretation of the results of sample-based hypothesis testing.

A relevant point to make here is the role of p-hacking. Christensen and Miguel (2018) deal with publication bias and how it is related to p-hacking, whereby researchers only report results with statistically significant effects at an arbitrary significance level. They suggest that if researchers stop searching across specifications or collecting data once the desired level of significance is achieved, the distribution of p-values would be left-skewed. A simple model of publication bias proposed by McCrary et al. (2016) suggests that, under some relatively strong assumptions regarding the rate of non-publication of statistically insignificant results, readers of research studies could potentially adjust their significance threshold to 'undo the distortion' by using a more stringent t-test statistic of 3.02 (rather than 1.96) to infer statistical significance at the 95 per cent confidence level. The underlying idea here is that what is significant at the 5 per cent level may not be significant at the 1 per cent level. If a researcher wants to reject (accept) a hypothesis, the 5 per cent (1 per cent) results will be reported.

Kim (2019) is sceptical of the false positive findings reported in empirical studies because 'researchers almost exclusively adopt the "p-value less than 0.05" criterion for statistical significance' without paying due attention to large-sample biases that can potentially mislead their research outcomes. He proposes that a statistical toolbox (rather than a single hammer) be used in empirical research, which offers researchers a range of statistical instruments, including a range of alternatives to the p-value criterion such as the Bayesian methods, optimal significance level, sample size selection, equivalence testing and exploratory data analyses. It is found that the positive results obtained under the p-value criterion cannot stand when the toolbox is applied to three notable studies in finance.

Confirmation and publication biases, coupled with the ability to manipulate empirical results, explain why the proposition that women are more risk-averse than men has, at least for some of us, become an undisputed fact of life. If, as Kim recommends, a statistical toolbox (rather than a single hammer) is used in empirical research, and if the results are reported objectively, then at least some results will show that women are not necessarily more risk-averse than men. It is a myth that women are necessarily more risk-averse than men.

7.4 COVERED INTEREST PARITY AS A TESTABLE HYPOTHESIS

Economics, the dismal science, is often criticized (by both outsiders and insiders) as being out of touch with reality. For example, one insider (an accomplished economist) once argued that 'economics today is in the situation that medicine was at the end of the Middle Ages' because 'it consists of a set of theories invented without reference to any actual systematic observation' (Bergmann, 1999). Rather than looking around the world to see what is actually going on, economists tend to think up some simple version of what might be going on, adopting what Bergmann (1999) calls the 'retire-to-your-study approach'.

On the empirical side of research, economists do not observe the actual decision-making process but rather look at some computer-generated numbers to find out whether they are consistent with the underlying theory. If the numbers are inconsistent with the theory, they either call it a 'puzzle' or manipulate the results to support the theory. Bergmann (1999) tells a story of when she suggested to a 'famous monetary economist' that monetary economists should make a habit of talking to bankers. The famous economist told Bergmann that she was wrong, because he talked to bankers all the time and never learned a thing. She inferred that he did not talk to bankers about their business, which was deciding when to make loans (and at what price), but rather about his view of the world, which is a product of the 'retire-to-your-study approach'. Sometimes, this is a reflection of superiority complex on the part of academic economists: they are smarter than practitioners because they can solve partial differential equations, a task that is far beyond the intellectual abilities of the practitioners.

Perhaps nothing vindicates Bergmann more than the widespread practice of testing covered interest parity (CIP) when in fact it is not a testable hypothesis. CIP is a deterministic equation that represents a mechanical operation used by bankers to calculate the forward exchange rate for a certain maturity and quoting that rate to a customer at a particular point in time, given the prevailing conditions. Instead of asking bankers how they determine the forward rate, economists write CIP as a stochastic equation then test for cointegration between the spot and forward rates (as the necessary condition) and for coefficient restrictions (as the sufficient condition) for the validity of CIP. Econometric extravaganza follows by adding more explanatory variables, using a member of the extended family of autoregressive conditional heteroscedasticity (ARCH) models and other fancy estimation techniques, only to conclude that deviations from CIP can be observed.

Things go further on the theoretical front when economists argue, on the basis of the unbiased efficiency hypothesis, that the forward rate can be used to forecast the spot rate expected to prevail on the maturity date of the forward contract. This issue was dealt with under the forward premium puzzle in Chapter 2. This so-called puzzle can be resolved quickly and easily by talking to a banker, who will tell us that the forward rate is not determined on the basis of the expected spot rate, which means that the forward rate has nothing to do with forecasting.

Inference on the validity of CIP is typically based not on the actual transaction data used by bankers but rather on published data obtained from public sources. A consequence of the use of published rather than transaction data is a typical measurement errors problem, which may lead to the wrong conclusion that deviations from CIP can be observed. Several reasons have been presented to explain deviations from CIP, from the very simple (such as transaction costs) to the very fancy (such as the peso problem). The fact of the matter is that CIP is a deterministic equation that must hold because of the very process used to determine the forward rate.

Covered interest parity is typically described as a 'theory' or 'theorem', which means that it can be formulated as a testable hypothesis. For example, S. Jones (2009) describes CIP as 'the theory that positive returns cannot be earned by borrowing the home or base currency to invest the commensurate amount in a foreign currency on a covered basis'. Fong et al. (2010) call CIP a 'theorem', postulating that 'the covered interest rate differential between two identical risk-free securities denominated in two different currencies should be equal to zero'. Szilagyi and Batten (2006) go further and call it a 'fundamental theorem'. It is ironic that CIP is a 'theorem' that does not hold precisely, yet not a single CIP guru left academia to make riskless arbitrage profit by exploiting deviations from the equilibrium condition implied by the 'theorem'. Yet, these gurus tell the audience in academic conferences and seminars how to make money from covered arbitrage without trying it themselves.

Testing CIP was a big industry in the 1970s and 1980s, when two types of tests were employed. The first is to determine whether profit opportunities can be arbitraged away; in other words, whether the actual forward premium deviates from what is implied by CIP by more than transaction costs. The second is to find out whether CIP holds on average, by testing the hypothesis that domestic and foreign interest rates and spot and forward exchange rates are bound by the CIP relation; cointegration was (and still is) used for this purpose. Invariably, empirical testing of CIP reveals deviations from CIP, which are explained in terms of several factors, particularly transaction costs.

In reality, deviations are bound to be found if the tests are based on published, non-transaction data. It is ironic that the use of non-transaction data is advocated on the grounds that transaction data are not available. For example, S. Jones (2009) suggests that 'it is often difficult to locate data on interest rates, spot foreign exchange rates and forward points at many time horizons that are synchronous'. If proper data are not available, it does not make sense to test a hypothesis on the basis of improper data and derive inference accordingly. In any case, transaction data are available, although they are not easy to obtain. Furthermore, the use of non-transaction data introduces measurement errors in the dependent and explanatory variables, which may lead to invalid inference.

Although Taylor (1987) calls CIP a 'theorem', his results indicate that it must hold as a truism if proper data are used. Taylor observes that earlier studies (for example, Officer and Willett, 1979) reported empirical deviations from CIP, but he argues that the results of those studies 'almost certainly reflect data imperfections rather than market inefficiencies'. He argues that it is essential that 'any data used to test covered interest parity should be contemporaneously sampled and be actual market data on which a trader could have dealt', and that 'previous empirical work on covered interest parity often makes use of data from published sources that are not contemporaneously sampled'. By using high-frequency data collected in the London foreign exchange market, he shows that 'the relevant markets are remarkably efficient in eliminating profitable arbitrage opportunities'; in other words, no deviations from CIP are observed.

Committeri et al. (1993) go even further than Taylor, arguing that a proper test of CIP should be based on data that have three properties: (1) market participants could have actually dealt with them; (2) sampled at the same instant in time; and (3) collected from independent sources. By using data satisfying these criteria, they obtain unambiguous results that support the validity of CIP. This point had been made earlier by Coulbois and Prissert (1974), who suggested that reported data could differ from transaction data, thereby explaining why deviations from CIP may be observed. The fact of the matter is that it does not make any difference whether or not data are available, because there is no point in testing a definitional equation.

Deviations from CIP are observed only because the wrong data are used for empirical testing. CIP must hold by design, as it is a representation of a mechanical banking operation; yet, testing CIP is still a thriving industry. It is business as usual for economists using published, non-transaction data and fancy econometrics to test CIP and find deviations, which are subsequently explained somehow (alternatively, a 'puzzle' is claimed). For example, Felmingham and Leong (2005) find that CIP fails if ordinary least squares (OLS) and fully modified OLS are applied. Akram et al. (2008) demonstrate the presence of short-lived deviations from CIP, which can be economically significant and persist for a long enough period to allow agents to exploit them. Fong et al. (2010) use a 'novel and unique dataset' and conclude that deviations exist to compensate for liquidity and credit risk. Baba and Packer (2009) identify 'sharp and persistent deviations from the CIP condition'. Thornton (1989) concludes that 'frequent violations of CIP occur, but do not persist'. In none of these cases are actual transaction data used to test CIP. Based on an empirical illustration, Moosa (2017c) concludes as follows:

> The results of this illustration have two implications. The first is that deviations from CIP are observed when non-transaction data are used, even if the bid–offer spreads are taken into consideration. The second is that deviations disappear when transaction data are used – in this case when the forward rate that would have been quoted by a bank is used. It seems that there is no point in testing CIP because we know the outcome in advance. If non-transaction data are used, we will invariably observe deviations. If transaction data are used, CIP fits very well, which is tautology because the quoted forward rate is calculated from CIP.

Only Post-Keynesian economists seem to have realized that CIP must hold by necessity. While the Post-Keynesian or cambist view on this issue can be found in Smithin (1994), it was Lavoie (2000) who invoked the proposition put forward by Coulbois and Prissert (1974) to formulate the Post-Keynesian view of the forward rate. The underlying proposition is that while CIP holds always perfectly by design, the forward exchange rate is not an expectation variable but rather the result of a 'simple arithmetic operation' (Lavoie, 2000). Llewellyn (1980) argues that the standard theoretical approach to the analysis of the forward exchange rate ignores the mechanism through which banks (which make the market) provide forward exchange facilities.

Instead of formulating a theory of the determination of the forward rate without reference to any actual systematic observation, it makes more sense to follow the advice of Bergmann (1999) and ask bankers what they do when they quote forward rates to their customers. For this purpose, it is not necessary to interview bankers or to survey them because the actual practice whereby the forward rate is determined is described in the professional literature, which can be found by using Google to search for 'how forward rates are determined in practice'. When they offer forward contracts to customers, bankers use a formula that represents CIP to calculate the forward rate. They may not even know what CIP is, but they adhere strictly to the formula. If they choose any rate other than the rate produced by the CIP formula, they will not be able to hedge their position, and end up on the wrong side of a profitable arbitrage operation. No banker will tell us that the forward rate is determined by a theory or that it can be used to forecast the spot rate. Unlike academics, practitioners do not have the luxury of theorizing because they deal in real money. And unlike academics, practitioners lose their jobs if they get it wrong.

Let us look at the description of forward contracts, forward rates and covered interest parity in the professional literature, where a forward contract is 'an agreement, usually with a bank, to exchange a specific amount of currencies sometime in the future for a specific rate – the forward exchange rate'. The question of how the forward rate is determined is answered as follows in a document published by Microfinance Currency Risk Solutions (MFX, 2016):

> How is this forward exchange rate calculated? It cannot depend on the [spot] exchange rate 1 year from now because that is not known. What is known is the spot price, or the exchange rate, today, but a forward price cannot simply equal the spot price, because money can be safely invested to earn interest, and, thus, the future value of money is greater than its present value. What seems reasonable is that if the current exchange rate of a quoted currency with respect to a base currency equalizes the present value of the currencies, then the forward exchange rate should equalize the future value of the quoted currency and the future value of the base currency.

The forward exchange rate maintains covered interest parity (equality of the interest rate differential and forward spread). A corollary that follows is that if the interest rates of the two countries are equal, the forward exchange rate is simply equal to the spot rate.

It is often claimed in the academic literature that deviations from CIP tend to arise in turbulent markets. For example, Baba and Packer (2009) find results indicating that 'sharp and persistent deviations from the CIP condition are observed during the turmoil'. S. Jones (2009) suggests that in tranquil markets, and given data of a contemporaneous nature, CIP tends to hold within a narrow bound consistent with transaction costs. However, he adds, during periods containing significant turbulence, there is evidence of larger deviations where arbitrage appears possible for a short period of time. He shows that since September 2008, breaches of CIP have been 'commonplace', and attributes deviations in turbulent markets to 'major financial events that raised bank counterparty risks and drained liquidity from the short-term money market'. This is nonsense, because bankers adhere strictly to the CIP formula when they calculate the forward rate, irrespective of whether conditions are tranquil or turbulent. Under bad conditions a bank may not offer a forward contract to a customer, but it will not offer a contract by quoting a forward rate that is different from what is implied by CIP. The views expressed by some academic economists reflect an attitude of a superiority complex, as 'we know more than bankers'. This is a triumph of wishful thinking over reason.

Covered interest parity holds by design because it represents a formula used by bankers to calculate the forward rates they quote to their customers. Deviations from CIP represent a 'free lunch', the ability to make money without bearing risk (at least, market risk). One can only wonder what has happened to the basic finance principle of 'no such thing as a free lunch', as riskless arbitrage profit is a free lunch that is available to anyone. CIP is not a 'theory' or a 'theorem', hence it is not a testable hypothesis.

7.5 CONCLUDING REMARKS

In this chapter we examined four myths in financial economics: the myth that credit rating agencies provide useful information about the default risk embodied in securities, the myth that some financial institutions are too big to fail, the myth that women are more risk-averse than men, and the myth that covered interest parity is a testable hypothesis. The last two myths result from either faulty empirical testing or (in the case of CIP) the very use of empirical testing. If some academic economists believe that women are more risk-averse than men, or that covered interest parity is a testable hypothesis, they would be wrong, but this kind of belief does not inflict extensive damage on society; in other words, it is benign.

On the other hand, believing that credit rating agencies provide useful information that can be used to buy securities was an important contributor to the materialization of the global financial crisis. The most damaging myth, however, is the myth of 'too big to fail', because it means that the government should channel taxpayers money to failed financial institutions, thus diverting resources from where they would produce more value for society (for example, health and education) to the pockets of the financial oligarchs. For example, the billions of dollars used to save a failed US insurance company in 2008 could have been put to a better use, such as preparing for something like Covid-19.

Governments in 'Western' countries do indulge in this kind of malpractice, but what is coming is worse. Many governments have adopted bail-in legislation, whereby failed banks will be saved by confiscating depositors' money. Needless to say, it is a joke that depositors will be compensated by getting, in return for their stolen money, shares in failed banks. As a contingency plan to meet the possibility that people abandon banks and keep their money under the mattress, some governments have declared war on cash and threatened to put behind bars any citizen who would dare settle a transaction by using an amount of cash that exceeds a predetermined limit (that will be reduced over time). For governments launching a war on cash, the coronavirus provides a good excuse for banning cash transactions in the name of public health. It is truly a mad, mad world.

8. The myths of macroeconomics

8.1 RELIABILITY OF THE REPORTED INFLATION FIGURES

We are repeatedly told that inflation is running at an annual rate of 1.5 per cent or so, presumably because the central bank is doing a good job, and this is why the governor should get a big bonus and a salary rise. However, a visit to the supermarket, hosting a dinner in a restaurant, and paying bills for utilities and health insurance show otherwise. Are we supposed to believe the government or our wallets?

A typical response to the claim that the inflation rate is higher than what is declared by the central bank is that just because the prices of a few items are rising, this does not necessarily imply a high inflation rate because the prices of other items are falling simultaneously. True, but a typical consumer does not buy a laptop or an iPad every other day, while spending repeatedly on items whose prices are rising, such as food, fuel, clothing, rent, transport, repair and maintenance, child care, health and education, and it is the prices of these items which rise rapidly. Weiner (2019) is right in saying the following: 'every time I see and hear someone talk about low inflation, I immediately think about everything that I purchase that costs more today than yesterday'. Furthermore, the demand for the items whose prices are rising is rather inelastic. This is why consumers observe that, as time goes by, they can save less and less of their stagnant incomes as a result of the rise in the cost of living (that is, inflation). And this is why Weiner (2019) wonders whether inflation is under control, or whether 'it is just a big lie'.

To find the truth, follow the money trail or look for the beneficiary. The government has strong motives for masking the actual inflation rate and reporting a lower rate instead. The first reason why governments under-report inflation is political gain, as keeping inflation under control sounds good in campaign speeches; it may even make the difference in a close election. In non-election years, fudging the inflation figures enables the government to avoid public pressure to do something about it. The second reason is that low reported inflation generates big savings for the government because social security payments are adjusted by the inflation rate. Boring (2014) argues that the consumer price index (CPI) is tied to the incomes of about 80 million Americans, including social security beneficiaries, food stamp recipients, military and federal civil service retirees and survivors, and children on school lunch programmes. The third reason is that low inflation justifies a policy of low interest rates that governments are pursuing for the benefit of banks and corporate interests. A central bank pursuing quantitative easing would always claim that it is not inflationary, in defiance of the quantity theory of money (and common sense). The last thing this central bank wants to hear is an announcement of high inflation. It is ironic that governments not only deny the presence of inflation but also claim that they are keeping interest rates low to entice mild inflation, which is required for economic recovery. This is a super-travesty.

Some observers believe that inflation is under-reported because the inflation figures are not compatible with the growth of the money supply as predicted by the quantity theory of money, and the very definition of inflation that it is a situation where too much money chases too few goods. It also follows from the official definition of inflation adopted by the United States (US) Bureau of Labor Statistics, that it is 'a process of continuously rising prices or equivalently, of a continuously falling value of money' (Boring, 2014). In this sense, Schiff (2013) mentions the impossibility of creating something out of nothing. His argument is that 'printing a dollar diminishes the value of all existing dollars by an aggregate amount equal to the purchasing power of the new dollar'.

Figure 8.1 shows a big gap between the monetary growth rate and the inflation rate in the US, which has been explained in various ways. The first explanation is that the gap is accounted for by changes in the velocity of circulation. However, since independent measures of velocity are not available, this proposition cannot be confirmed or refuted. Another explanation is that a significant portion of the US money supply, particularly currency, is held abroad. Yet another explanation is that monetary growth has been reflected mostly in house prices, and perhaps financial prices, rather than the prices of goods and services. If this explanation is valid, rising financial and house prices should lead to goods price inflation through the wealth effect. Still, inflation is invisible in official statistics.

Claims that governments under-report inflation are common. Mauldin (2013) suggests that the US Bureau of Labor Statistics (BLS), which compiles the consumer price index, 'has engaged in methodological shenanigans over the past couple decades'. He adds the following:

> The upshot of all their monkeying with the numbers is that the official rate of inflation may be two to four times lower than the actual rate (which is rather

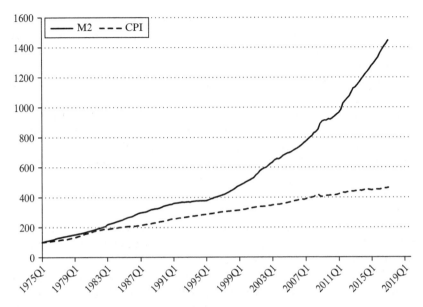

Figure 8.1   US money supply (M2) and CPI (1975: 1 = 100)

convenient if you're a government bureaucrat trying to hold down interest costs
and Social Security payments).

Fernet (2016) and Cavallo et al. (2016) examine the under-reporting of
inflation in Argentina. Fernet (2016) argues that what is more troubling
than persistently high and rising inflation is 'the government's flippant
and dismissive treatment of how difficult it will be to quash inflation and
just how much it is affecting the lives of Argentina's people'. Cavallo et al.
(2016) suggest that during the period from 2007 to 2015, the Argentine
government manipulated economic statistics in an attempt to fool the
public into believing that inflation was lower than what it actually was.
Ordinary people did not buy it, showing instead a remarkable aptitude for
contesting the official claims. Cavallo et al. explain in detail the 'Argentine
statistics sham' and note that 'it holds lessons even for the United States
and Europe, where some segments of the public see bias in government
statistics even where none exists'.

Manipulating the inflation figures is not a 'Western' malpractice that
only Argentina has embraced. The Chinese authorities also indulge in
the manipulation of the inflation figures. Moosa (1997) examines the
behaviour of the Chinese official CPI relative to a market-based index
and shows that the official index underestimates the actual inflation rate

with time-varying bias. The biasedness of the official index is attributed to covert price rises induced by the presence of price controls and quantity rationing.

Governments have both the motive and the means to manipulate the inflation figures. As far as the means are concerned, Boring (2014) argues that the government has a few resources at its disposal to manipulate the CPI. To start with, the process of calculating the CPI is 'top secret'; for example, the raw data used to calculate the CPI are not available to the public. Boring (2014) did ask the Bureau of Labor Statistics (BLS) why the data were not made publicly available; the answer was, 'so companies can't compare prices'. This, according to Boring, makes very little sense because companies can easily compare prices with publicly available data. Secrecy makes it impossible to audit the reported inflation figures. Statistical agencies have the habit of changing the way they calculate the CPI under the pretext of 'methodological improvements'. For example, the BLS has changed the way it calculates inflation more than 20 times in 30 years (Boring, 2014). These changes are convenient for producing low inflation figures by including or excluding certain items in the CPI. Given the lack of transparency, there is no way to know what goes on behind the closed doors of statistical agencies.

It is a myth that the reported inflation figures reflect the facts on the ground, particularly in this age of quantitative easing and ultra-low interest rates. Governments justify these destructive policies in terms of low inflation and the desire to revive the economy or avoid the next recession. However, we know that the inflation rate is higher than what is announced, simply because inflation is something that we can feel. We can feel it by the big annual increases in the premiums for health insurance. We can feel it by shopping in a supermarket or having a meal in a restaurant. We can feel it by asking a handyman to do a small job at home. We can feel it by paying utility and school bills. And we can feel it when we dig into our savings to meet current expenditure.

8.2 THE EFFECT OF INTEREST RATES ON GROWTH

I like the proverb (or adage), 'you can lead a horse to water but you can't make him drink'. It means that you can give someone an opportunity but you cannot force them to take it. In economics it means that the central bank can reduce interest rates but it cannot force individuals and companies to borrow and invest. This means that a policy of low interest rates aimed at reviving the economy may or may not work. It will not work if financial institutions are not willing to extend credit to the private sector, fearing the risk of default. And it will not work if the private sector is not willing to borrow because the economic outlook is bearish. After all, it takes two to tango.

Let us start with the second possibility that the private sector is not willing to borrow and invest. The rationale behind the belief that low interest rates are conducive to growth is the perceived positive effect on consumption and investment. Low interest rates are supposed to encourage consumers to borrow and spend on consumer durables, households to borrow and invest in housing, and businesses to borrow and invest in plant and equipment as well as inventory. Since these are components of aggregate demand, the level of output will rise, and consequently growth kicks in and accelerates. So, the question is whether or not consumption and investment expenditure are interest-sensitive. When the economic outlook is bleak, households anticipate declining incomes and the possibility of joblessness. A person expecting a loss of income or experiencing signs of job insecurity, triggered by a slowdown in economic activity, is unlikely to borrow to replace the old car or fridge. This person is unlikely to borrow to buy a bigger house. Business firms sensing diminishing economic activity will not borrow to expand productive capacity or invest in inventory. Firms do not indulge in capital investment just because interest rates are low, as they expect positive net present value or an internal rate of return that is higher than the cost of funding. Low interest rates do not represent either a necessary or a sufficient condition for capital investment. Investment is more profit-sensitive than interest-sensitive.

In recent years central banks adopted quantitative easing as a policy whereby new money is produced (out of thin air) and used to buy securities (of various kinds and maturities) from financial institutions. In the process, security prices rise while yields decline; in other words, the objective of quantitative easing is to maintain low interest rates across a range of maturities. The declared objective is to boost the real sector of the economy by pushing down the cost of borrowing to a lower level than what can be achieved by using conventional interest rate policy, which targets a particular short-term rate (typically the federal funds rate in the US and the corresponding rates in other countries). However, even if households and business firms are willing to borrow and invest, banks may not be willing to extend credit, at least not by as much as is required to revive the economy. Banks may very well choose to accumulate reserves rather than extend credit if they believe that the risk of default is high.

In January 2008, US banks held $15.4 billion in reserves, giving a reserve ratio of 0.027 or 2.7 per cent. In October 2008, quantitative easing was initiated, and by the end of the month reserves had risen to $284.6 billion, producing a reserve ratio of 0.46. At the end of March 2010, they held reserves amounting to $1.15 trillion, with a reserve ratio of 1.47; that is, they held more reserves than deposits. Wheelock (2010) attributes disparity between the growth rates of the monetary base and the money supply to the lack of willingness of banks to lend, due to scepticism about the perceived creditworthiness of potential borrowers. McTeer (2010) contends that the large expansion of the Fed's balance sheet remains as excess reserves, which are not used for money-creating lending and investing. Ben Bernanke is quoted as saying that 'scarred banks curtail their lending to companies after financial crises even if they have sufficient funds, inhibiting economic growth' (*The Economist*, 2015a).

The accumulation of reserves by US banks can be attributed to: (1) fear about the creditworthiness of borrowers in the aftermath of the global financial crisis and the great recession; and (2) the fact that reserves no longer represent a non-interest-bearing asset. Since October 2008, the Fed has been paying interest on the reserves of commercial banks held with it, which means that banks will accumulate reserves as long the interest paid on reserve accounts is high enough to deter banks from converting their new reserves to interest-earning assets by extending loans to households and firms. It is rather odd to adopt quantitative easing to encourage banks to give loans while simultaneously discouraging them from doing so by paying them interest on reserves.

Another point to bear in mind is that even if the central bank cuts the official rate, there is no guarantee that banks will follow suit and cut their lending rates to encourage households and firms to borrow. This happens quite often in Australia, where banks fail to match the cuts to the cash rate announced by the Reserve Bank of Australia (RBA). In October 2019, the RBA cut the official cash rate by a quarter of a percentage point to a new record low of 0.75 per cent and declared that further cuts were possible to boost employment and 'lift stubbornly low inflation back into the 2–3% target band' (Karp, 2019). As we saw in the previous section, no one believes the bogus claim that inflation is below 2 per cent. In March 2020, the RBA went for another record low of 0.5 per cent to alleviate the economic effects of the outbreak of the coronavirus; which is ridiculous, to say the least.

Tagliaferro (2019) does not believe that the intention of the RBA is to boost the economy by cutting interest rates, as he argues that 'the truth is that the RBA has joined the world's central banks in conducting an experiment'. He adds the following:

> Their paradigm is that the economy will benefit from policies based on economic theories that, in reality, have previously resulted in major imbalances

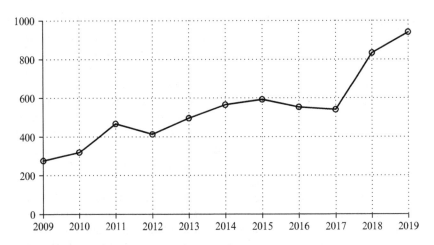

Figure 8.2   Stock buy-backs by US shareholding companies

and have frequently ended in crises: the technology boom and bust, the housing boom and mortgage financing bust in the US followed by a global financial crisis, and several other booms and busts such as those experienced in Iceland, Spain, and Ireland. The common theme in all these events is easy access to very cheap credit.

He goes on to criticize the low interest rate policy by suggesting that 'lower interest rates have not been encouraging investment but rather share buy backs'. This can be seen in Figure 8.2, which depicts stock buy-backs in the US since 2009. It is not only that low interest rates do not boost the economy, but they also have serious adverse consequences. When interest rates are extremely low, prudent savers are penalized and encouraged to take on more risk. If the policy is sustained over a long period of time, it provides support only for overleveraged inefficient companies that would otherwise fail. Low interest rates maintain bubbles in the housing and stock markets. On a macroeconomic level, the policy hurts economic growth because growth needs capital accumulation that is financed through savings. Households are reluctant to lend their savings to the government when Treasury bond yields are low, in which case the government finds it tantalizing, perhaps inevitable, to go down the slippery slope of monetizing the budget deficit by 'printing' money.

In his outgoing speech, Mario Draghi, who has retired as the head of the European Central Bank, said that interest rate cuts may not have the same power that they once did (Schrager, 2019). This is how he expresses this point of view:

Today, we are in a situation where low interest rates are not delivering the same degree of stimulus as in the past, because the rate of return on investment in the economy has fallen. Monetary policy can still achieve its objective, but it can do so faster and with fewer side effects if fiscal policies are aligned with it.

It is interesting to see that Draghi is advocating the use of fiscal policy, given that he was a champion of quantitative easing. However, he makes a valid point that was made earlier: low interest rates on their own cannot trigger real capital investment, because what matters is the cost of borrowing relative to return on real capital. It is therefore a myth that the economy can be revived by cutting interest rates, even by Draghi's admission.

Using interest rates to revive the economy is a policy prescription that is based on the assumption that only the private sector can propel the economy, because the government's fiscal stimulus does not work, or so the myth goes. Cochrane (2013) disputes the traditional and New Keynesian explanations of how the fiscal stimulus works. This is how he represents the traditional Keynesian view:

> More government spending, even if on completely useless projects, 'puts money in people's pockets.' Those people in turn go out and spend, providing more income for others, who go out and spend, and so on. We pull ourselves up by our bootstraps. Saving is the enemy, as it lowers the marginal propensity to consume and reduces this multiplier.

And this is how he represents the New Keynesian view:

> The government should spend money, even if on totally wasted projects, because that will cause inflation, inflation will lower real interest rates, lower real interest rates will induce people to consume today rather than tomorrow, we believe tomorrow's consumption will revert to trend anyway, so this step will increase demand.

It is not clear why Cochrane emphasizes the term 'useless projects'; I assume because anything the (allegedly) inefficient public sector does is useless, and anything the (allegedly) efficient private sector does is useful. Yes, the government can and does waste money on stuff like paying private sector consultants for simple tasks that can be performed more efficiently by the underlying government department, or spending $100 million on a postal referendum to legalize the killing of possums operating in private family homes. Even worse, the government may decide to spend billions of dollars of taxpayers' money fighting a war of aggression in a far-away country, typically as a member of a 'coalition of the willing'. Billions are wasted on the military–industrial complex in the name of 'national security'. On the other hand, building a new road, an airport or a hospital can hardly be a waste, and there is always the capacity to have more. Housing the homeless is useful, not wasteful. Investing in health and education is useful, not wasteful.

Then, who said that the private sector does not waste money by indulging in useless projects? Recall the agency problem, where managers make decisions in their own interest, not in the interest of shareholders; that is, the project may be useless for shareholders but profitable for managers. The private sector indulges in wasteful expenditure by hiring the unneeded services of consultants, just because they are cronies of the chief executive officer (CEO) or the chief financial officer (CFO). Private sector companies waste money paying high salaries to executives who would do the best job for their companies by staying at home. They pay incompetent, greedy and corrupt executives millions of dollars in golden parachutes to thank them for destroying shareholders' equity and bringing the companies to their knees. Private sector companies waste money on unwarranted luxury and perks for the CEO and their inner circle such as private jets and helicopter rides from the top of the building to the golf course. They waste billions on mergers and acquisitions intended exclusively for empire-building. In 2008, the Royal Bank of Scotland wasted some $50 billion on an acquisition that eventually brought its fall from grace.

As usual, someone like me who thinks that the fiscal stimulus can work may resort to the con art of econometrics to produce supportive empirical evidence. Likewise, a free marketeer who thinks that the fiscal stimulus is useless can use the con art of econometrics to produce empirical evidence supporting their point of view. However, unreliable and subjective empirical evidence can be done without when common sense tells us that fiscal stimulus can be useful. It is intuitive and makes sense to suggest that fiscal stimulus works if the resources are allocated properly. For example, building a road using local contractors, materials and labour is bound to be stimulating. In this case, the traditional Keynesian mechanism works very well. A road project needs workers who get paid and subsequently spend at a least a fraction of their income, which will be someone else's income, who spends some of it, and so on. This process works, without the complications of the New Keynesian view, even if some of those workers spend money on more tattoos. If, however, the government decides not to build a road because resources have to be allocated to fighting a war requiring imported arms, then this kind of fiscal stimulus will not work.

It is interesting to note that the International Monetary Fund (IMF), which is guided by the free market principles of the Washington Consensus, advocates the use of fiscal stimulus to counter the effects of the coronavirus outbreak. The IMF recommends the use of public money to 'save lives'. In an IMF blog, Vitor Gaspar and Paolo Mauro (2020) argue that 'developing an effective vaccine also requires public money'. They add:

> Governments should protect people from the economic impact of this global health crisis. Those who are hit the hardest should not go bankrupt and lose their livelihood through no fault of their own. A family-operated restaurant in a tourism-reliant country, or the employees of a factory shut down because of a local quarantine will need support to weather the crisis.

They go on to describe how governments can help by 'spending money to prevent, detect, control, treat, and contain the virus'; 'providing timely, targeted, and temporary cash flow relief to the people and firms that are most affected'; 'giving wage subsidies to people and firms to help curb contagion'; and 'expanding and extending transfers – both cash and in-kind, especially for vulnerable groups'. Likewise, the Organisation for Economic Co-operation and Development (OECD) (2020) recommends the use of fiscal policy to counter the adverse effects of the coronavirus outbreak, with emphasis on the need to enhance fiscal support via stronger public investment.

It is therefore a myth that reducing interest rates boosts the economy, because low interest rates are neither a necessary nor a sufficient condition for capital expenditure. And it is a myth that the fiscal stimulus does not work, because it does if government funds are spent properly on infrastructure and projects that utilize local labour and materials. If the fiscal stimulus takes the form of cutting taxes for the rich, it will not work, which brings us to the two myths that will be discussed next.

8.3 THE EFFECT OF TAX CUTS ON ECONOMIC GROWTH

The myth we are concerned with here is that reducing the corporate income tax rate and the personal tax rate for the rich is conducive to economic growth. The myth is used to justify tax cuts for the benefit of the oligarchy at the expense of the majority. Tax cuts reduce the funds required to finance government expenditure. Free marketeers argue that tax cuts leave more money to be invested by the private sector in employment-creating projects, which will benefit everyone through the trickledown effect. This sounds cool, but in reality the surplus cash received by companies and the billionaires who own the companies is not invested in job creation; rather, it is used to finance stock buy-backs, invested in parasitic financial activities or funnelled to tax havens.

Since the late 1970s, supply-side economists have been telling us that tax cuts stimulate economic growth to such a degree that tax revenue would rise rather than fall. However, the empirical evidence for this hypothesis is rather thin. In a study of the Joint Committee on Taxation (2005) on the economic effects of reducing marginal tax rates, it is suggested that 'growth effects eventually become negative ... because accumulating federal government debt crowds out private investment'. The study concludes that 'lowering marginal tax rates is likely to harm the economy over the long run if the tax reductions are deficit financed'.

If high taxes are bad for the economy, we should expect robust economic growth during periods characterized by low tax rates, and vice versa. This is not the conclusion reached by Aaron et al. (2004), who found that 'historical evidence shows no clear correlation between tax rates and economic growth', and that 'comparisons across countries confirm that rapid growth has been a feature of both high- and low-tax nations'. Allard and Lindert (2006) find that a higher ratio of tax revenue to gross domestic product (GDP) leads to an improvement in economic performance, because the additional revenue is used to undertake growth-promoting activities such as investment in public education, infrastructure and public health. Similar conclusions are reached by Mazerov (2010), the Congressional Budget Office (CBO) (2005, 2008) and the Congressional Research Service (Gravelle et al., 2009).

A variety of tax cuts were enacted under President George Bush Junior between 2001 and 2003 (commonly referred to as the 'Bush tax cuts') through the Economic Growth and Tax Relief Reconciliation Act of 2001, and the Jobs and Growth Tax Relief Reconciliation Act of 2003. Kogan (2003) evaluated the claims that the Bush tax cuts of 2001 would boost growth, and found 'little support for claims made by Administration officials and other proponents of these tax cuts that either the 2001 tax cut or the new "growth" package would generate substantial improvements in long-term economic growth', that 'these tax cuts would have only a small effect on the economy over the long term', and that 'the effect is as likely to be negative as positive'. On the same issue, the CBO (2001) concluded that 'the cumulative effects of the new tax law on the economy are uncertain but will probably be small'. Likewise, Gale and Potter (2002) found that the effect on long-term economic growth was more likely to be a small negative than a small positive. Similar conclusions are reached by Elmendorf and Reifschneider (2002) and Auerbach (2002). Kogan (2003) argues that 'the proposition that tax cuts can pay for themselves – like most claims of a "free lunch" – is too good to be true', and that 'it does not withstand scrutiny'.

In 2003, 450 economists, including ten Nobel Prize laureates, signed a statement opposing the Bush tax cuts (available at http://www.epi.org/

page/-/old/stmt/2003/statement_signed. pdf). They expressed the view that economic growth had not been sufficient to generate jobs and prevent unemployment from rising, but that 'the tax cut plan proposed by President Bush is not the answer to these problems'. The statement made it clear that 'passing these tax cuts will worsen the long-term budget outlook, adding to the nation's projected chronic deficits', and that 'this fiscal deterioration will reduce the capacity of the government to finance Social Security and Medicare benefits as well as investments in schools, health, infrastructure, and basic research'. Moreover, it was suggested that 'the proposed tax cuts will generate further inequalities in after-tax income'. Those who signed the statement include Nobel Prize winners George Akerlof, Kenneth Arrow, Lawrence Klein, Daniel McFadden, Franco Modigliani, Robert Solow, Joseph Stiglitz, Paul Samuelson and William Sharpe.

Krugman (2007) argues that 'supply side doctrine, which claimed without evidence that tax cuts would pay for themselves, never got any traction in the world of professional economic research, even among conservatives'. Roubini (2010) suggests that the Republican Party is 'trapped in a belief in voodoo economics, the economic equivalent of creationism'. Buffett (2003) commented on the proposed reduction in taxes on dividends by arguing that 'when you listen to tax-cut rhetoric, remember that giving one class of taxpayer a "break" requires – now or down the line – that an equivalent burden be imposed on other parties'. In other words, he said, 'if I get a break, someone else pays', which means that 'government can't deliver a free lunch to the country as a whole'. David Walker, former comptroller general of the United States, stated in January 2009 in a documentary film called *IOUSA* (available at http://www.iousathemovie. com): 'you can't have guns, butter and tax cuts' because 'the numbers just don't add up'.

Let us now turn to the myth of trickledown, a term that is identified with critics of 'Reaganomics'. The underlying idea is that policies designed to benefit the wealthy, such as financial deregulation and favourable tax treatment of capital income, will ultimately benefit everybody. It is the proposition that the benefits of growth will eventually trickle down even to the poor, or that a 'high tide carries all boats'. This notion, according to Quiggin (2009), is one of the casualties of the global financial crisis. The problem is that 'eventually' may never come, even though we are told that under the free market system all of us will 'eventually be billionaires'.

The notion of trickledown has been criticized severely. In the 1992 US presidential election, independent candidate Ross Perot called trickledown economics 'political voodoo'. In a video for the 2011 general election in New Zealand, Labour Party MP Damien O'Connor described trickledown economics as 'the rich pissing on the poor'. A 2012 study by the Tax Justice

Network indicates that wealth of the super-rich does not trickle down to improve the economy, but tends to be amassed and sheltered in tax havens, with a negative effect on the tax base of the home economy (Stewart, 2012). Chang (2011) criticizes trickledown policies, citing examples of slowing job growth and rising income inequality in most of the rich countries. In a 2015 report published by the International Monetary Fund, Dabla-Norris et al. (2015) dismiss the trickledown effect, as the rich get richer. This is what the report says:

> If the income share of the top 20 percent (the rich) increases, then GDP growth actually declines over the medium term, suggesting that the benefits do not trickle down. In contrast, an increase in the income share of the bottom 20 percent (the poor) is associated with higher GDP growth.

The financial sector is the obvious test case for the trickledown theory because incomes in the financial sector have risen more rapidly than in any other part of the economy. According to the theory, the growth in income accruing to the financial sector has benefits for the population as a whole in three main ways (Quiggin, 2009). First, the facilitation of takeovers, mergers and buyouts by private equity firms offers the opportunity to boost the efficiency with which capital is used and the productivity of the economy as a whole. Second, expanded provision of credit to households is conducive to higher standards of living, as households could ride out fluctuations in income, bring forward the benefits of future income growth and draw on the capital gains associated with rising asset prices. Third, the wealth of the financial sector generates demand for luxury goods and services of all kinds, thereby benefiting workers in general, or at least those in cities with high concentrations of financial centre activity such as London and New York.

Nothing can be further from the truth. The explosion in the pay of the financial elite contributed to the advent of the global financial crisis, which has left no less than 50 million people living below the poverty line in the US alone. There is no evidence for enhanced productivity growth as a result of mergers and acquisitions, which is invariably a parasitic activity. The expansion in credit and diversity of financial services offered to consumers has produced nothing but enormous private debt; the alleged beneficiaries live on a day-to-day basis by borrowing on one credit card to pay the bill for another. There is certainly no evidence for a rising standard of living, as real wages for the majority have been stagnant at a time when financial innovation has produced bubbles, crashes and crises that have made the poor poorer. As for the third travesty of demand for luxury goods, the concentration of wealth has an adverse effect on consumption. How many Rolex watches does an individual buy? Are we supposed to believe that when the financial oligarchs get bonuses out of taxpayers, depositors or shareholders, these stakeholders will be better off eventually? The beneficiaries will be tax havens and Swiss banks, as the oligarchs have a marginal propensity to consume of zero.

It seems, therefore, that the case against the proposition that tax cuts boost growth is strong. For free marketeers this is not a myth, because tax cuts deprive the government of financial resources that would otherwise be wasted. On the other hand, this means that fewer resources are available for investment in infrastructure, health and education. On balance, it is a myth that tax cuts boost growth. It is also a myth that tax cuts pay for themselves, simply because they do not generate growth. And it is a myth that tax cuts for corporations and the rich benefit the poor as wealth trickles down. What we see is that the rich get richer and the poor get poorer, particularly in the 'plutonomies' of English-speaking countries.

8.4 WHO CONTROLS THE MONEY SUPPLY?

If the central bank can control the money supply, regulation should be directed at enhancing its ability to execute this function by using tools such as capital ratios, reserve ratios and interest rates. If, however, it is believed that banks can create money out of thin air, the appropriate policy action would be to overhaul the system by depriving bankers of the power of money creation. This is because excessive and erratic monetary growth, which is likely to be a product of the procyclical profit-maximizing behaviour of commercial banks, leads to inflation and boom–bust cycles; in which case an overhaul of the system is required. It is a myth that the central bank controls the money supply under a fractional reserve banking system, and it is a myth that commercial banks lend excess reserves, or that they cannot lend without having the reserves first.

Jakab and Kumhof (2015) identify two models of commercial banking, with implications for the ability of commercial banks to create money and the ability of the central bank to control the money supply. The first model is what they describe as the 'highly misleading' intermediation of loanable funds model, which dates to the 1950s–1960s and back to the 19th century. The other model is the financing through money creation model, which is consistent with the 1930s view of the economists associated with the Chicago School, including Irving Fisher. On the other hand, Werner (2016) distinguishes among three different theories of banking. The first is the financial intermediation theory, postulating that banks collect deposits and subsequently lend them out, in which case they are not different from non-bank financial intermediaries. The second theory is the fractional reserve theory, which says that individual banks cannot create money, but the banking system collectively can through multiple deposit expansion. The third theory is the credit creation theory of banking, according to which individual banks create credit and money when they grant loans. The financing through money creation model of Jakab and Kumhof (2015) and the credit creation theory of banking of Werner (2016) are at odds with the money multiplier model, and support the proposition that the central bank cannot control the money supply.

The money multiplier model is increasingly considered to be a misleading description of the money creation process. The model portrays a bank as accepting deposits of cash from a customer, holding back a certain fraction of the cash as reserves, and then lending out the remainder to another customer. It follows that the central bank should have ultimate control over the amount of money in the economy, given that it is in a position to control the required reserves ratio and the monetary base (high-powered money). The model has three implications: (1) a commercial bank has to wait until someone deposits cash before it can make a loan; (2) the central bank has ultimate control over the total amount of money in the economy; and (3) the money supply cannot grow out of control, unless the central bank allows it to do so. In short, the money supply is a multiple (that is determined by the reserve ratio) of the monetary base.

In the 1960s, Philip Cagan (1965) demonstrated, by using the money multiplier model, that all big, sustained changes in the money supply were due to policy. This is how he described the money multiplier model:

> Given the quantity of high-powered [base] money, the public and the commercial banks jointly determine its division between public holdings [of cash] and bank reserves. The public determines the fraction of total money balances it wants to hold in the form of high-powered money . . . The banking system determines the volume of monetary liabilities it is willing to create, through loans and investment, per unit of high powered money it holds (that is, its reserves).

Cagan went on to describe the money multiplier model as expressing the money supply in terms of the monetary base, the currency to deposits ratio and the reserves to deposits ratio, which he called the 'determinants of the money stock'. By analysing movements of the money supply and its determinants over the period 1875–1960, he concluded that 'the secular growth in the money stock has depended primarily on additions to high-powered money'.

Despite the implication of Cagan's (1965) analysis that the money supply can be controlled by the central bank because it has a direct control over the monetary base, he admitted that 'the contribution of the two ratios to variations about the growth trend of the money stock has at certain times been substantial'. In the post-crisis period, the ability of commercial banks to affect the money supply by changing the reserve ratio was demonstrated vividly. On this occasion, the Fed wanted to see rapid monetary growth by expanding the monetary base. During the period September 2008 to November 2014, the monetary base grew at a compound annualized growth rate of 24 per cent, while the money supply (M2) grew at the rate of 7 per cent only (Moosa, 2016). That was mainly due to the accumulation of reserves by commercial banks, instead of using them to expand credit. This is not the only historical episode in which commercial banks, rather than the central bank, drove the money supply.

Goodhart (1984) describes the money multiplier model used in economics textbooks as 'an incomplete way of describing the process of the determination of the stock of money'. This view is shared by economists working at the Bank of England who suggest that the model is an 'inaccurate description of reality and a misconception'. In a study published in the *Bank of England Quarterly Bulletin*, McLeay et al. (2014) state the following:

> Another common misconception is that the central bank determines the quantity of loans and deposits in the economy by controlling the quantity of central bank money – the so-called 'money multiplier' approach. In that view, central banks implement monetary policy by choosing a quantity of reserves. And, because there is assumed to be a constant ratio of broad money to base money, these reserves are then 'multiplied up' to a much greater change in bank loans and deposits. For the theory to hold, the amount of reserves must be a binding constraint on lending, and the central bank must directly determine the amount of reserves. While the money multiplier theory can be a useful way of introducing money and banking in economic textbooks, it is not an accurate description of how money is created in reality.

If this is what the Bank of England believes, it follows that this is an admission that the money supply is not under its control. McLeay et al. go on to explain the money creation process as follows:

> Commercial banks create money, in the form of bank deposits, by making new loans. When a bank makes a loan, for example to someone taking out a mortgage to buy a house, it does not typically do so by giving them thousands of pounds worth of banknotes. Instead, it credits their bank account with a bank deposit of the size of the mortgage. At that moment, new money is created . . . Money creation in practice differs from some popular misconceptions – banks do not act simply as intermediaries, lending out deposits that savers place with them, and nor do they 'multiply up' Central Bank money to create new loans and deposits.

Speaking on a panel at a conference held in Toronto in April 2014, Adair Turner (Chairman of the Financial Services Authority until its abolition in March 2013) described the money multiplier model as 'mythological' and explained how banks create new money when they make loans. This is some of what he said:

> If you pick up most undergraduate textbooks . . . and you see how they describe the role of the banking system, they make two mistakes. First of all they describe a system which takes money from savers, and lends it to borrowers, failing to realise that the banking system creates credit, money and purchasing power *ab inicio*, *de novo*, and with an important role therefore within the economy. But also, again and again, [the textbooks] say 'Well what banks do is they take deposits from households and they lend money to businesses, making the capital allocation process between alternative capital investments.' As a description of what modern advanced economy banking systems do, this is completely mythological.

Likewise, Vítor Constâncio, a former vice-president of the European Central Bank, describes the money multiplier model as the 'old theoretical view'. Constâncio (2011) states the following:

> It is argued by some that financial institutions would be free to instantly transform their loans [of reserves] from the central bank into credit to the non-financial sector. This fits into the old theoretical view about the credit multiplier according to which the sequence of money creation goes from the primary liquidity created by central banks to total money supply created by banks via their credit decisions. In reality the sequence works more in the opposite direction with banks taking first their credit decisions and then looking for the necessary funding and reserves of central bank money.

A similar view has been expressed by Benes and Kumhof (2012), who argue that 'the deposit multiplier is simply, in the words of Kydland and Prescott, a myth' and that 'private banks are almost fully in control of the money creation process'. Mian and Sufi (2014) provide evidence indicating that quantitative easing had no effect on the stock of broad money.

The fundamental implication of the credit creation theory is that commercial banks, rather than the central bank, determine the money supply. The central bank is obliged to support the lending decisions of banks by providing sufficient reserves to ensure that all payments are settled. Contrary to the prediction of the money multiplier model, Holtemoller (2002) suggests that 'the money stock and the monetary base are determined endogenously by the optimizing behaviour of commercial banks and private agents like households and firms'. He presents empirical evidence that contradicts the money multiplier model and supports a model of the 'money creating sector'.

Sigurjonsson (2015) expresses the view that the central bank has a limited ability to control the money supply by deploying tools such as capital requirements, reserve requirements and interest rates. Capital requirements do not fully constrain bank lending, for various reasons. The first reason stems from the fact that retained earnings are a component of equity, implying that a bank can expand credit by retaining part of its earnings (which are generated by credit expansion to start with). The second reason is that banks can raise capital by issuing new stock. The third reason is that they can free up capital via securitization. The fourth reason is that the Basel rules allow banks to calculate regulatory capital requirements by using internal models, which means that they are in a position to manipulate their models and change regulatory capital in such a way as to be able to lend more (Moosa, 2008). Banks can also use creative (read 'fraudulent') accounting to minimize regulatory capital.

According to the money multiplier model, the central bank can control the money supply by adjusting the quantity of reserves via changes in the reserve ratio, which is not entirely under its control. The total amount of loans that commercial banks can extend is limited to a certain multiple of central bank reserves (which is the reciprocal of the reserve ratio set by the central bank). In practice, however, banks make loans and look for reserves later. As a lender of last resort, the central bank provides reserves on demand; otherwise, a liquidity crisis may be triggered or interest rates rise to high levels. If the central bank refused to provide more reserves, the commercial bank needing reserves would be unable to make payments to other banks, forcing it to sell some of its assets to obtain the reserves it needs. This means that a liquidity problem may become a solvency problem, which may cause a cascade of bankruptcies throughout the banking system. If this course of events materializes, the central bank would be accused of putting financial stability in jeopardy.

Another reason why reserves may not constrain bank lending is that if payments are made between customers of the same bank, no extra reserves will be required. This is because payment by one customer (reduction of reserves) will be offset by the deposit made by the receiver of the payment. Naturally, payments are not made exclusively by the customers of one bank, but this also means that if the banking system is dominated by a few large banks, a big fraction of the payments will be offset by deposits made by the receivers without any need for central bank reserves. Furthermore, if credit expansion by various banks runs at similar rates and the flows of deposits are fairly balanced, banks can expand lending activity considerably without needing a significant amount of reserves. Keynes (1930) suggested that 'there is no limit to the amount of bank money which the banks can safely create provided they move forward in step'.

What about using interest rate policy to control the money supply? The underlying idea here is that if the central bank wants to reduce the ability of commercial banks to expand credit and the money supply, it raises the policy rate (which represents the cost of borrowing reserves from the central bank), forcing commercial banks to raise their lending and deposit rates. The view of the Bank of England on this issue, as expressed by McLeay et al. (2014), is as follows:

> The interest rate that commercial banks can obtain on money placed at the central bank influences the rate at which they are willing to lend on similar terms in sterling money markets – the markets in which the Bank and commercial banks lend to each other and other financial institutions . . . Changes in interbank interest rates then feed through to a wider range of interest rates in different markets and at different maturities, including the interest rates that banks charge borrowers for loans and offer savers for deposits. By influencing the price of credit in this way, monetary policy affects the creation of broad money.

However, higher rates may not curb lending, particularly when the economy is booming and asset price bubbles are present; these are exactly the same conditions under which curbing bank lending is necessary. We know from elementary microeconomics that the price of a commodity is not the only factor that affects the demand for that commodity; by the same token, the price of credit is not the only factor that determines the demand for credit. For example, Pilkington (2014) suggests that the demand for credit can be driven by speculative excesses in the property or stock market, inflationary wage-price spirals, and economic growth. Furthermore, higher deposit rates attract more deposits, perhaps even from foreigners. If higher interest rates lead to domestic currency appreciation, foreign goods become cheaper, which would boost the demand for credit to finance imports. Central banks are reluctant to raise interest rates for fear of the potential adverse consequences for economic growth. A tool of last resort is the imposition of quantitative restrictions on credit, which is politically unacceptable.

It is a myth that commercial banks cannot affect the money supply because they can only lend excess reserves. It is a myth that the central bank can control the money supply by controlling the monetary base and reserve ratio. The central bank can influence, but not control, the money supply. Commercial banks have the ability and the incentive to affect the money supply by granting credit. After all, the money supply in a modern economy is predominantly in the form of bank deposits.

8.5 BOOSTING GROWTH BY REDUCING THE TRADE DEFICIT

On 28 June 2016 Donald Trump was speaking at a campaign rally in Pennsylvania, where he laid out plans to counter the 'unfair trade practices' of China and threatened to apply tariffs under sections 201 and 301 of US trade legislation, which he subsequently did. During the same rally, Trump suggested that China's membership of the World Trade Organization (WTO) enabled the 'greatest jobs theft in history'. On 3 March 2017 President Trump signed two executive orders, calling for tighter tariff enforcement in anti-subsidy and anti-dumping trade cases, and ordered a review of US trade deficits and their causes. A tit-for-tat trade war ensued, hurting both countries, to the extent that a way out was being sought until the coronavirus outbreak forced those endeavours to pale into insignificance, even oblivion.

The declared reason for the imposition of tariffs is the desire, on part of the US, to reduce or eliminate the bilateral trade deficit with China, on the grounds that a trade deficit is bad for growth and employment. This proposition is supported by economic analysis prepared in 2016 by Trump's economic advisers (Navarro and Ross, 2016). They attribute the decline in the growth rate of the US economy from 3.5 per cent in 1947–2001 to 1.9 per cent since then (in part) to 'China's entry to the WTO', which 'opened America's markets to a flood of illegally subsidized Chinese imports, thereby creating massive and chronic trade deficits'. They go on to explain 'how nations grow and prosper' by suggesting that GDP growth (and consequently the ability to generate additional income and tax revenues) is 'driven' by growth in consumption, investment, government spending and net exports. It follows, according to them, that negative net exports (a deficit in the balance of trade) exert an adverse effect on growth. Therefore, they argue, 'reducing this "trade deficit drag" would increase GDP growth'. This analysis is flawed, reflecting considerable lack of understanding of the basic principles of macroeconomics.

The Navarro–Ross narrative is based on a misunderstanding of the national income identity, which is known to anyone with elementary knowledge of macroeconomics. This misunderstanding can be attributed to the failure to recognize the difference between an identity and a causal relation, and between 'explaining' and 'accounting for'. The national income identity is written as follows:

$$Y = C + I + G + (X - M) \tag{8.1}$$

which says that GDP (Y) is measured as the sum of four components: personal consumption expenditure (C), private investment expenditure (I), government expenditure (G), and net exports (the difference between exports, X, and imports, M). Navarro and Ross seem to believe that because M has a minus sign in the identity, an increase in imports reduces GDP, hence a causal effect runs from net exports to GDP. The fact of the matter is that causation runs the other way round, from GDP to imports.

Both consumption and imports are endogenous variables, in the sense that they depend on income. Consider the consumption and imports functions, which can be written as $C = \alpha_0 + \alpha_1 Y$ and $M = \beta_0 + \beta_1 Y$. Substituting into equation (8.1) yields:

$$Y = \alpha_0 + \alpha_1 Y + \bar{I} + G + \bar{X} - (\beta_0 + \beta_1 Y) \qquad (8.2)$$

where a bar denotes 'autonomous' components of aggregate demand that do not depend on income. Hence:

$$Y = \frac{\alpha_0 - \beta_0}{1 - \alpha_1 + \beta_1} + \left(\frac{1}{1 - \alpha_1 + \beta_1}\right)\bar{E} \qquad (8.3)$$

where $\bar{E} = \bar{I} + \bar{G} + \bar{X}$ is autonomous expenditure; that is, the expenditure components that do not depend on GDP. Consumption and imports do not appear in the reduced-form equation (8.3) because they are endogenous variables that depend on income. According to this equation, GDP is determined by autonomous expenditure and subsequently determines the endogenous variables, consumption and imports. Navarro and Ross got it wrong with respect to the direction of causation.

Let us now look at the national income identity in a different form, representing the equilibrium condition of equality of injections into and withdrawals from the circular flow of income. Hence:

$$I + G + X = S + T + M \qquad (8.4)$$

where S is saving and T is tax revenue. By rearranging (8.4), we obtain:

$$(X - M) = (T - G) + (S - I) \qquad (8.5)$$

where $(T - G)$ is the budget deficit and $(S - I)$ is the saving–investment balance. This identity holds for any level of GDP. Reducing the trade deficit (that is, raising the value of the trade balance) is bound to affect $(T - G)$ and/or $(S - I)$, with consequences for Y. A rise in the value of $(X - M)$ must be associated with one or more of the following: a rise in T, a fall in G, a rise in S (hence a fall in C) and a fall in I. Therefore, raising the value of $(X - M)$ will not necessarily boost the value of GDP because the other components of autonomous expenditure will change in the opposite direction.

Navarro and Ross (2016) do not seem to understand why imports have a negative sign in the national income identity; that is, why imports are subtracted from the sum of consumption, investment, government expenditure and exports. Apparently, they believe in something ominous about the negative sign. This is a misinterpretation of the national income identity, resting on the flawed reasoning that a higher level of imports implies that goods that might have been produced at home are now being produced abroad. This misinterpretation of the national income identity leads to the belief that slower growth of GDP is caused by rapid growth of imports.

A negative sign is assigned to imports in the national income identity to avoid double counting as imports constitute elements of other components of aggregate expenditure. Consumption, investment, government expenditure and exports are measured without accounting for where the purchased goods are made. Consumption is spending to acquire both domestic and foreign goods. The same goes for investment, government expenditure and exports (re-exporting goods purchased from abroad). Without subtracting imports, GDP would look much bigger than it actually is. The national income identity can be rewritten by distinguishing between domestic and foreign goods as follows:

$$Y = (C + C^*) + (I + I^*) + (G + G^*) + (X + X^*) - M \quad (8.6)$$

where an asterisk denotes spending on foreign goods. Since imported goods are parts of consumption, investment, government expenditure and exports, it follows that:

$$M = C^* + I^* + G^* + X^* \quad (8.7)$$

By substituting (8.7) into (8.6), we obtain the equation:

$$Y = C + I + G + X \quad (8.8)$$

which means that GDP does not depend on imports. The fear of the negative sign on imports is unwarranted.

It is a myth that reducing the trade deficit boosts economic growth. Believing otherwise stems from misunderstanding of basic macroeconomics and the national income identity. Unfortunately, it is believing otherwise that has triggered the trade war between the US and China, which hurts both countries and the world economy at large.

8.6   CONCLUDING REMARKS

In March 2020, as the spread of the coronavirus intensified, central banks responded by cutting interest rates to revive stock markets and fend off recession. The economic and financial effects of the coronavirus outbreak are conspicuous. It is disrupting international supply chains and having an adverse effect on the travel industry and international trade. A downturn in China would have adverse effects on Australia because the latter cannot sell raw materials. Factories around the world buying parts from China, and subsequently exporting final products to China, can see their business decline, but the only thing they can do is hope that the virus will be contained.

One can only wonder how lower interest rates reverse retrenchment in economic activity. Will a factory in England dealing with China borrow to expand production, knowing that it cannot get the parts from China at the right amount and time? Will Australian producers borrow and expand production, knowing that they cannot sell much to China? Will airlines borrow to expand their fleets at a time when they have grounded almost all of their planes, having cancelled several, if not all, routes? Will people borrow to go on a cruise, having witnessed how passengers on the *Diamond Princess* were locked in their cabins at the port of Yokohama? The answer to all of these questions is 'no'.

It is therefore a puzzle why central banks believe that they can counter the coronavirus by cutting interest rates. Given that the decline in economic activity is a consequence of the coronavirus outbreak, the only way the trend will be reversed is through the containment of the outbreak. Needless to say, central banks are not in a position to do that. A commentator on the Consumer News and Business Channel (CNBC), Jim Cramer, hit the spot when he said that, 'unless the Fed can create a vaccine or beat the virus, then it really doesn't matter' (Stankiewicz, 2020). Likewise, in an interview which aired on the Al Jazeera channel on 5 March 2020, Patrick Perret-Green, an international economist, said: 'cutting interest rates is like putting sticking plaster on a gaping wound'. He also wondered why governments spent billions of dollars to save banks in 2008, but they are reluctant to spend billions of dollars to save people from the coronavirus. If anything, governments should raise interest rates to be able to borrow from the public for the purpose of financing fiscal stimulus, rather than doing that by creating money out of thin air.

It is a myth that interest rate cuts can revive the economy, because spending decisions depend on the economic outlook, such that no matter how low interest rates are, spending will not be affected if the outlook is bearish, as it is now (in April 2020). Interest rate cuts will not work, neither will other measures based on the myths discussed in this chapter. Governments might resort to other weapons to combat the effects of the coronavirus, including tax cuts and protectionism (to reduce the trade deficit). These will not work, because they are based on myths. In the meantime, governments will keep on lying about inflation, and under-report the inflation figures.

9. The mother of all myths: do the royals attract tourists?

9.1 INTRODUCTION

The debate on whether or not the British royals attract tourists is largely emotional, involving little or no formal, and perhaps not even circumstantial, evidence. It is a 'he said, she said' debate, based primarily on political beliefs. For example, Joseph (2017) suggests that 'the royals draw millions of tourists every year', referring as evidence to the observation that 'in 2016, over 2.7 million tourists visited Buckingham Palace, Windsor Castle, the Palace of Holyroodhouse and other key royal attractions'. He goes on to claim that the royal family provides a £1.76 billion annual boost to the British economy, far in excess of the cost of maintaining the monarchy, which is about £292 million per year. It is not obvious from the claim made by Joseph (2017) how the royals attract tourists. Is it simply the desire of foreign tourists to experience a glimpse of a member of the royal family? Is it the desire to witness royal events, such as weddings, births and anniversaries? Or is it the mere fact that tourists pay for the privilege of visiting royal estate or monarchy-related places of attraction?

It is, however, a myth that the British royals attract tourists and that they pay for themselves (that is, that they generate more tourism revenue than what is required to cover their massive expenses). While this is not a myth for royalists such as Piers Morgan, it is definitely a myth for British republicans such as Arthur Scargill, Dennis Skinner, Ken Livingstone and Richard Dawkins. Welsh nationalists refer to 'that royal myth about tourism', and to a 'myth that is ever present in the English media and spouted at every opportunity by unionist MPs' (Welshnotbritish.com, 2014). In this chapter an argument is put forward that this myth is indeed a myth; perhaps the mother of all myths.

9.2 THE ROYAL FAMILY AS A SOURCE OF TOURIST ATTRACTION

Monarchists claim that the royal family is a major reason why foreign tourists visit Britain, but it is not clear how the attraction works. Three explanations can be detected from the debate: (1) no reason is given, in which case it is assumed that the attraction lies in the royal persona; (2) visitors are attracted by royal events such as weddings and births; and (3) they are attracted by the desire to visit royal landmarks. In this section the first two explanations are considered, while the third explanation is discussed in the following section.

Those suggesting that the royals draw millions of tourists every year may or may not say whether tourists visit Britain because of royalty per se or because of the spectacle of royal events. For example, Haven-Tang (2017) refers explicitly to royal events by saying: 'Love it or hate it, the pomp and pageantry associated with British royalty, whether routine events such as trooping the colour or anniversaries such as the Queen's Diamond Jubilee in 2012, are rarely found in any other country'. Baird (2017) quotes a spokesperson for VisitLondon as saying that 'the royal family are so important for tourism in London'. He goes on to predict that Prince Harry's wedding would deliver a £2 billion boost to the British economy, pointing out that 'street parties, tourism and pub takings could boost UK economy when the couple tie the knot next spring'.

Khazan (2013) suggests that 'there's at least some evidence that the monarchy brings in heaps of tourism revenue', and that 'the monarchy appears to bring in as much in tourist revenue as they cost, at least in years with familial events like births'. In fact, Khazan (2013) attributes the attraction of tourists to the personal appeal of the royal family by arguing that 'the royal family acts as a sort of charismatic megafauna for the entire royalty-tourism ecosystem'. While he mentions the word 'evidence', Khazan does not produce any evidence. Likewise, Riggins (2014) asserts that 'royals don't merely give the public excuses to spend; they also single-handedly attract new business into the country'. These arguments suggest that the royals attract tourists both individually and collectively (hence, the 'family is' and the 'family are').

Strong and largely unsubstantiated statements are made by Long and Palmer (2008), who assert that 'as institutions and as individuals, royalty attracts considerable public interest among the subjects of monarchies and the citizens of non-monarchical republics alike'. They even mention a figure of 10 per cent, which they do not attribute to any source, as the percentage of all visitors who are attracted by a 'general feeling that Britain is a unique and glorious heritage centre to which the monarchy makes an inestimable contribution'. Yet they admit that 'little work has explored the broad and specific relationships between royalty and tourism'.

While Haven-Tang (2017) admits that 'there is an absence of data as to whether tourists go to the UK specifically because of the royal family' and that 'tourists might not be primarily attracted to the UK solely by the monarchy', she refers to 'the spectacle of royal events', which 'enable VisitBritain and other national tourism agencies to build on Britain's tourism appeal which blends heritage, pageantry and the contemporary'. In this way, she concludes, 'the relationship between royalty and tourism has an important economic and destination marketing dimension'. A Bedfordshire Tory MP, Nadine Dorries, once declared that 'not only are they [the royals] a very important part of our constitution, but they are a huge attraction for tourists around the world – the royal family generates a huge revenue for this country' (Welshnotbritish.com, 2014).

Riggins (2014) attributes to PricewaterhouseCoopers (PWC) the claim that the British royal family is the reason for a 'whopping £107m per year through tourism and memorabilia sales in London alone', citing 'unidentified researchers' as saying that 'this figure goes up to £620m nationwide'. He refers to 'Elizabeth's grandchildren', who 'continue to fill their diaries with juicy public engagements'. A particular royal event that is emphasized by Riggins (2014) is 'the arrival of Prince William and Kate Middleton's baby', to which he attributes a £243 million bump in retail sales, 'including an extra £62m on celebratory booze, and £80m on royal souvenirs'. A report produced by PWC (2011) attributes the commercial benefit to London arising out of the royal wedding (of William and Kate) to the 560 000 visitors expected to travel to London from around the UK for the wedding. Two-thirds of those visitors were expected to go shopping while they were in London, and well over half would visit bars, clubs, restaurants and tourist attractions.

Let us see how these claims fare under scrutiny. The claim that the royals attract tourists because of the magic of the royal persona is typically made by monarchists on purely emotional grounds without any evidence; perhaps because the evidence does not exist. It is hard to imagine that a tourist from Vietnam decides to spend a big amount of money hoping to have a glimpse of a member of the royal family so that they can boast about it back home. Furthermore, seeing a member of the royal family (unlike a pop star or an athlete) is far away from being certain, and no one is going to sit in front of one of the royal palaces hoping to see Prince Charles and the Duchess of Cornwall pass by. Members of the royal family do not sit inside Buckingham Palace from 9 am to 5 pm every day, posing for pictures with tourists. It remains to be said that it is not implausible to imagine that in the past people travelled long distances to have a glimpse of Elvis Presley, John Lennon, Pele, Bobby Charlton or George Best. Neither is it implausible to believe that these days people travel to faraway places to see the likes of Lionel Messi, Cristiano Ronaldo, Roger Federer, Tom Cruise or Leonardo DiCaprio. This proposition may even be valid for Justin Bieber, but whether or not it is valid for members of the royal family is open to debate.

Now we turn to the proposition that visitors to Britain are attracted by the spectacle of royal events. We have to bear in mind that what we are concerned with here is not those travelling from the north of England to cheer the royals; rather, the focus is on foreign visitors, as tourism is an export industry. We have to assume that the British people are more enthusiastic than foreigners about seeing the royals in the flesh. For this reason the analysis presented by PWC about how London would benefit from the royal wedding is irrelevant for the issue under consideration. Moreover, the same effect could materialize as a result of an international football match at Wembley, a pop star performing in the same venue, or the Notting Hill Carnival. Foreign tourists visit Britain all year round, and not only during royal events.

Without survey evidence it is impossible to prove that tourists visit Britain because of the royal family. It is not possible to find out what percentage of the money spent by tourists has something to do with the attraction of the royal family. Therefore, these seemingly precise pound amounts do not pass the test of scrutiny. People do not visit a country because it is a monarchy or a republic. And even if the royals have a special appeal, why is it that the British royal family is special, as similar claims are rarely made in conjunction with any other royal family? It is therefore not clear why Haven-Tang (2017) believes that the events associated with the British royal family are 'rarely found in any other country'.

The figures presented by Tourism Alliance (2017) about the value of UK events do not have an item related to the royal family, as shown in Figure 9.1. Conferences and meetings are worth £19.2 billion, while exhibitions and trade fairs bring in £11 billion. Music and sporting events generate £2.3 billion each. This spending pattern has nothing to do with the royal family. European countries were monarchies for a long time, some of which are still monarchies and some are republics. No evidence is available for the proposition that tourists choose the countries to visit on the basis of whether they are kingdoms or republics. The fastest-growing inbound tourism can be found in republics that used to be monarchies. According to the figures supplied by Tourism Alliance (2017), the fastest-growing inbound tourism can be found in Serbia (48 per cent), Romania (47 per cent), China (46 per cent), Latvia (45 per cent) and Lithuania (37 per cent). None of these countries are kingdoms.

Factors other than the royal family attract tourists to Britain, as an endless list of attractions can be put forward to justify the desire to visit Britain. The country has a multi-layered history involving prehistoric Britons, Gaels, Celts and Picts through Vikings, Romans and Normans, all of whom have left fascinating traces for visitors to explore. The

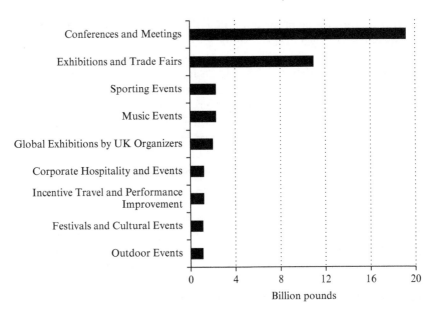

Figure 9.1   Spending on UK events by foreign visitors

scenery can be breathtaking: examples include the Lake District, the White Cliffs of Dover and the Scottish Highlands. A wide range of urban adventures are available in various cities and towns, and there is the attraction of British pubs, which are landmarks of continuity that have existed in the same spot for hundreds of years (their names tell stories, often linked to local history, outlaws, wars and customs). People visit Britain to watch unorthodox traditions such as cheese rolling in Gloucestershire, fireball whirling in Scotland, Morris men dancing and banging sticks, and hobby horses terrorizing villages on May Day. There are also magnificent gardens such as RHS Garden Wisley, Fountains Abbey and Studley Royal Water Garden, the Glorious Gardens of Argyll and Bute, Bodnant Garden, Powis Castle and Garden, and Blenheim Palace and Park.

People might want to visit Britain to find out how such a small country managed to rule the world for such a long time, in which case Westminster and 10 Downing Street matter more than Buckingham Palace. People visit Britain to see places like where the D-Day operation started, where the evacuees of Dunkirk arrived, where the *Titanic* began its first and last voyage, where the *Mayflower* started its voyage to the new world, and the path taken by the Jarrow marchers in 1936. Britain is the country where the industrial revolution was born, football was invented (and so were ping pong and rugby), the first grand slam tennis tournament was staged, and the first underground railway system was built.

Britain is the country where the computer, radar and the test-tube baby were invented. It is the country that hosts the largest foreign exchange centre and eurocurrency centre in the world. It is the country of Isaac Newton, Charles Darwin, Stephen Hawking, Michael Faraday, Edmond Halley, Alexander Graham Bell, Alexander Fleming and Robert Boyle. It is the country of William Shakespeare, Charles Dickens, Graham Greene, Somerset Maugham, Agatha Christie and Arthur Conan Doyle. It is the country of James Bond, Dixon of Dock Green, Sherlock Holmes, Robin Hood, Harry Potter and Winnie the Pooh. It is the land of the Beatles, the Rolling Stones, Queen and Mungo Jerry. For economists, the country has appeal because it is the land of great economists such as J.M. Keynes, Adam Smith, Alfred Marshall, John Hicks, John Stuart Mill, Arthur Pigou and Thomas Malthus. Last, but certainly not least, it is the land of the great invention: fish and chips, once wrapped in page 3 of the *Sun* (preferably with mushy peas). One must not forget other delights such as Bramley apple pie, Cheddar cheese, Cheshire cheese, Lancashire hot pot, Yorkshire pudding and the great Scottish invention, haggis.

One part of British history that is not known to many people is that Britain was a republic over the period 1649–1660, following the end of the Second English Civil War and the trial and execution of Charles I. One may ask: if Britain had remained a republic, would fewer people be eager to visit the country these days? The same question may arise if Britain became a republic in the near future, an idea that is entertained by many. Will people be less prepared to visit Britain when the head of state is President Smith rather than King Charles? Some people believe that it is the other way round: that tourism will benefit from the abolition of the monarchy. For example, *The Economist* (2015b) suggests that 'the royals may not be entirely good for the country's image abroad or its view of itself', and that 'Britain still has a reputation as a snooty, class-obsessed place'. British republicans believe that a republican Britain will give a 'huge boost to "brand Britain"' and that 'our nation's image abroad will be of the modern, confident and forward-looking country we really are'. They refer to a statement by VisitBritain saying in their guide to promoting Britain that 'we can avoid the cliché-ridden imagery of the past and promote our heritage as a living part of a dynamic, positive and modern nation'. They describe the claim that royalty is good for tourism as 'untrue and irrelevant', arguing that 'even VisitBritain, our national tourist agency, can't find any evidence for it' (www.republic.org.uk).

9.3   THE ROYAL ESTATE AS A SOURCE OF ATTRACTION

The third explanation for the attraction power of the royal family is that tourists pay to visit the royal estate, perhaps to feel what it is like to be a British king or queen. Khazan (2013) attributes figures to the British tourism agency indicating that the royal family generates close to £500 million every year by drawing visitors to historic royal sites such as the Tower of London, Windsor Castle and Buckingham Palace. He also quotes the tourism agency as saying that of the 30 million foreigners who visited Britain in 2010, 5.8 million visited a castle. Haven-Tang (2017) suggests that the estates owned by the royal family are important in attracting tourists. Baird (2017) quotes a spokesperson for VisitLondon as saying that 'amongst the wealth of history and heritage on offer across the capital, the Royal palaces and parks are a firm favourite among visitors', and that '2016 was a record year for the number of international visitors into London, and Royal heritage was a big part of driving that'.

Long and Palmer (2008) suggest that 'the value of the monarchy for tourism can be argued on the basis [of] royal ownership of, association with, and patronage of palaces, properties and landscapes'. Royal sites include Buckingham Palace, Hampton Court (home to Henry VIII), Kensington Palace (where Princess Diana lived), Kew Palace (with its botanical gardens and historic kitchens), the Tower of London (with 900 years' worth of history as a royal palace), Windsor Castle (a residence of the Queen), Balmoral Castle (the Scottish home to the royal family), Sandringham House (the Queen's country retreat), St James's Palace (where important events throughout the royal family's history have taken place), and Somerset House.

Again, let us see how these claims stand up to scrutiny. Historical places are visited whether or not they are associated with the reigning monarchy. Foreign tourists do not only visit Buckingham Palace and Windsor Castle, but also Stonehenge, the Neolithic Orkney United Nations Educational, Scientific and Cultural Organization (UNESCO) World Heritage Site, the castles of William the Conqueror, Roman baths and ruins, Big Ben, Canterbury Cathedral, Durham Cathedral and the National Memorial Arboretum. Furthermore, most castles in Britain have nothing to do with the royal family. Wales, for example, has more castles per square mile than any other country in Europe, with a history that has left a landscape scattered with Iron Age hill forts, Roman ruins and castles from Medieval Welsh rulers. It is not clear why monuments like the Tower of London derive their attraction from the royal family, given that the monuments attracting tourists are not necessarily owned by the royal family. The Queen owns Balmoral and Sandringham, both of which were inherited from her father, but the royal family does not own the Crown Jewels, official royal residences and the vast majority of art: these belong to the nation rather than being the private property of the Queen. Attributing the attraction of the touristic value of the Tower of London to the reigning royal family seems to be a gross misrepresentation of reality.

If tourists visit Britain to see Buckingham Palace or the Tower of London, is the desire to do so due to the current monarchy or is it to do with history per se? Again, if Britain became a republic, would tourists stop visiting Buckingham Palace and the Tower of London? If the answer to this question is in the affirmative, then it would be rather difficult to explain why tourists visit the Palace of Versailles near Paris and Dolmabahçe Palace in Istanbul. This is why it is rather strange that Khazan (2013) is 'skeptical that England's attractions could still draw the same numbers of tourists without the physical monarchs in place'. To substantiate this statement, Khazan argues that 'people would still visit African savannas if they didn't have elephants, but probably not as many, or as often'. Perhaps, but perhaps not: tourists are just as likely to visit the savannas to watch lions and hyenas. They may still visit the savannas to see where elephants used to live. People still visit Mauritius to see the environment where the dodo thrived at one time. And it is doubtful that the number of tourists visiting Tasmania fell as a result of the extinction of the Tasmanian tiger. It remains to be said that most people who visit Australia never see a kangaroo, a wallaby, a koala or an emu.

If anything, it could be that visitor numbers and revenue would rise in the absence of the royal family. In a republic, royal properties such as Buckingham Palace would be open all year round, thus generating more income. Fathers (1992) suggests a scenario as to what could happen in a British republic: 'Buckingham Palace would be open to the public as it would be turned into an art gallery to display the former monarch's collection of paintings, which it was announced last week she was giving to the new republic as part of a long-delayed tax settlement'.

Let us now examine the facts and figures about the attractions visited by tourists. According to the figures provided by VisitBritain, visitors are more interested in restaurants, shopping, gardens, museums and pubs than the royal estate (Figure 9.2). In Figure 9.3, we see the revenue (in million pounds) derived from ticket admissions to the royal estate; the numbers are nowhere near the alleged hundreds of millions of pounds. No royal estate appears on the list of top 20 attractions arranged by the number of visitors (the Tower of London appears as number 9, but this landmark is not owned or occupied by the royal family). As we can see in Figure 9.4, the British Museum comes out on top with over 6 million visitors per year.

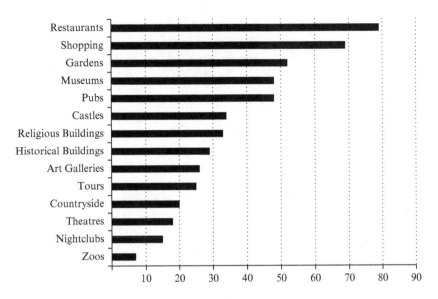

Figure 9.2 Activities of visitors to the UK (%)

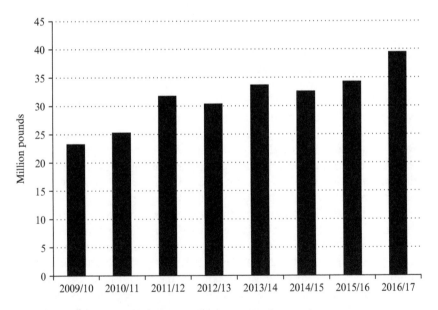

Figure 9.3 Income from ticket admissions to the royal estate (million pounds)

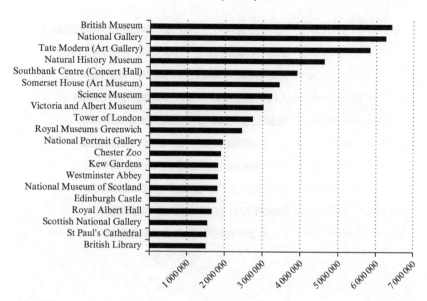

Figure 9.4   Number of visitors to top 20 attractions

Even Chester Zoo, which not many people have heard of, appears in the top 20 list. Windsor Castle appears as number 23, as shown in Figure 9.5, which displays attractions ranked 21–30. Buckingham Palace appears as number 66, as shown in Figure 9.6.

9.4   DO OTHER MONARCHIES ATTRACT TOURISM?

The claim that the monarchy attracts tourists seems to be reserved for the British royal family; at least, it is made more often in conjunction with British royalty than otherwise. For example, Haven-Tang (2017) suggests that the events associated with the British royal family are 'rarely found in any other country'. Long and Palmer (2008) argue that 'the British monarchy is perhaps pre-eminent, if certainly not unique, in illustrating the connection between royalty and tourism'. This is because 'the monarchy in the UK performs major, ongoing and complex roles in maintaining and personifying traditional British national identities and values'. However, there is no logical reason why the proposition that the British royal family attracts tourists is not equally valid for other (at least, European) monarchies. Is there a reason why the Dutch, Swedish and Danish monarchies are less efficient in performing 'complex roles' and hence are not as good at attracting tourism?

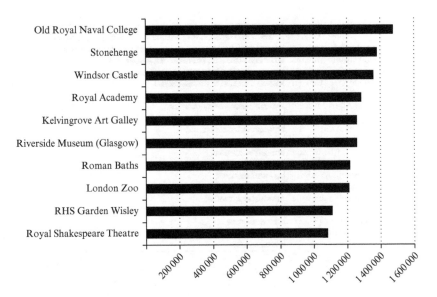

Figure 9.5   Number of visitors to attractions ranked 21–30

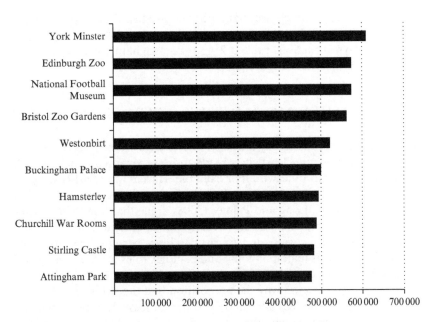

Figure 9.6   Number of visitors to attractions ranked 61–70

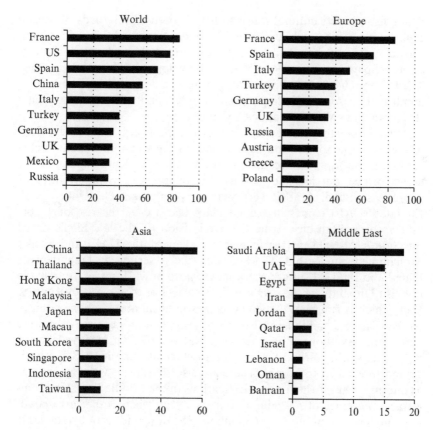

Figure 9.7 Top tourist destinations (million tourists)

As a matter of fact, similar claims have been made for the Dutch and Swedish royal families by Riggins (2014) and Deutsche Welle (DW) (2009), respectively. If what is true for the British monarchy is also true for other monarchies, then kingdoms in general should attract more tourists than republics. This cannot be further away from the truth. Consider Figure 9.7, which shows the top ten recipients of inbound tourism in the world, Europe, Asia and the Middle East. On the world stage, France and the United States (US) receive most tourists, and seven republics attract more tourists than the UK. In the top three, we find one kingdom, Spain, but it is doubtful that Spain would be receiving fewer tourists had it not reinstated the royal family in 1978. As in the case of Britain, people visit Spain for reasons other than the monarchy. The Mediterranean climate attracts millions of tourists from Northern Europe, including Britain.

Spain also attracts cultural tourism, having been a crossroads of several civilizations. Cities such as Seville, Granada, Santander, Oviedo, Gijon, Bilbao and San Sebastian have historical landmarks and a lively cultural agenda. Spain also offers Real Madrid, Barcelona and flamenco dancing. The US does not have a king or long history, but it attracts tourists for a number of reasons, including natural wonders and entertainment venues (Broadway, Las Vegas, Atlantic City, and so on).

Perhaps the most interesting case for comparison is the Middle East, where six of the top ten tourist destinations are kingdoms. Saudi Arabia comes out on top, not because tourists want to see King Salman or the crown prince, but for one reason only: religious tourism. Millions of people visit Saudi Arabia every year for pilgrimage. The United Arab Emirates (UAE) comes in second place because of the rise of Dubai as a cosmopolitan city. True, the royal vision of the late Sheik Zayed bin Sultan Al-Nahyan (the former president of the UAE) and Sheikh Mohammed bin Rashid Al Maktoum (the governor of Dubai) made Dubai and the UAE in general what they are now. However, tourists do not visit Dubai to see the royals or their palaces or to witness royal events. Iran, which is run by a theocracy, comes in at number 4 as the country receives some 5 million tourists every year, mainly because of culture and history, symbolized by Persepolis, Naghsh-e Rosta, Nagshe Jahan as well as 22 world cultural heritage sites (which at one time US President Trump threatened to bomb). There are also those who visit the country as pilgrims. Out of the top ten destinations in the Middle East, kingdoms attract an average of 6.9 million tourists a year, whereas the corresponding number for republics is 4.65 million. The difference is not statistically significant (a t statistic of 0.67).

9.5 THE MONARCHY AS A DETERMINANT OF TOURISM IN BRITAIN

Research on the determinants of tourism seems to recognize tourism as a normal good, the demand for which depends on price and income. Some other factors include the ease of obtaining a visa, accessibility (in terms of the availability of frequent flights to the destination) and turmoil (terrorism and political uncertainty).

Blake and Cortes-Jiménez (2007) identify the main drivers of demand for inbound tourism in the UK as income and price: that is, income in the source country (a positive relation), and relative prices, which may be proxied by the real exchange rate. They also mention taste and marketing, with some reservations, as well as extraordinary events such as the Olympic

Games (positive effect) and terrorism (negative effect). There is no mention of royal events. Likewise, Durbarry and Sinclair (2001) measure the sensitivity of the demand for tourism in the UK to changes in prices, exchange rates and expenditure.

The British Tourist Authority (2001) found that 98 per cent of the variation in Britain's receipts from foreign tourists could be explained by the gross domestic product (GDP) of Organisation for Economic Co-operation and Development (OECD) countries (as a proxy for the income of foreign tourists) and the trade weighted exchange rate of the pound (as a proxy for the price or cost of visiting Britain). The study revealed that foreign demand for tourism in Britain is highly cost-sensitive, where cost is determined primarily, but not exclusively, by the exchange rate. The exchange rate elasticity of tourism was found to be -1.3; that is, earnings from foreign tourists decline by 13 per cent for a 10 per cent appreciation of the pound, which makes a visit to Britain more expensive in foreign currency terms. On the other hand, an income elasticity of 0.6 means that tourism earnings go up by 6 per cent in response to a 10 per cent rise in the income of foreign tourists.

Britain stands very well in terms of accessibility, in the sense that numerous flights arrive in British airports from all around the world. However, the difficulty of obtaining a British visa hampers the growth of tourism. VisitBritain (2012) suggests that 'the UK visitor visa regime has been singled out as a major factor inhibiting Britain's competitiveness as a destination for international tourism', particularly because Britain is not a member of the Schengen area (and now no longer a member of the European Union). The requirements for a British visa application are more elaborate than those of other European countries. In addition to the standard documents showing evidence for financial status and travel plans, original documents are required to verify permission to be in the country of application, evidence of marital status, and the sponsor's immigration status if the individual is visiting a friend or relative. Tourism Alliance (2017) suggests that while there has been an improvement in the visa offering over the last five years, the fact remains that, since the biometric visa was introduced in 2008, the UK's share of outbound tourism from China, Russia and India has declined by 30 per cent.

9.6 CONCLUDING REMARKS

The monarchists arguing for the ability of the royal family to attract tourism do not seem to be sure of the mechanism whereby the royals manage to attract tourism. While republicans tend to reject this proposition outright, because they resent the very idea of monarchy, one must say that the burden of proof should fall on the monarchists who believe that the royal family pay for themselves by attracting tourists. It has occurred to me that those believing in the power of the royal family to attract tourists have changed their minds in the aftermath of the Jeffrey Epstein scandal involving Prince Andrew and the withdrawal of Prince Harry from public life. Those events have made some royalists furious, but no one mentions the implications for tourism.

Three explanations are presented for the ability of the royal family to attract tourists. The first is the attraction of the royal persona: that tourists are eager to have a glimpse of one or more royals. In the absence of survey evidence on this proposition, it is hard to sell. The second explanation is that foreign tourists are attracted by royal events. Again, only survey evidence, which is unavailable, can give credibility to this argument. Tens of good reasons, which are more plausible than the desire to see the royals or experience the spectacle of royal events, can be suggested to explain why people want to visit Britain. The third explanation is that tourists are attracted to Britain because they want to see royal estate such as Buckingham Palace and Windsor Castle. The revenue generated from what tourists pay to visit the royal estate pales into insignificance compared to the billions of pounds generated from foreign tourists. Then there is no reason to regard such landmarks as the Tower of London as royal estate, neither is there any reason to suggest that tourists would stop visiting this landmark and others if Britain became a republic.

Being counterfactual can be useful for this kind of debate. For example, if in a futuristic world the United Kingdom became the Republic of Britain, would inbound tourism drop just because foreigners like to visit the United Kingdom but not the Republic of Britain? Definitely, if the government of President Smith decided to impose more stringent visa restrictions, or to ban alcohol and shut down pubs, like the 1920s prohibition in the US. If, however, the government of President Smith relaxed visa restrictions and subsidized pubs, more tourists would visit the Republic of Britain than the United Kingdom.

The attractiveness of the Tower of London will not be affected by a change from a kingdom to a republic, as the present system of governing a country is irrelevant to its heritage. Tourists visit particular countries for a number of reasons including, but not limited to, history, heritage, entertainment, natural beauty and adventure, irrespective of whether that country is run by a king, a queen, an emperor, a sultan, a president, a prime minister, a chancellor, a sheikh or a mulla. It is more likely that tourists visit Britain not because of the Queen but perhaps because of the heritage left by Queen, the band that in 1975 performed the queen of all songs: 'Bohemian Rhapsody'. And there is much more where Queen and 'Bohemian Rhapsody' came from. It is therefore a myth that the British royals cover their expenses by attracting foreign tourists.

10. Epilogue: puzzles and myths in economics and finance

10.1 RECAPITULATION

Puzzles and myths in various areas of economics and finance were examined throughout Chapters 2–9. The puzzles cover the fields of international finance, international economics, macroeconomics and finance. Paradoxes in economics and finance, which were examined in Chapter 1, are essentially puzzles. The myths cover the fields of econometrics, laissez-faire, financial economics and macroeconomics. In Chapter 9, the mother of all myths was discussed: the myth that the British royals attract tourists, which makes them self-funded.

The discussion of puzzles and paradoxes is aimed at demonstrating that they are not really paradoxes or puzzles, because logical and plausible explanations can be put forward for all of them. Myths, on the other hand, are perceived as such by some economists, while others consider them to be undisputed facts of life. They arise primarily in normative economics, where value judgement plays an important role in determining how the state of affairs ought to be. Whether a myth is truly a myth or otherwise depends on the strength of arguments and evidence for one claim or another. For example, an argument was presented in Chapter 6 that the private sector is not necessarily more efficient than the public sector. For me, the superiority of the private sector is a myth; for free marketeers, on the other hand, it is the truth, the whole truth and nothing but the truth. For most of the profession, econometrics provides useful tools for empirical research, but for a minority (including this author) econometrics is a con art that can be used to prove anything; hence, it is useless at best and dangerous at worst. One myth, however, is not about ideological or intellectual differences, but rather about the controversy over whether or not the government tells the truth about inflation.

In Chapter 1, the characteristics of a puzzle in general terms were identified. A puzzle baffles and confuses, it represents an unanswered question or unsolved problem, it is fun, it has a right answer, it is a form of play, it is some sort of amusement, its solution requires ingenuity and patience, it is written by someone, and it is recreational. The puzzles of economics and finance exhibit some, but not all, of these properties. This point warrants some elaboration.

Do the puzzles of economics and finance baffle and confuse? No, even though their originators and those who believe them think otherwise. They do not baffle and confuse because plenty of plausible explanations can be presented for each puzzle. Look no further than the Meese–Rogoff puzzle, which has been blown out of proportion in glorification of its originators. Do economic puzzles represent unanswered questions or unsolved problems? No, because answers and solutions are plentiful. Are they fun, and do they provide amusement, and are they recreational? Yes, they provide entertainment, as we are going to see in some of the comments posted online on the so-called Shimer puzzle. Do they have right answers? Yes, more than one right, logical, sensible and plausible answer. Are they a form of play? No, because they are supposed to be taken seriously. Does the solution require ingenuity and patience? Definitely not: ingenuity and patience are not required to realize why pensioners cut their spending through retirement, which is the rule rather than the exception (the exception being billionaire pensioners). Are economics puzzles written? Yes, they are written by the originators. The Meese–Rogoff puzzle was written by Richard Meese and Ken Rogoff; the presidential puzzle was written by Pedro Santa-Clara and Rossen Valkanov; and the idiosyncratic volatility puzzle was written by Andrew Ang, Robert Hodrick, Yuhang Xing and Xiaoyan Zhang. The puzzles of economics and finance, I must add, bring glory to the originators, and this is why I am so eager to create a puzzle, which I will try in the following section.

10.2   BAKING YOUR OWN PUZZLE

In this section, I demonstrate how anyone can 'bake' their own puzzle by following a step-by-step procedure. While solving an existing puzzle in economics and finance does not require ingenuity and patience, the baking of a new puzzle requires ingenuity and patience, or at least one of these. Ingenuity is needed to construct a complex mathematical model that, with the help of an incredible set of assumptions, gives a result that forms the basis of the puzzle. Patience is required in looking for a data set that produces empirical results to corroborate the theoretical results. While some puzzles are based on the theoretical results (such as the equity premium puzzle) or empirical results (such as the Meese–Rogoff puzzle), a puzzle based on both of them is more credible. I will now illustrate how to bake a puzzle for my own glory.

I start by constructing a complex mathematical model that only a few can understand. To make it look sophisticated and impressive, I throw in a few partial differential equations, some stochastic calculus and elements of measure theory. The model predicts that when interest rates go up, stock prices go up as well; the process works through several channels. First, when interest rates go up, holders of bank deposits get a windfall gain, which they invest in the stock market, leading to rising stock prices. Second, banks and other financial institutions benefit from higher loan rates; consequently, they propel the stock market. Third, when interest rates go up, bond prices go down, in which case investors shift to stocks. Fourth, high interest rates depress inflation, which is good for the stock market. This is the ingenuity part of the baking process. The patience part is that I have to come up with empirical evidence to support the predictions of the theoretical model. After a thorough search I find a particular case – preferably the United States (US) – where over a particular period of time interest rates and stock prices are positively correlated. I get the paper published in a top journal, and the findings become an established fact of life.

Subsequent research on the relation between stock prices and interest rates reveals negative correlation, but this cannot be right, because my fancy model, which is supported by empirical evidence, predicts otherwise; and my model must be right because it follows the principles of neoclassical economics (and because it is my model). Economists finding negative correlation do not say that their results make sense; rather, they say that their results represent a puzzle. However, some of them show courage by challenging the predictions of my model. They present explanations for why correlation between interest rates and stock prices should be negative, including the following: (1) interest rate is the discount factor used for stock valuation according to the dividend discount model; (2) high interest rates depress the economy, adversely affecting corporate profitability; (3) interest rate is the cost of borrowing to invest in the stock market; (4) bond yields are long-term interest rates, which means that as they rise, investors shift to the stock market; and (5) high interest rates depress inflation, which is bad for the stock market.

When these brave economists submit their papers to journals they get rejected by referees who happen to be myself, or those who have confirmed my results and pledged loyalty to the puzzle. Some of the brave economists will get their papers published (most likely, in low-ranked journals) even though their results defy the predictions of my model, because they are lucky enough not to have me or one of my supporters as a referee. I will deal with those who challenge the status quo, and argue that my puzzle is solvable, by writing comments, replies, rejoinders, blogs, op-eds, and so on to undermine their work; I will even smear them and call them 'conspiracy theorists', because ends justify the means. I will cast doubt on the validity of reasons (1)–(5) above, and find some loopholes in the methodology or sample. And I will write new papers to support the results in my original paper (and assign to the bin new results that do not confirm the original ones). My puzzle will survive the test of time because it is more puzzling than other people's puzzles.

10.3 A SILLY PUZZLE AND A DUMB PUZZLE

The silly puzzle I am going to talk about is the retirement–consumption puzzle, which arises from contradiction between the theory of life-cycle consumption (perceived by some economists to be a law of physics) and the observation that consumption expenditure declines in retirement. It is a puzzle because some theory allegedly portrays an accurate picture of consumption behaviour, predicting that individuals indulge in consumption smoothing, which they are good at. According to the simple one-good model of life-cycle consumption, the trajectory of consumption by an individual should be continuous in time. If the trajectory is not continuous, a reallocation of consumption is undertaken so as to reduce the size of the discontinuity and boost lifetime utility without an increase in the use of resources.

While unnecessarily sophisticated explanations have been put forward for this puzzle, some simple explanations can be suggested. A basic assumption of the underlying model, which is required for consumption smoothing, is divorced from reality: the assumption that consumers are forward-looking planners. For the majority of people, retirement income is lower than the income earned while working, which leads to a drop in consumption during retirement. Some workers retire earlier than anticipated because of health issues or unemployment, resulting in an unexpected reduction in lifetime financial resources, again leading to a concurrent reduction in consumption.

People retire when they get old. Old people consume less food, less beverages, less travel and less clothing. They consume less food because their digestive systems are not as good as they used to be. They consume fewer beverages because their livers are not as powerful as they were once. They spend less on travel, either because they have been everywhere or because they do not want to die or get injured while they are away; and surely they cannot put up with long queues in airports and long flights. Another explanation is the cessation of work-related expenses, such as transport and clothing. Yet another explanation is that retired people have considerably more leisure than working people. Retirees have more leisure, which can be used to purchase goods more efficiently or to substitute home-produced goods for purchased goods. In this interpretation, spending declines but actual consumption does not. This is a silly puzzle because it can be explained even by those without knowledge of economics. If you ask anyone why retired people consume less, they will tell you one or more of the answers given above, and they will do it without using a model.

A dumb puzzle is the Shimer puzzle; it is dumb in the sense that some economists justifiably wonder why it is considered a puzzle at all. The origin of the puzzle is Shimer's (2005) paper (invariably described as 'influential') in which he argues that the Mortensen–Pissarides (MP) search model of unemployment lacks an amplification mechanism because it generates less than 10 per cent of the observed business cycle fluctuations in unemployment. This presumably happens in the presence of labour productivity shocks of plausible magnitude (for example, Barnichon, 2008).

Why is this a puzzle? Humorous answers to this question can be found in a discussion on the website of Economics Job Market Rumors (https://www.econjobrumors.com/topic/why-is-the-shimer-puzzle-a-puzzle). Using fake names, the participants commented on the Shimer puzzle, starting with the following comment:

> I don't really get why it's so special it has its own name. So DMP [Diamond–Mortensen–Pissarides model] relying on labor productivity shocks no good. Where's the puzzle there? That'd be like calling the Phillips curve failtacular in the 70s the 'Friedman puzzle'.

Other comments include the following:

- 'Why is the Shimer puzzle a puzzle? A puzzle' – meaning that it is a puzzle that the Shimer puzzle is a puzzle.
- 'Puzzling indeed' – again, it is puzzling why this is a puzzle.
- 'Seriously, why should the fact that a model does not fit the data be called a puzzle?'
- '[It is a puzzle] because Shimer is too stupid to figure it out'. These are not my words, but the words of a commentator who knows their economics.
- 'Model fits some data but not other. We so confused. We so confused.'
- 'I agree that labeling as a "puzzle" the inability of a model to fit the data is quite awkward and somewhat pretentious. It is like saying "How the reality dare to disagree with our beloved model!"'
- 'Is there a prestigious field where they call this kind of thing a puzzle? Like in physics, do they run an experiment and find out it falsifies a model or conventional wisdom, then call it a puzzle?'

- 'It is such a joke that tens of thousands of papers have been written on the DMP/Shimer model. The model has bad out-of-sample properties, it is not used in the private sector for forecasting, and it is certainly not used in serious policy circles. Do you think Obama has heard of the DMP model?'
- 'Over-fitting a bunch of cherry-picked "stylized facts" IN SAMPLE is not evidence of external validity or usefulness.
- 'Name one success of these models beyond fitting cherry-picked "facts" in sample? Give me one reason to use/believe-in the model.'

These comments say it all on why the Shimer puzzle is a dumb puzzle. Apparently the commentators reject the myth of puzzles in economics.

10.4 ECONOMIC PUZZLES BASED ON ECONOMIC MYTHS: AN EXAMPLE

In a publication of the World Bank entitled *Puzzles of Economic Growth*, the following questions are raised and portrayed (at least implicitly) as being puzzles pertaining to observed cross-country differences in economic growth (Balcerowicz and Rzońca, 2015):

1. Why has Australia got so much ahead of New Zealand, in spite of the latter being held up as a paragon of free market reform?
2. How is it possible that Austria, with its persistently oversized state enterprise sector, has managed to (nearly) catch up with Switzerland, which in the early 1970s boasted per capita national income that was more than 50 per cent higher?
3. How can we account for differences in economic growth between Estonia and Slovenia, and which of these two countries has been more successful at systemic transformation?
4. Why is Mexico so much poorer than Spain, despite having been wealthier all the way into the 1960s?
5. Why has Venezuela, which in 1950 had a per capita income higher than that of Norway and remains a major exporter of oil, slipped behind Chile? How is it possible that its currency, considered one of the most stable currencies in the world until the 1970s, has lost its lustre even for Venezuelans?
6. Why has 'communist' China outstripped 'capitalist' India?
7. Why has Pakistan's growth lagged behind that of Indonesia, even though the latter was exposed to recurrent bouts of state interventionism, and

suffered one of the deepest crises in world economic history in the years 1997–98?
8. Why, even before the 2010 earthquake, has the Dominican Republic been visited by tourists many more times than Haiti, despite being situated on the same island?

These puzzles are based on myths: the myths that under all conditions free market 'reforms' are conducive to growth, that an oversized state retards growth, that 'systemic transformation' (meaning moving towards laissez-faire, I assume) boosts growth, and that capitalist countries should grow faster than communist countries. They are no different from the 'puzzle' of why the United Kingdom (UK) has 42 times the number of confirmed Covid-19 cases as Egypt, even though Egypt does not have as free an economy as that of the UK. The growth-related myths have already been debunked in the discussion of the myths of laissez-faire in Chapter 6, but more will be said in what follows.

The Heritage Foundation subscribes to these ideas, putting forward the view that economic freedom makes an economy grow and prosper, and that the free market system, which is rooted in economic freedom, 'has fuelled unprecedented economic growth and development around the world' (Miller et al., 2019). Peet (1992) sees a myth in the concept of freedom as envisaged by those holding a 'mainstream market liberal political-economic viewpoint' who believe that freedom is entirely an economic construct, which exists in an unfettered market. The implication of this view is that freedom has a meaning that is akin to choice, the availability of alternatives. It is the freedom to do things without being hindered by government intervention. It is freedom from restrictions that prevent the oligarchy from getting on with whatever they want to do to accumulate wealth. One of the measures of economic freedom, as envisaged by the Heritage Foundation, is property rights. Even natural resources must be in private hands, which is a tradition that goes back to imperialism, as the colonial powers introduced these ideas to the colonies and enforced them by laws, whips and machine guns.

Peet argues that for most people in society, freedom has entirely different meanings, such as freedom from hunger, freedom of speech and of association, freedom from arbitrary constraints, and freedom to be creative and artistic. While deregulation is conducive to the free market concept of freedom, this trend has been accompanied by a deterioration in freedom from poverty, freedom of speech and association, freedom from arbitrary constraints, and freedom to be creative and artistic. Look no further than the war on whistleblowers in the name of a hoax called 'national security', and if in doubt remember two names: Julian Assange and Edward

Snowden. It does not make sense to claim that freedom from regulation is conducive to growth, whereas freedom from poverty, illiteracy and sickness are not so because these freedoms require government spending. Freedom from the coronavirus must be far more conducive to growth than freedom from regulation, even if the former requires massive government spending.

The fact of the matter is that growth is affected by a large number of factors besides economic freedom, government size and free market reform. For example, Barro (1996) found that for a given starting level of real per capita gross domestic product (GDP), the growth rate is enhanced by higher initial schooling and life expectancy, lower fertility, lower government consumption, better maintenance of the rule of law, lower inflation, and improvements in the terms of trade. For given values of these and other variables, growth is negatively related to the initial level of real per capita GDP, which provides support for the catch-up hypothesis. Political freedom has only a weak effect on growth, but there is some indication of a non-linear relation in the sense that an expansion of political rights from a low level stimulates economic growth, but once a moderate amount of democracy has been attained, a further expansion reduces growth. While Barro's results show a negative effect of government consumption on growth, the Heritage Foundation condemns all kinds of government spending.

In a review of the literature, Chirwa and Odhiambo (2016) find that the key determinants of economic growth in developing countries include foreign aid, foreign direct investment, fiscal policy, investment, trade, human capital development, monetary policy, natural resources and reforms, as well as geographic, regional, political and financial factors. In developed countries, the study reveals that the key determinants of economic growth include physical capital, fiscal policy, human capital, trade, demographics, monetary policy, and financial and technological factors. Nothing is said about economic freedom, but significant support is found for human capital, which typically requires government spending on health and education.

The results of empirical work in economics and finance depend, *inter alia*, on which technique is used to analyse the data. Levine and Renelt (1992) used extreme bounds analysis, as suggested by Leamer (1983), and found that 'almost all results are fragile'. On the other hand, Sala-i-Martin (1997) used another version of extreme bounds analysis and found 22 out of 59 variables to be robust. These include regional variables, political variables, religious variables, market distortions, market performance, types of investment, primary sector production, openness, type of economic organization, and whether or not the underlying country is a former Spanish colony. In a similar study using Bayesian averaging of classical estimates (BACE), Sala-i-Martin et al. (2004) examined 67 explanatory variables and found 18 to be 'significantly and robustly partially correlated with long-term growth'. These variables are East Asian dummy, primary schooling, GDP in 1960, fraction of tropical area, population density, malaria prevalence, life expectancy, fraction Confucian, African dummy, Latin American dummy, fraction of GDP in mining, Spanish colony, years open, fraction Muslim, fraction Buddhist, ethnolinguistic fractionaliza-tion, and share of government consumption.

It is therefore a gross simplification to view growth as being dependent on the adoption or otherwise of free market policies. Kenny and Williams (2001) examine cross-country econometric studies of economic growth and conclude that 'the results are disappointing in that no model has proven robust to trial by repeated regression'. They refer to two articles of Jeffrey Sachs (1996, 1997) that reach 'markedly different conclusions', thus providing 'an illustration of the problems facing even the best development economists'. In general, they argue that 'attempts to divine the cause or causes of long-term economic growth, testing a wide range of possible determinants using statistical techniques, have produced results that (like the two Sachs articles) are frequently contradictory to results reported elsewhere'. They also note that 'empirical evidence is hardly unanimous in support of a particular view of the growth process'. Because of the variability of results and the diversity of views on the growth process, they contend that 'review of the available evidence suggests that the current state of understanding about the causes of economic growth is fairly poor'.

Likewise, Levine and Zervos (1993) suggest that 'it is conceptually difficult to interpret the coefficients on regressions that involve data for over 100 countries averaged over 30 years during which time business cycles, policy changes, and political disturbances have influenced economic activity'. By analysing the results of cross-country regressions, they find indicators of financial development to be strongly associated with long-run growth, and that it is extremely difficult to identify believable links between a wide assortment of indicators of individual policies and long-run growth. They could not find robust ties between indicators of monetary or fiscal policy and long-run growth.

Now, we turn to the questions about Mexico, Haiti and Venezuela, none of which represents a puzzle as is claimed. Mexico's growth has been lacklustre, even though (or perhaps because) Mexico has, since the 1980s, opened up to foreign trade and investment, achieved fiscal discipline and privatized state-owned enterprises, the very recipe for growth according to the Heritage Foundation and free marketeers. It is not difficult to explain why Mexico's performance has been inferior to that of Spain. Hanson (2010) reviews the arguments put forward to explain this phenomenon, which he attributes to: (1) poorly functioning credit markets; (2) distortions in the supply of non-traded inputs; (3) perverse incentives for informality, which create a drag on productivity growth; and (4) the bad luck of exporting goods that China sells, rather than goods that China buys. This is not a puzzle, as adequate explanations are provided by Hanson (2010).

Then comes the question why Venezuela, which is flush with oil, is strapped for cash (and the same goes for Iraq and Libya). Free marketeers attribute the dire situation in Venezuela to the economic system introduced by Hugo Chavez and sustained by his successor, Nicolas Maduro. In his first address to the United Nations in September 2017, Donald Trump said that 'the problem with Venezuela is not that socialism has been poorly implemented, but that socialism has been *faithfully* implemented'. On that occasion he paused for a response but he was met with awkward silence, before sounds of murmured laughter could be heard, and eventually weak clapping (*The Independent*, 2017). Trump said what he said to justify the crippling economic sanctions imposed on Venezuela, and attempts aiming at regime change by supporting the self-declared president, Juan Guaido. Naturally, all of that was to defend the people of Venezuela by starving them to death. For free marketeers, Venezuela is in a dire situation because Chavez and Maduro channelled oil revenues to the provision of food subsidies, healthcare and education. The fact of the matter is that Venezuela had to be punished for what Kathleen Schuster (2017) describes as 'the expropriation of the oil industry in the name of nationalization', and for refusing to say 'how high?' when the US says 'jump'. Does this ring a bell? Recall the regime change in Iran in 1953, which was orchestrated by the US's Central Intelligence Agency (CIA) and the UK's MI6 in response to 'the expropriation of the oil industry in the name of nationalization'.

Kiger (2019) describes the situation in Venezuela now and then as follows:

> It wasn't that long ago that Venezuela, which possesses the world's largest crude oil reserves, was a relatively stable democracy with one of Latin America's fastest-rising economies . . .
>
> But starting in 2014, the South American nation began suffering a startling collapse. With Venezuela's gross domestic product plummeting even more than the United States during the Great Depression, many of its nearly 32 million inhabitants became unable to afford food, and resource-starved hospitals did not have enough soap and antibiotics.

Well, it is no surprise that Venezuela's GDP plummeted even more than the US's during the Great Depression, because the US was not under sanctions and siege. It is not that Venezuela was a shining example of economic success before Chavez and Maduro. The economy, which was run by an oligarchy, was at the mercy of fluctuations in oil prices. Following the plummeting of oil prices due to the late 1980s glut, Venezuela was forced to accept a bailout by the International Monetary Fund (IMF) in 1989. Naturally, that was followed by sharply rising prices of consumer goods and fares for public transport, leading to violent demonstrations, to which the authorities responded by declaring a nationwide curfew and suspension of civil liberties. The grotesque inequality was maintained.

Why is it a puzzle that an economy collapses because of sanctions, destabilization by foreign powers and threats of military invasion? Even worse, on 26 March 2020 (while the world was reeling under the hammer of the coronavirus) it was announced that the US Department of Injustice had charged Maduro with narco-terrorism and drug trafficking, offering a $15 million reward for information leading to his arrest. It would be a puzzle if, despite these hostilities, Venezuela had a prosperous economy and cash. Is it a puzzle that the economy of Iraq shrank in the 1990s following the destruction of the infrastructure and the imposition of crippling sanctions by the US (to defend the people of Iraq, of course)? Those who claim that the situation in Venezuela represents a puzzle want to distract attention from the devastating effects of the sanctions (by the way, the imposition of sanctions is considered an act of war). A report, published by the Centre for Economic Policy Research (CEPR) and co-authored by Jeffrey Sachs, reveals that 'as many as 40 000 people may have died in Venezuela as a result of US sanctions that made it harder for ordinary citizens to access food, medicine and medical equipment' (Buncombe, 2019). It is not a puzzle that Venezuela is in a dire situation.

The last puzzle to be examined in this chapter is that even before the 2010 earthquake, the Dominican Republic has been visited by tourists many more times than Haiti, even though they share an island. This puzzle resembles a similar puzzle: that more people visit Switzerland than Afghanistan. A more perplexing puzzle is that more people visit Switzerland than Albania, even though the two countries are located on the same continent. Sharing an island does not mean that Haiti and the Dominican Republic should have the same number of tourists, or else that would be a puzzle.

Haiti and the Dominican Republic share an island, but they could not be more different. While the Dominican Republic has proper streets, one needs an hour to travel just a few kilometres in Haiti. Only about 50 per cent of Haitians can read and write (as opposed to nearly 90 per cent in the Dominican Republic). The child mortality rate in Haiti is three times higher than in the Dominican Republic. The weak infrastructure in Haiti hampers quick delivery of aid and emergency help during natural catastrophes. No Haitian city has a regular electricity supply. Are these not good enough reasons for tourists to prefer the Dominican Republic to Haiti? Where is the puzzle?

10.5   WORDS OF WISDOM FROM EINSTEIN

A genius by the name of Albert Einstein once said that 'we cannot solve our problems with the same thinking we used when we created them'. He also described futile repetitive behaviour as 'insanity: doing the same thing over and over again and expecting different results'. Allegedly, though not confirmed, he once said 'everything should be made as simple as possible, but no simpler'. For example, the effect of the fiscal stimulus can be explained intuitively with reference to the traditional Keynesian view of the multiplier, in which case there is no need to go through the New Keynesian explanation, which makes the matter overly complicated.

Economists like complexity; never mind that no one can understand their models, including policy-makers. However, the complexity brought about by the excessive mathematization of economic theory, or the extravaganza of econometrics, has not enhanced our understanding of the working of the economy and financial markets as we move from one crisis to another, from bad to worse. Puzzles arise and persist because of belief in the power of econometrics, ideological bias, confirmation bias, failure to pay attention to reality, flaws in empirical work and the elevation of economics to the status of physical science. Myths arise because of dogmatic thinking.

Unnecessary complexity brings with it overconfidence and whatever comes with overconfidence. Romer (2020) expresses this view by suggesting that economists work 'from the basement' because 'they don't know their own limitations, and they have a far greater sense of confidence in their analyses than I have found to be warranted'. Romer has something to say about the connection between myths and normative economics, as explained in Chapter 1. He refers to a 'system that delegates to economists the responsibility for answering normative questions', arguing that this system 'will fail and cause enormous damage when powerful industries are brought into the mix'. He also says that 'in their attempt to answer normative questions that the science of economics could not address, economists open the door to economic ideologues who lacked commitment to scientific integrity'.

On the bright side, puzzles bring glory to the originator. Therefore, I will close by saying, 'long live my puzzle that interest rates and stock prices should be positively correlated when they appear otherwise'. I remain committed to the defence of this puzzle, no matter what, even at the expense of ignoring Albert Einstein's words of wisdom or acting as an economic ideologue, as suggested by Paul Romer.

References

Aaron, H.J., Gale, W.G. and Orszag, P.R. (2004) Meeting the Revenue Challenge, in M. Rivlin and I. Sawhill (eds) *Restoring Fiscal Sanity*, Washington, DC: Brookings Institution.

Abhyankar, A., Sarno, L. and Valente, G. (2005) Exchange Rates and Fundamentals: Evidence on the Economic Value of Predictability, *Journal of International Economics*, 66, 325–348.

Adair, P. and Adaskou, M. (2015) Trade-off-Theory vs. Pecking Order Theory and the Determinants of Corporate Leverage: Evidence From a Panel Data Analysis upon French SMEs (2002–2010), *Cogent Economics and Finance*, 3, 1–12.

Afxentiou, P.C. and Serlitis, A. (1993) International Capital Mobility and the Long Run Investment and Saving in Canada, *Economia Internazionale*, 46, 147–167.

Aggarwal, R., Lucey, B.M. and Mohanty, S.K. (2009) The Forward Exchange Rate Bias Puzzle is Persistent: Evidence from Stochastic and Nonparametric Cointegration Tests, *Financial Review*, 44, 625–645.

Aggarwal, R. and Zong, S. (2008) Behavioral Biases in Forward Rates as Forecasts of Future Exchange Rates: Evidence of Systematic Pessimism and Under-Reaction, *Multinational Finance Journal*, 12, 241–277.

Akerlof, G.A. and Shiller, R.J. (2015) The Dark Side of Free Markets, *Conversation*, 21 October. https://theconversation.com/the-dark-side-of-free-markets-48862.

Akram, Q.F., Rime, D. and Sarno, L. (2008) Arbitrage in the Foreign Exchange Market: Turning on the Microscope, *Journal of International Economics*, 76, 237–253.

Alexakis, A. and Apergis, S. (1992) The Feldstein–Horioka Puzzle and Exchange Rate Regimes: Evidence From Cointegration Tests, *Journal of Policy Modelling*, 16, 459–472.

Al-Jassar, S. and Moosa, I.A. (2020) Empirical Evidence on International Capital Immobility: A Consumption-Based Approach, *International Review of Applied Economics*, 34, 175–192.

Allard, G.J. and Lindert, P.H. (2006) Euro-Productivity and Euro-Job Since the 1960s: Which Institutions Really Mattered?, NBER Working Papers, No. 12460.

Allen, H.L. and Taylor, M.P. (1989) Chart Analysis and the Foreign Exchange Market, *Bank of England Quarterly Bulletin*, November.

Allen, H.L. and Taylor, M.P. (1990) Charts, Noise and Fundamentals in the London Foreign Exchange Market, *Economic Journal*, 100, 49–59.

Al-Najjar, B. and Hussainey, K. (2011) Revisiting the Capital-Structure Puzzle: UK Evidence, *Journal of Risk Finance*, 12, 329–338.

Al-Nakeeb, B. (2016) *Two Centuries of Parasitic Economics: The Struggle for Economic and Political Democracy on the Eve of the Financial Collapse of the West*, New York: (Private Publication).

Al-Nakeeb, B. (2017) The Case for Taxing Interest, *Real-World Economics Review*, 81, 63–75.

Alworth, J. and Arachi, G. (2001) The Effect of Taxes on Corporate Financing Decisions: Evidence from a Panel of Italian Firms, *International Tax and Public Finance*, 8, 353–376.

Amadeo, K. (2019) Democrats vs. Republicans: Which is Better for the Economy?, *Balance*, 7 December. https://www.thebalance.com/democra ts-vs-republicans-which-is-better-for-the-economy-4771839.

Anderson, J.E. and van Wincoop, E. (2003) Gravity with Gravitas: A Solution to the Border Puzzle, *American Economic Review*, 93, 170–192.

Ang, A. and G. Bekaert (2002) International Asset Allocation with Regime Shifts, *Review of Financial Studies*, 15, 1137–1187.

Ang, A., Hodrick, R.J., Xing, Y. and Zhang, X. (2006) The Cross-Section of Volatility and Expected Returns, *Journal of Finance*, 61, 259–299.

Arano, K., Parker, C. and Terry, R. (2010) Gender-Based Risk Aversion and Retirement Asset Allocation, *Economic Inquiry*, 48, 147–155.

Asness, C.S., Israelov, R. and Liew, J.M. (2010) International Diversifica-tion Works (in the Long Run). http://www.retailinvestor.org/pdf/For Diversify.pdf.

Auerbach, A.J. (2002) The Bush Tax Cut and National Saving, NBER Working Papers, No. 9012.

Baba, N. and Packer, F. (2009) Interpreting Deviations from Covered Interest Parity During the Financial Market Turmoil of 2007–08, *Journal of Banking and Finance*, 33, 1953–1962.

Bacchetta, P. and van Wincoop, E. (2006) Can Information Heterogeneity Explain the Exchange Rate Determination Puzzle?, *American Economic Review*, 96, 552–576.

Backus, D.K., Kehoe, P.J. and Kydland, F.E. (1992) International Real Business Cycles, *Journal of Political Economy*, 100, 745–775.

Backus, D.K., Kehoe, P.J. and Kydland, F.E. (1995) International Business Cycles: Theory and Evidence, in T. Cooley (ed.) *Frontiers of Business Cycle Research*, Princeton, NJ: Princeton University Press.

Baird, R. (2017) Meghan Markle and Prince Harry Wedding to Deliver £2bn Boost to UK Economy, *International Business Times*, 27 November.

Baker, M., Ruback, R. and Wurgler, J. (2004) Behavioral Corporate Finance: A Survey, in E. Eckbo (ed.) *Handbook of Corporate Finance*, Part III, Amsterdam: North-Holland.

Balcerowicz, L. and Rzońca, A. (eds) (2015) *Puzzles of Economic Growth*, Washington, DC: World Bank.

Bali, T.G. and Cakici, N. (2008) Idiosyncratic Volatility and the Cross-Section of Expected Returns, *Journal of Financial and Quantitative Analysis*, 43, 29–58.

Bali, T.G., Cakici, N. and Whitelaw, R. (2011) Maxing Out: Stocks as Lotteries and the Cross Section of Expected Returns, *Journal of Financial Economics*, 99, 427–446.

Baltagi, B.H. (2002) *Econometrics* (3rd edition), New York: Springer.

Banton, C. (2020) Efficiency Definition, *Invetopedia*, 6 February. https://www.investopedia.com/terms/e/efficiency.asp.

Barberis, N., Huang, M. and Thaler, R.H. (2006) Individual Preferences, Monetary Gambles, and Stock Market Participation: A Case for Narrow Framing, *American Economic Review*, 96, 1069–1090.

Barnett, S. (2000) Evidence on the Fiscal and Macroeconomic Impact of Privatization, IMF Working Papers, No. 130.

Barnhart, S.W., McKnown, R. and Wallace, M.S. (1999) Non-Informative Tests of the Unbiased Forward Exchange Rate, *Journal of Financial and Quantitative Analysis*, 34, 265–291.

Barnichon, R. (2008) The Shimer Puzzle and the Identification of Productivity Shocks, Federal Reserve Board, Finance and Economics Discussion Papers.

Barro, R.J. (1996) Determinants of Economic Growth: A Cross-Country Empirical Study, NBER Working Papers, No. 5698.

Barro, R.J. (2005) Rare Events and the Equity Premium, NBER Working Papers, No. 11310.

Barro, R.J. (2006) Rare Disasters and Asset Markets in the Twentieth Century, *Quarterly Journal of Economics*, 121, 823–866.

Baxter, M. and Crucini, M.J. (1993) Explaining Saving–Investment Correlations, *American Economic Review*, 83, 416–436.

Baxter, M. and Jermann, U.J. (1997) The International Diversification Puzzle is Worse Than You Think, *American Economic Review*, 87, 170–180.

Bayoumi, T. (1990) Saving–Investment Correlations: Immobile Capital, Government Policy or Endogenous Behaviour?, *IMF Staff Papers*, 37, 360–387.

Beard, T.R., Ford, G.S., Kim, H. and Spiwak, L.J. (2011) Regulatory

Expenditures, Economic Growth and Jobs: An Empirical Study, Phoenix: Center Policy Bulletin No. 28. http://www.phoenix-center.org/PolicyBul letin/PCPB28Final. pdf.

Becker, T.A. and Shabani, R. (2010) Outstanding Debt and the Household Portfolio, *Review of Financial Studies*, 23, 2900–2934.

Bel, G., Fageda, X. and Warner, M.E. (2010) Is Private Production of Public Services Cheaper than Public Production? A Meta-Regression Analysis of Solid Waste and Water Services, *Journal of Policy Analysis and Management*, 29, 553–577.

Beloa, F. Galab, V.D. and Lic, J. (2013) Government Spending, Political Cycles, and the Cross Section of Stock Returns, *Journal of Financial Economics*, 107, 305–324.

Benartzi, S. and Thaler, R. (1995) Myopic Loss Aversion and the Equity Premium Puzzle, *Quarterly Journal of Economics*, 110, 73–92.

Benes, J. and Kumhof, M. (2012) The Chicago Plan Revisited, IMF Working Papers, No. WP12/202.

Bennett, J., Estrin, S. and Urga, G. (2007) Methods of Privatization and Economic Growth in Transition Economies, *Economics of Transition*, 15, 661–683.

Bergin, P. and Feenstra, R. (2001) Pricing-to-Market, Staggered Contracts, and Real Exchange Rate Persistence, *Journal of International Economics*, 54, 333–359.

Bergmann, B. (1999) Abolish the Nobel Prize for Economics, *Challenge*, 42, 52–57.

Bernasconi, M., Marenzi, A. and Pagani, L. (2005) Corporate Financing Decisions and Nondebt Tax Shields: Evidence From Italian Experiences in the 1990s, *International Tax and Public Finance*, 12, 741–773.

Bernasek, A. and Shwiff, S. (2001) Gender, Risk, and Retirement, *Journal of Economic Issues*, 35, 345–356.

Bernstein, P.L. (1996) Dividends: The Puzzle, *Journal of Applied Corporate Finance*, 9, 16–22.

Biger, N. (1979) Exchange Risk Implications of International Portfolio Diversification, *Journal of International Business Studies*, 10, 63–74.

Bini-Smaghi, L. (1991) Exchange Rate Variability and Trade: Why is it so Difficult to Find any Empirical Relationship?, *Applied Economics*, 23, 927–935.

Black, F. (1976) The Dividend Puzzle, *Journal of Portfolio Management*, 2, 5–8.

Black, F. (1990) Why Firms Pay Dividends, *Financial Analysts Journal*, 46, 5.

Blake, A. and Cortes-Jiménez, I. (2007) The Drivers of Tourism Demand in the UK, Christel DeHaan Tourism and Travel Research Institute, University of Nottingham, December.

Blommestein, H.J. (2009) The Financial Crisis as a Symbol of the Failure of Academic Finance (A Methodological Digression), *Journal of Financial Transformation*, 27, 3–8.

Bodman, P.M. (1995) National Savings and Domestic Investment in the Long Term: Some Time Series Evidence from the OECD, *International Economic Journal*, 9, 37–60.

Bogan, V. (2008) Stock Market Participation and the Internet, *Journal of Financial and Quantitative Analysis*, 43, 191–211.

Booth, A.L. and Nolen, P. (2012) Gender Differences in Risk Behaviour: Does Nurture Matter?, *Economic Journal*, 122, F56–F78.

Booth, L., Aivazian, V., Demirguc-Kunt, A. and Maksimovic, V. (2001) Capital Structure in Developing Countries, *Journal of Finance*, 56, 87–130.

Borghans, L., Golsteyn, B.H.H., Heckman, J.J. and Meijers, H. (2009) Gender Differences in Risk Aversion and Ambiguity Aversion, *Journal of the European Economic Association*, 7, 649–658.

Boring, P. (2014) If You Want to Know the Real Rate of Inflation, Don't Bother with the CPI, *Forbes*, 3 February.

Boubakri, N., Smaoui, H. and Zamiti, M. (2009) Privatization Dynamics and Economic Growth, *Proceedings of Annual London Conference on Money, Economy and Management*, 9–10 July, Imperial College, London.

Boyer, B., Mitton, T. and Vorkink, K. (2010) Expected Idiosyncratic Skewness, *Review of Financial Studies*, 23, 169–202.

Brennan, M.J. and Cao, H.H. (1997) International Portfolio Investment Flows, *Journal of Finance*, 52, 1581–1880.

Bresciani-Turroni, C. (1934) The Purchasing Power Parity Doctrine, *L'Egypte Contemporaine*, 25, 433–464.

British Tourist Authority (2001) *The Price Sensitivity of Tourism in Britain*. www.niassembly.gov.uk/. . ./british-tourist-authority-price-sensitivity-of-tourism-to-britain.

Brook, Y. (2016) Free Market, 13 November. http://serious-science.org/free-market-7407.

Brown, S., Veld, C. and Veld-Merkoulova, Y. (2017) Why Do Individuals not Participate in the Stock Market?, Paper Presented at the Risk Forum, Paris, March.

Buettner, T., Overesch, M., Schreiber, U. and Wamser, G. (2008) The Impact of Thin Capitalization Rules on Multinational Financing and Investment Decisions, Deutsche Bundesbank Discussion Papers, No. 03/2008.

Buffett, W. (2003) Dividend Voodoo, *Washington Post*, 20 May.

Buncombe, A. (2019) US Sanctions on Venezuela Responsible for 'Tens of Thousands' of Deaths, *Independent*, 26 April.

Burns, W.C. (1997) Spurious Correlations. https://hbr.org/2015/06/beware-spurious-correlations.

Business Insider (2012) The Dividend Puzzle – or Why the Dividend Emperor May Have no Clothes!, 1 June. https://www.businessinsider.com/the-dividend-puzzle-or-why-the-dividend-emperor-may-have-no-clo thes-2012-6/?r=AU&IR=T.

Cagan, P. (1965) The Money Stock and its Three Determinants, in P. Cagan (ed.) *Determinants and Effects of Changes in the Stock of Money, 1875–1960*, Cambridge, MA: National Bureau of Economic Research.

Calvet, L.E., Campbell, J.Y. and Sodini, P. (2007) Down or Out: Assessing the Welfare Costs of Household Investment Mistakes, *Journal of Political Economy*, 115, 707–747.

Calvet, L.E., Campbell, J.Y. and Sodini, P. (2009) Measuring the Financial Sophistication of Households, *American Economic Review*, 99, 393–398.

Cannon, B. (2015) The Idiosyncratic Volatility Puzzle: A Behavioral Explanation. https://digitalcommons.usu.edu/gradreports/466.

Cao, J. and Han, B. (2016) Idiosyncratic Risk, Costly Arbitrage, and the Cross-Section of Stock Returns, *Journal of Banking and Finance*, 73, 1–15.

Carmichael, B. and Coën, A. (2003) International Portfolio Choice in an Overlapping Generations Model with Transaction Costs, *Economic Letters*, 80, 269–275.

Casey, K.L. (2009) In Search of Transparency, Accountability, and Competition: The Regulation of Credit Rating Agencies, Speech by SEC Commissioner, Washington, DC, 6 February.

Cassel, G. (1916) The Present Situation of the Foreign Exchange, *Economic Journal*, 26, 62–65.

Cassel, G. (1922) *Money and Foreign Exchange After 1914*, New York: Constable & Co.

Cavallo, A., Cruces, G. and Perez-Truglia, R. (2016) Learning from Potentially Biased Statistics, *Brookings Papers on Economic Activity*, Spring, 59–108.

CBO (2001) The Budget and Economic Outlook: Update, August. ftp://ftp.cbo.gov/30xx/doc 3019/EntireReport.pdf.

CBO (2005) Analyzing the Economic and Budgetary Effects of a 10 per cent Cut in Income Tax Rates, *Economic and Budget Issue Briefs*, 1 December.

CBO (2008) Options for Responding to Short-Term Economic Weakness, January. https://www.cbo.gov/sites/default/files/110th-congress-2007-20 08/reports/01-15-econ_stimulus.pdf.

Chabi-Yo, F. and Yang, J. (2009) Default Risk, Idiosyncratic Coskewness and Equity Returns, Working Paper, Ohio State University.

Chaney, T. (2013) The Gravity Equation in International Trade: An Explanation, NBER Working Papers, No. 19285.

Chang, H.J. (2011) *23 Things They Don't Tell You About Capitalism*, New York: Bloomsbury Press.

Chari, V., Kehoe, P. and McGrattan, E. (1998) Monetary Shocks and Real Exchange Rates in Sticky Price Models of International Business Cycles, Federal Reserve Bank of Minneapolis, Research Department Staff Reports, No. 223.

Chen, J.J. (2004) Determinants of Capital Structure of Chinese-Listed Companies, *Journal of Business Research*, 57, 1341–1351.

Chen, Z. and Petkova, R. (2012) Does Idiosyncratic Volatility Proxy for Risk Exposure?, *Review of Financial Studies*, 25, 2745–2787.

Cheung, Y. and Chinn, M. (1998) Integration, Cointegration, and the Forecast Consistency of Structural Exchange Rate Models, *Journal of International Money and Finance*, 17, 813–830.

Chinn, M.D. and Meredith, G. (2004) Monetary Policy and Long-Horizon Uncovered Interest Parity, *IMF Staff Papers*, 51, 409–430.

Chirwa, T.G. and Odhiambo, N.M. (2016) Macroeconomic Determinants of Economic Growth: A Review of International Literature, *East European Journal of Economics and Business*, 11, 33–47.

Choi, C.Y., Mark, N.C. and Sul, D. (2004) Unbiased Estimation of the Half-Life to PPP Convergence in Panel Data, NBER Working Papers, No. 10614.

Chowdhury, A.R. (1993) Does Exchange Rate Volatility Depress Trade Flows? Evidence from Error-Correction Models, *Review of Economics and Statistics*, 75, 700–706.

Christ, C.F. (1951) A Test of an Econometric Model for the United States, 1921–1947, in *Conference on Business Cycles*, National Bureau of Economic Research.

Christ, C.F. (1956) Aggregate Econometric Models: A Review Article, *American Economic Review*, 46, 385–408.

Christensen, G. and Miguel, E. (2018) Transparency, Reproducibility, and the Credibility of Economics Research, *Journal of Economic Literature*, 56, 920–980.

Cieslik, A. and Tarsalewska, M. (2013) Privatization, Convergence, and Growth, *Eastern European Economics*, 51, 5–20.

Clark, P.B., Tamirisa, N., Wei, S.J., Sadikov, A. and Rajan, R. (2004) Exchange Rate Volatility and Trade Flows – Some New Evidence, *IMF Occasional Papers*, No. 235.

Clarke, K. (2005) The Phantom Menace: Omitted Variable Bias in Econometric Research, *Conflict Management and Peace Science*, 22, 341–352.

Cochrane, J. (2013) New vs. Old Keynesian Stimulus, *Grumpy Economist*, 8 November. https://johnhcochrane.blogspot.com/2013/11/new-vs-old-keynesian-stimulus.html.

Cocquemas, F. and Whaley, R.E. (2016) Still No Presidential Puzzle for the Stock Market, *Journal of Portfolio Management*, Summer, 4–7.

Committee on the Judiciary (1961) Hearings before the Subcommittee on Antitrust and Monopoly, Washington, DC: US Government Printing Office.

Committeri, M., Rossi, S. and Santorelli, A. (1993) Tests of Covered Interest Parity on the Euromarket with High-Quality Data, *Applied Financial Economics*, 3, 89–93.

Conover, C.M. Jensen, G.R. and Johnston, R.R. (2002) Emerging Markets: When are They Worth it?, *Financial Analyst Journal*, March/April, 86–95.

Constâncio, V. (2011) Challenges to Monetary Policy in 2012, Speech at the 26th International Conference on Interest Rates, Frankfurt.

Constantinos, G. (2010) Home Bias Puzzle: Is it a Puzzle or Not?, *Economic Analysis*, 43, 7–14.

Cook, P. and Uchida, Y. (2003) Privatization and Economic Growth in Developing Countries, *Journal of Development Studies*, 39, 121–154.

Cooper, I. and Kaplanis, E. (1994) Home Bias in Equity Portfolios, Inflation Hedging, and International Capital Market Equilibrium, *Review of Financial Studies*, 7, 45–60.

Coulbois, P. and Prissert, P. (1974) Short Term Capital Flows and Monetary Policy, *De Economist*, 122, 283–308.

Council on Foreign Relations (2015) The Credit Rating Controversy. http://www.cfr.org/ financial-crises/credit-rating-controversy/p22328.

Croson, R. and Gneezy, U. (2009) Gender Differences in Preferences, *Journal of Economic Literature*, 47, 448–474.

Dabla-Norris, E., Kochhar, K., Suphaphiphat, N., Ricka, F. and Tsounta, E. (2015) Causes and Consequences of Income Inequality: A Global Perspective, IMF Staff Discussion Note, June.

Danesi, M. (2018) What is a Puzzle?, *Psychology Today*, 17 March.

Dar, A., Amirkhalkhali, S. and Amirkhalkhali, S. (1994) On the Fiscal Policy Implications of Low Capital Mobility: Some Further Evidence from Cross-Country, Time-Series Data, *Southern Economic Journal*, 61, 169–190.

Davidson, P. (1982) Rational Expectations: A Fallacious Foundation for Studying Crucial Decision Making Processes, *Journal of Post Keynesian Economics*, 5, 182–198.

DeAngelo, H. and Masulis, R.W. (1980) Optimal Capital Structure under Corporate and Personal Taxation, *Journal of Financial Economics*, 8, 3–29.

Deaton, A. and Muellbauer, J. (1980) An Almost Ideal Demand System, *American Economic Review*, 70, 312–336.

De Rugy, V. (2011) The Perils of Economic Forecasting, *National Review*, 3 November. https://www.nationalreview.com/corner/perils-economic-forecasting-veronique-de-rugy/.

Dixon, H. (1999) Controversy: Exchange Rates and Fundamentals, *Economic Journal*, 109, 652–654.

Doganlar, M. (2002) Estimating the Impact of Exchange Rate Volatility on Exports: Evidence From Asian Countries, *Applied Economics Letters*, 9, 859–863.

Donohue, J.J. and Levitt, S.D. (2001) The Impact of Legalized Abortion on Crime, *Quarterly Journal of Economics*, 116, 379–420.

Dooley, M., Frankel, J. and Mathieson, D. (1987) International Capital Mobility: What Do Saving–Investment Correlations Tell Us?, *IMF Staff Papers*, 34, 503–530.

Dorfman, J. (2016) Ten Free Market Economic Reasons To Be Thankful, *Forbes*, 23 November.

Dowd, K. (1999) Too Big to Fail? Long-Term Capital Management and the Federal Reserve, Cato Institute Briefing Papers, No. 52, September.

Durbarry, R. and Sinclair, M.T. (2001) *Tourism Taxation in the UK*, Report for the Tourism Action Group, Confederation of British Industry.

DW (2009) Sweden Gets a Boost from Upcoming Royal Wedding, 14 September. http://www.dw.com/en/sweden-gets-a-boost-from-upcoming-royal-wedding/a-4663974.

The Economist (1998), The Perils of Prediction, 1 August.

The Economist (2003) The Dividend Puzzle, 9 January.

The Economist (2005) Who Rates the Raters?, 26 May.

The Economist (2013) Free Speech or Knowing Misrepresentation?, 5 February.

The Economist (2015a) As Safe as Houses, 31 January.

The Economist (2015b) Should Britain Abolish the Monarchy?, 8 September.

Ehrbar, H.G. (2000) Irrealist Lines of Defense in Econometrics, Working Paper, Economics Department, University of Utah.

Ellsberg, D. (1961) Risk, Ambiguity, and the Savage Axioms, *Quarterly Journal of Economics*, 75, 643–669.

Elmendorf, D.W. and Reifschneider, D.L. (2002) Short-Run Effects of Fiscal Policy with Forward-Looking Financial Markets, *National Tax Journal*, September, 357–386.

Engel, C. (1994) Can the Markov Switching Model Forecast Exchange Rates? *Journal of International Economics*, 36, 151–165.

Engel, C. (1999) Accounting for US Real Exchange Rate Changes, *Journal of Political Economy*, 107, 507–538.

Engel, C. and Kletzer, K. (1989) Saving and Investment in an Open Economy with Non-Traded Goods, *International Economic Review*, 34, 503–530.

Engel, C., Mark, N. and West, K. (2008) Exchange Rate Models are Not as Bad as You Think, *NBER Macroeconomics Annual*, 22, 381–441.

Evans, C.L. (1999) Do National Borders Matter?, Doctoral dissertation, Harvard University.

Evans, C.L. (2001) Home Bias in Trade: Location or Foreign-ness?, Federal Reserve Bank of New York, Working Paper.

Evans, M. and Lyons, R. (2005) Meese–Rogoff Redux: Micro-Based Exchange Rate Forecasting, *American Economic Review*, 965, 405–414.

Fair, R. (2008) Estimating Exchange Rate Equations Using Estimated Expectations, Yale University ICF Working Papers, No. 07-18.

Falk, G. (1995) How Does Econometrics Contribute, If at All, to the Scientific Status of Economics? https://www.tcd.ie/Economics/assets/pdf/SER/1995/Gavin_Falk.html.

Fama, E.F. (1981) Stock Returns, Real Activity, Inflation, and Money, *American Economic Review*, 71, 545–565.

Fathers, M. (1992) The Great British Republic, *Independent*, 29 August.

FCIC (2011) *The Financial Crisis Inquiry Report*, Washington, DC: US Government Printing Office.

Feidakis, A. and Rovolis, A. (2007) Capital Structure Choice in European Union: Evidence from the Construction Industry, *Applied Financial Economics*, 17, 989–1002.

Feldstein, M. (1983) Domestic Saving and International Capital Movements in the Long Run and the Short Run, *European Economic Review*, 21, 129–151.

Feldstein, M. and Bachetta, P. (1991) National Saving and International Investment, in D. Bernheim and J. Shoven (eds) *National Saving and Economic Performance*, Chicago, IL: University of Chicago Press.

Feldstein, M. and Horioka, C. (1980) Domestic Saving and International Capital Flows, *Economic Journal*, 90, 314–329.

Felmingham, B. and Leong, S. (2005) Parity Conditions and the Efficiency of the Australian 90- and 180-Day Forward Markets, *Review of Financial Economics*, 14, 127–145.

Fernet, B. (2016) Is Argentina Lying About Inflation Again?, 27 April. https://www.thebubble.com/is-argentina-lying-about-inflation-again.

Fieleke, N. (1982) National Saving and International Investment, *Saving and Government Policy*, Federal Reserve Bank of Boston Conference Series, No. 25.

Financial Times (2001) Why an Accident like Hatfield was Waiting to Happen, 22 February.

Fisher, I. (1930) *The Theory of Interest*, New York: Macmillan.

Flood, R. and Rose, A.K. (1999) Understanding Exchange Rate Volatility without the Contrivance of Macroeconomics, *Economic Journal*, 109, F660–F672.

Flood, R. and Rose, A.K. (2002) Uncovered Interest Parity in Crisis, *IMF Staff Papers*, 49, 252–266.

Flood, R. and Rose, A.K. (2008) Why So Glum? The Meese–Rogoff Methodology Meets the Stock Market, CEPR Discussion Papers, 6714.

Fong, W.M., Valente, G. and Fung, J.K.W. (2010) Covered Interest Arbitrage Profits: The Role of Liquidity and Credit Risk, *Journal of Banking and Finance*, 34, 1098–1107.

Foote, C. and Goetz, C. (2008) The Impact of Legalized Abortion on Crime: Comment, *Quarterly Journal of Economics*, 123, 407–423.

Frank, A.G. (1976) Economic Genocide in Chile: Open Letter to Milton Friedman and Arnold Harberger, *Economic and Political Weekly*, 11, 880–888.

Frankel, J.A. (1993) Quantifying International Capital Mobility in the 1980s, in D.K. Das (ed.) *International Finance: Contemporary Issues*, New York: Routledge.

Frankel, J.A. (2011) Over-optimism in Forecasts by Official Budget Agencies and its Implications, NBER Working Papers, No. 17239.

Frankel, J.A. and Dornbusch, R. (1988) The Flexible Exchange Rate System: Experience and Alternatives, in S. Boner (ed.) *International Finance and Trade*, London: Macmillan.

Frankel, J.A. and Froot, K. (1990) Chartists, Fundamentalists and the Demand for Dollars, in A.S Courakis and M.P. Taylor (eds) *Private Behaviour and Government Policy in Interdependent Economies*, Oxford: Oxford University Press.

Frankel, J.A. and MacArthur, A. (1988) Political vs. Currency Premia in International Real Interest Differentials, *European Economic Review*, 32, 1083–1121.

Frankel, J.A. and Rose, A. (1995) Empirical Research on Nominal Exchange Rates, *Handbook of International Economics*, 3, Amsterdam: Elsevier.

Frankfurter, G.M. (1999) What is the Puzzle in 'The Dividend Puzzle'?, *Journal of Investing*, Summer, 8, 76–85.

French, K. and Poterba, J. (1991) Investor Diversification and International Equity Markets, *American Economic Review*, 81, 222–226.

Friberg, R. and Paterson, R.W. and Richardson, A.D. (2011) Why is There a Home Bias? A Case Study of Wine, *Journal of Wine Economics*, 6, 37–66.

Frydenberg, S. (2008) Theory of Capital Structure: A Review. http://papers.ssrn.com/sol3/ papers.cfm?abstract_id=556631.

Fu, F. (2009) Idiosyncratic Risk and the Cross-Section of Expected Returns, *Journal of Financial Economics*, 91, 24–37.

Gailliot, H.J. (1970) Purchasing Power Parity as An Explanation of Long-Term Changes in Exchange Rates, *Journal of Money, Credit and Banking*, 2, 384–357.

Gale, W.G. and Potter, S.R. (2002) An Economic Evaluation of the Economic Growth and Tax Relief Reconciliation Act of 2001, *National Tax Journal*, 55, 133–186.

Gaspar, V. and Mauro, P. (2020) Fiscal Policies to Protect People During the Coronavirus Outbreak, IMF Blog, 5 March. https://blogs.imf.org/20 20/03/05/fiscal-policies-to-protect-people-during-the-coronavirus-out break/.

Gehrig, T. (1993) An Information Based Explanation of the Domestic Bias in International Equity Investment, *Scandinavian Journal of Economics*, 95, 97–109.

Geske, R. and Roll, R. (1983) The Fiscal and Monetary Linkage between Stock Returns and Inflation, *Journal of Finance*, 38, 1–33.

Geweke, J.F., Horowitz, J.L. and Pesaran, M.H. (2006) Econometrics: A Bird's Eye View, IZA Discussion Papers, No. 2458.

Gill, A. and Mathur, N. (2011) Factors that Influence Financial Leverage of Canadian Firms, *Journal of Applied Finance and Banking*, 1, 19–37.

Global Centre for Public Service Excellence (2015) *Is the Private Sector more Efficient? A Cautionary Tale*, Singapore: UNDP.

Godrej, D. (2015) Myth 5: The Private Sector is More Efficient than the Public Sector, *New Internationalist*, 1 December.

Goertzel, T. (2002) Econometric Modeling as Junk Science, *Skeptical Inquirer*, 26, 19–23.

Goetzmann, W.N., Li, L. and Rouwenhorst, K.G. (2005) Long-Term Global Market Correlations, *Journal of Business*, 78, 1–38.

Goldstein, M., Mathieson, D. and Lane, T. (1991) Determinants and Systematic Consequences of International Capital Flows, IMF Occasional Papers, No. 77.

Goodhart, C. (1984) *Monetary Policy in Theory and Practice*, London: Macmillan.

Goodhart, C. (1988) The Foreign Exchange Market: A Random Walk with a Dragging Anchor, *Economica*, 55, 437–480.

Goodwin, B. and Grennes, T.J. (1994) Real Interest Equalization and the Integration of International Financial Markets, *Journal of International Money and Finance*, 13, 107–124.

Gorman, L.R. and Jorgensen, B.N. (2002) Domestic versus International

Portfolio Selection: A Statistical Examination of the Home Bias, *Multinational Finance Journal*, 6, 131–166.

Gorman, S.A. (1998) *The International Equity Commitment*, Charlottesville, VA: Institute of Chartered Financial Analysts.

Granger, C.W.J. (1969) Investigating Causal Relations by Econometric Models and Cross-Spectral Methods, *Econometrica*, 37, 424–438.

Granger, C.W.J. (1986) Developments in the Study of Cointegrated Economic Variables, *Oxford Bulletin of Economics and Statistics*, 48, 213–228.

Granger, C.W.J. and Newbold, P. (1974) Spurious Regression in Econometrics, *Journal of Econometrics*, 2, 111–120.

Gravelle, J.G., Hungerford, T.L. and Labonte, M. (2009) Economic Stimulus: Issues and Policies, Congressional Research Service, 10 November.

Greenwood, V. (2018) What Makes Downsizing so Hard to Swallow?, *BBC Worklife*, 18 May. https://www.bbc.com/worklife/article/2018051 0-the-food-you-buy-really-is-shrinking.

Griliches, Z. (1986) Economic Data Issues, in Z. Griliches and M.D. Intriligator (eds) *Handbook of Econometrics*, Vol. III, Amsterdam: North-Holland.

Grubel, H.G. (1968) Internationally Diversified Portfolios: Welfare Gains and Capital Flows, *American Economic Review*, 58, 1975–1999.

Grubel, H.G. and Fander, K. (1971) The Interdependence of International Equity Markets, *Journal of Finance*, 26, 89–94.

Guisan, M.C. (2001) Causality and Cointegration between Consumption and GDP in 25 OECD Countries: Limitations of the Cointegration Approach, *Applied Econometrics and International Development*, 1, 39–61.

Guiso, L. and Jappelli, T. (2005) Awareness and Stock Market Participation, *Review of Finance*, 9, 537–567.

Guiso, L., Sapienza, P. and Zingales, L. (2008) Trusting the Stock Market, *Journal of Finance*, 63, 2557–2600.

Guo, H. (2001) A Simple Model of Limited Stock Market Participation, *Federal Reserve Bank of St Louis Review*, May/June, 37–47.

Han, B. and Kumar, A. (2013) Speculative Retail Trading and Asset Prices, *Journal of Financial and Quantitative Analysis*, 48, 377–404.

Han, Y. and Lesmond, D. (2011) Liquidity Biases and the Pricing of Cross-Sectional Idiosyncratic Volatility, *Review of Financial Studies*, 24, 1590–1629.

Hansen, L.P. (2005) Comment: On Exotic Preferences for Macroeconomics, by D.K. Backus, B.R. Routledge and S.E. Zin, *NBER Macroeconomics Annual*, 2004, 418–421.

Hansen, L.P. (2007) Behers, Doubts and Learning: Valuing Macroeconomic Risk, Richard T. Ely Lecture, *American Economic Review*, 97, 1–30.

Hansen, L.P. and Hodrick, R.J. (1980) Forward Exchange Rates as Optimal Predictors of Future Spot Rates: an Econometric Analysis, *Journal of Political Economy*, 88, 829–853.

Hanson, G.H. (2010) Why isn't Mexico Rich?, *Journal of Economic Literature*, 48, 987–1004.

Harberger, A. (1980) Vignettes on the World Capital Markets, *American Economic Review*, 70, 331–337.

Harris, M. and Raviv, A. (1991) The Theory of Capital Structure, *Journal of Finance*, 46, 297–355.

Harvey, J.T. (1993) Daily Exchange Rate Variance, *Journal of Post Keynesian Economics*, 15, 515–540.

Harvey, J.T. (1999) The Nature of Expectations in the Foreign Exchange Market: A Test of Competing Theories, *Journal of Post Keynesian Economics*, 21, 181–200.

Haven-Tang, C. (2017) Do Tourists visit Britain Because of the Royal Family?, 1 December. https://www.walesonline.co.uk/news/news-opin ion/fact-check-tourists-visit-britain-13984339.

Hawkins, J. and Turner, P. (2000) International Financial Reform: Regulatory and other Issues, Paper Presented at a Conference on International Financial Contagion, Washington DC, 3–4 February.

Hays, J. (2016) Russian Privatization and Oligarchs. http://factsandde tails.com/russia/ Economics_Business_Agriculture/sub9_7b/entry-5169. html.

Head, K. and Mayer, T. (2014) Gravity Equations: Workhorse, Toolkit, and Cookbook, in G. Gopinath, E. Helpman and K. Rogoff (eds) *Handbook of International Economics*, Amsterdam: Elsevier.

Heckman, J. (2000) Causal Parameters and Policy Analysis in Economics: A Twentieth Century Retrospective, *Quarterly Journal of Economics*, 115, 45–97.

Heckman, J. (2001) Econometrics and Empirical Economics, *Journal of Econometrics*, 100, 3–5.

Heckman, J. (2005) The Scientific Model of Causality, *Sociological Methodology*, 35, 1–97.

Hedges, C. (2017) Speech. https://www.youtube.com/watch?v=Ycuw9Cv h6W4.

Helliwell, J. (1998) *How Much Do National Borders Matter?*, Washington, DC: Brookings Institution.

Herman, M. (2009) Corruption Helped Cause Financial Crisis, *The Times*, 23 September.

Hicks, J.R. (1980) *Causality in Economics*, Canberra: ANU University Press.

Hill, C. (2010) Why Did Rating Agencies Do Such a Bad Job Rating Subprime Securities?, *Pitt Law Review*, 71, 585–608.

Ho, D., Imai, K., King, G. and Stuart, E. (2007) Matching as Nonparametric Preprocessing for Reducing Model Dependence in Parametric Causal Inference, *Political Analysis*, 15, 199–236.

Hodge, G.A. (1996) *Contracting out Government Services: A Review of International Evidence*, Melbourne: Montech Pty.

Holmes, J.M. (1967) The Purchasing Power Parity Theory: In Defence of Gustav Cassel as a Modern Theorist, *Journal of Political Economy*, 75, 686–695.

Holtemoller, O. (2002) Money and Banks: Some Theory and Empirical Evidence for Germany, Humboldt University of Berlin, Interdisciplinary Research Project 373.

Hoover, K.D. (2006) Causality in Economics and Econometrics. https://ssrn.com/abstract =930739.

Hoque, H., Silvapulle, P. and Moosa, I.A. (2007) A Threshold Cointegration Approach to the Stock-Price Inflation Puzzle, *International Journal of Economic Perspectives*, 1, 83–101.

Houa, K. and Loh, R.K. (2016) Have We Solved the Idiosyncratic Volatility Puzzle?, *Journal of Financial Economics*, 121, 167–194.

Huang, R. and Ritter, J.R. (2005) Testing the Market Timing Theory of Capital Structure, Working Paper. http://bear.warrington.ufl.edu/ritter/TestingOct2805(1).pdf.

Hume, D. (1739) *A Treatise of Human Nature*, London: John Noon.

Hume, D. (1742) *Essays: Moral, Political, and Literary*, London: A. Millar.

Hume, D. (1777) *An Enquiry Concerning Human Understanding*, Oxford: Clarendon Press.

Independent (2017) Donald Trump Makes Joke about Socialism at UN General Assembly, is Met with Awkward Silence, 20 September.

Institute of Medicine (2012) Best Care at Lower Cost: The Path to Continuously Learning Health Care in America. http://www.iom.edu/Reports/2012/Best-Care-at-Lower-Cost-The-Path-to-Continuously-Learning-Health-Care-in-America.aspx.

International Monetary Fund (2016) United Kingdom – Selected Issues, IMF Country Report, No. 16/169.

Ito, T. (1990) Foreign Exchange Rate Expectations: Micro Survey Data, *American Economic Review*, 80, 434–449.

Jakab, Z. and Kumhof, M. (2015) Banks are not Intermediaries of Loanable Funds – and why this Matters, Bank of England Working Papers, No. 529.

Jiang, G., Xu, D. and Yao, T. (2009) The Information Content of Idiosyncratic Volatility, *Journal of Financial and Quantitative Analysis*, 44, 1–28.

Jobert, A., Platania, A. and Rogers, L.C.G. (2005) A Bayesian Solution to the Equity Premium Puzzle, Statistical Laboratory, University of Cambridge.

Johnson, T. (2004) Forecast Dispersion and the Cross-Section of Stock Returns, *Journal of Finance*, 59, 1957–1978.

Joint Committee on Taxation (2005) Macroeconomic Analysis of Various Proposals to Provide $500 Billion in Tax Relief, JCX-4-05, 1 March. http://www.house.gov/jct/x-4-05.pdf.

Jones, A. (2009) A First Amendment Defense for the Rating Agencies?, *Wall Street Journal*, 21 April. http://blogs.wsj.com/law/2009/04/21/a-first-amendment-defense-for-the-rating-agencies/.

Jones, S. (2009) Deviations from Covered Interest Parity During the Credit Crisis, Working Paper, Leonard N. Stern School of Business. http://web-docs.stern.nyu.edu/ glucksman/docs/Jones2009.pdf.

Joseph, A. (2017) One is Worth £67bn!, *Daily Mail*, 20 November.

Jošić, H. and Jošić, M. (2016) Alternative Measures of Internal Distance in Estimating Home, *Economic Research*, 29, 380–394.

Joyce, T. (2009) A Simple Test of Abortion and Crime, *Review of Economics and Statistics*, 91, 112–123.

Kalra, R., Stoichev, M. and Sundaram, S. (2004) Diminishing Gains from International Diversification, *Financial Services Review*, 13, 199–213.

Karp, P. (2019) Reserve Bank Cuts Interest Rates to Historic Low of 0.75% to Boost Weak Economy, *Guardian*, 1 October.

Kearns, A. (1995) Econometrics and the Scientific Status of Economics: A Reply. https://www.tcd.ie/Economics/assets/pdf/SER/1995/Allan_Kearns.html.

Kennedy, P.E. (2002) Sinning in the Basement: What are the Rules? The Ten Commandments of Applied Econometrics, *Journal of Economic Surveys*, 16, 569–589.

Kenny, C. and Williams, D. (2001) What Do We Know About Economic Growth? Or, Why Don't We Know Very Much?, *World Development*, 29, 1–22.

Keynes, J.M. (1930) *A Treatise on Money*, London: Macmillan.

Khan, A.J., Azim, P. and Syed, S.H. (2014) The Impact of Exchange Rate Volatility on Trade: A Panel Study on Pakistan's Trading Partners, *Lahore Journal of Economics*, 19, 31–66.

Khazan, O. (2013) Is the British Royal Family Worth the Money?, *Atlantic*, 23 July.

Kiger, P.J. (2019) How Venezuela Fell from the Richest Country in South America into Crisis, 9 May. https://www.history.com/news/venezuela-chavez-maduro-crisis.

Kilian, L. and Taylor, M. (2003) Why is it so Difficult to Beat the Random Walk Forecast of Exchange Rates?, *Journal of International Economics*, 60, 85–107.

Kim, J.H. (2019) Tackling False Positives in Business Research: A Statistical Toolbox with Applications, *Journal of Economic Surveys*, 33, 862–895.

Kim, S. (2006) What is a Puzzle? http://cs.wellesley.edu/~cs215/Lectures/L17-IntroGamesJigsawPuzzle/ScottKim-What_is_a_Puzzle.pdf.

Klees, S.J. (2016) Inferences from Regression Analysis: Are they Valid?, *Real-World Economics Review*, 74, 85–97.

Kliger, D. and Sarig, O. (2002) The Information Value of Bond Ratings, *Journal of Finance*, 55, 2879–2902.

Knyazeva, A., Knyazeva, D. and Stiglitz, J.E. (2013) Ownership Change, Institutional Development and Performance, *Journal of Banking and Finance*, 37, 2605–2627.

Kocherlakota, N.R. (1996) The Equity Premium: It's Still a Puzzle, *Journal of Economic Literature*, 34, 42–71.

Kogan, R. (2003) Will Tax Cuts Ultimately Pay for Themselves? Center on Budget and Policy Priorities, 3 March.

Koutsoyiannis, A. (1977) *Theory of Econometrics: An Introductory Exposition of Econometric Methods*, London: Macmillan.

Koyuncu, J.Y. (2016) Does Privatization Affect Economic Growth? An Evidence From Transition Economies, *Anadolu University Journal of Social Sciences*, 16, 51–57.

Kräussl, R., Lucas, A. Rijsbergenc, D.R., van der Sluis, P.J. and Vrugtd, E.B. (2014) Washington Meets Wall Street: A Closer Examination of the Presidential Cycle Puzzle, *Journal of International Money and Finance*, 43, 50–69.

Krugman, P. (2007) *The Conscience of a Liberal*, New York: Norton.

Kunieda, S., Takahata, J. and Yada, H. (2012) Japanese Firms' Debt Policy and Tax Policy. http://hermes-ir.lib.hitu.ac.jp/rs/bitstream/10086/21194/1/070econDP11-11.pdf.

Laker, D. (2003) Benchmark Rebalancing Calculations, *Journal of Performance Measurement*, 7, 8–23.

Lane, T.D. (1991) Empirical Models of Exchange Rate Determination: Picking up the Pieces, *Economia Internazionale*, 44, 210–226.

Lassard, D.R. (1976) World, Country and Industry Relationships in Equity Returns: Implications for Risk Reduction Through International Diversification, *Financial Analysts Journal*, 32, 32–38.

Lavoie, M. (2000) A Post Keynesian View of Interest Parity Theorems, *Journal of Post Keynesian Economics*, 23, 163–179.

Leamer, E. (1983) Let's Take the Con out of Econometrics, *American Economic Review*, 73, 31–43.

Leblang, D. and Mukherjee, B. (2005) Government Partisanship, Elections, and the Stock Market: Examining American and British Stock Returns, 1930–2000, *American Journal of Political Science*, 49, 780–802.

Lee, B. and Veld-Merkoulova, Y. (2016) Myopic Loss Aversion and Stock Investments: An Empirical Study of Private Investors, *Journal of Banking and Finance*, 70, 235–246.

Leontief, W. (1971) Theoretical Assumptions and Nonobserved Facts, *American Economic Review*, 61, 1–7.

Levine, R. and Renelt, D. (1992) A Sensitivity Analysis of Cross-Country Growth Regressions, *American Economic Review*, 82, 942–963.

Levine, R. and Zervos, S.J. (1993) What We Have Learned about Policy and Growth from Cross-Country Regressions? *American Economic Review*, 83 (Papers and Proceedings), 426–430.

Levy, H. and Sarnat, M. (1970) International Diversification of Investment Portfolios, *American Economic Review*, 60, 668–675.

Lewis, M. (2010) *The Big Short: Inside the Doomsday Machine*, New York: Norton.

Li, K., Yue, H. and Zhao, L. (2009) Ownership, Institutions, and Capital Structure: Evidence from China, *Journal of Comparative Economics*, 37, 471–490.

Lin, Z. and Brannigan, A. (2003) Advances in the Analysis of Non-Stationary Time Series: An Illustration of Cointegration and Error Correction Methods in Research on Crime and Immigration, *Quality and Quantity*, 37, 151–168.

Lippert, J. (2010) Credit Ratings Can't Claim Free Speech in Law Giving New Risks, *Bloomberg Markets Magazine*, 7 December.

Liu, Y., Ren, J. and Zhuang, Y. (2009) An Empirical Analysis on the Capital Structure of Chinese Listsed IT Companies, *International Journal of Business and Management*, 4, 46–51.

Llewellyn, D.T. (1980) *International Financial Integration: The Limits of Sovereignty*, London: Macmillan.

Long, P. and Palmer, N. (eds) (2008) *Royal Tourism: Excursions around Monarchy*, Clevedon: Channel View Publications.

Love, D. and Phelan, G. (2015) Hyperbolic Discounting and Life-Cycle Portfolio Choice, *Journal of Pension Economics and Finance*, 14, 492–524.

Lui, Y.H. and Mole, D. (1998) The Use of Fundamental and Technical Analyses by Foreign Exchange Dealers: Hong Kong Evidence, *Journal of International Money and Finance*, 17, 535–545.

Lyons, R.K. (2001) *The Microstructure Approach to Exchange Rates*, Cambridge, MA: MIT Press.

Madura, J. (2011) *Financial Markets and Institutions*, Mason, OH: South-Western Cengage Learning.

Magoulick, M. (2015) What is Myth? https://faculty.gcsu.edu/custom-website/mary-magoulick/defmyth.htm.

Mark, N. (1995) Exchange Rates and Fundamentals: Evidence on Long-Horizon Predictability, *American Economic Review*, 85, 201–218.

Markowitz, H.M. (1952) Portfolio Selection, *Journal of Finance*, 7, 77–91.

Mauldin, J. (2013) Is the Government Lying To Us About Inflation? Yes!, 22 March. https://www.mauldineconomics.com/outsidethebox/is-the-government-lying-to-us-about-inflation-yes.

Mauricas, Ž., Darškuvienė, V. and Mariničevaitė, T. (2017) Stock Market Participation Puzzle in Emerging Economies: The Case of Lithuania, *Organizations and Markets in Emerging Economies*, 9, 225–243.

Mazerov, M. (2010) Cutting State Corporate Income Taxes is Unlikely to Create Many Jobs, Centre on Budget and Policy Priorities, 14 September.

McAleer, M., Pagan, A.R. and Volker, P.A. (1985) What will Take the Con out of Econometrics?, *American Economic Review*, 75, 293–307.

McCallum, B.T. (1994) A Reconsideration of the Uncovered Interest Parity Relationship, *Journal of Monetary Economics*, 33, 105–132.

McCallum, J. (1995) National Borders Matter: Canada–US Regional Trade Patterns, *American Economic Review*, 85, 615–623.

McCrary, J., Christensen, G. and Fanelli, D. (2016) Conservative Tests under Satisficing Models of Publication Bias, *PLOS One*, 11 (2). https://journals.plos.org/plosone/article?id=10.1371/journal.pone.0149590.

McDowell, J. (1998) Perspectives on What is Myth, *Folklore Forum*, 29, 75–89.

McLean, B. and Nocera, J. (2010) *All the Devils are Here*, New York: Penguin Publishing Group.

McLeay, M., Radia, A. and Thomas, R. (2014) Money Creation in the Modern Economy, *Bank of England Quarterly Bulletin*, First Quarter. https://www.bankofengland.co.uk/quarterly-bulletin/2014/q1/money-creation-in-the-modern-economy.

McTeer, R. (2010) Monetary Policy, Deflation and Quantitative Easing, *Forbes*, 30 July.

Meadowcroft, J. (2019) The Economists and the General, *Features Magazine*, 30 May.

Meese, R. and Rogoff, K. (1983) Empirical Exchange Rate Models of the Seventies: Do They Fit Out-of-Sample?, *Journal of International Economics*, 14, 3–24.

Mehra, R. (2003) The Equity Premium: Why is it a Puzzle?, *Financial Analysts Journal*, January/February, 54–69.

Mehra, R. and Prescott, E.C. (1985) The Equity Premium: A Puzzle, *Journal of Monetary Economics*, 15, 145–161.

Mehra, R. and Prescott, E.C. (1988) The Equity Risk Premium: A Solution?, *Journal of Monetary Economics*, 22, 133–136.

Meng, S. (2019) *Patentism Replacing Capitalism: A Prediction from Logical Economics*, New York: Palgrave-Macmillan.

Merkellos, R.N. and Siriopoulous, C. (1997) Diversification Benefits in the Smaller European Markets, *International Advances in Economic Research*, 3, 142–153.

Meyssan, T. (2020) The Fabrication of the Myth of the 'Syrian Revolution' by the United Kingdom, 2 March. http://www.informationclearing house.info/53059.htm.

MFX (2016) Understanding FX Forwards: A Guide for Microfinance Practitioners. http://www.microrate.com/media/docs/investment/V-Gui de-to-FX-Fowards.pdf.

Mian, A. and Sufi, A. (2014) Money Creation in the Modern Economy, *Quarterly Bulletin*, 54, 14–27.

Mika, A. (2017) Home Sweet Home: The Home Bias in Trade in the European Union, European Central Bank Working Papers, No. 2046.

Mill, J.S. (1848) *Principles of Political Economy with Some of Their Applications to Social Philosophy*, London: George Routledge & Sons.

Miller, D. (1992) The Icarus Paradox: How Exceptional Companies Bring about Their Own Downfall, *Business Horizons*, 35, 24–35.

Miller, M.H. (1977) Debt and Taxes, *Journal of Finance*, 32, 261–275.

Miller, T., Kim, A.B. and Roberts, J.M. (2019) *Index of Economic Freedom*, Washington, DC: Heritage Foundation.

Mitchell, W.C. (1937) *Quantitative Analysis in Economic Theory*, New York: McGraw-Hill.

Modigliani, F. and Miller, M.H. (1958) The Cost of Capital, Corporation Finance and the Theory of Investment, *American Economic Review*, 48, 261–297.

Modigliani, F. and Miller, M.H. (1963) Corporate Income Taxes and the Cost of Capital: A Correction, *American Economic Review*, 53, 433–443.

Moosa, I.A. (1997) Does the Chinese Official CPI Underestimate Inflation?, *Applied Economics Letters*, 4, 301–304.

Moosa, I.A. (1999) Testing the Currency-Substitution Model under the German Hyperinflation, *Journal of Economics*, 70, 61–78.

Moosa, I.A. (2000) *Exchange Rate Forecasting: Techniques and Applications*, London: Macmillan.

Moosa, I.A. (2002a) A Test of the Post Keynesian Hypothesis on

Expectation Formation in the Foreign Exchange Market, *Journal of Post Keynesian Economics*, 24, 443–457.

Moosa, I.A. (2002b) Exchange Rates and Fundamentals: A Microeconomic Approach, *Economia Internazionale*, 53, 97–106.

Moosa, I.A. (2004) What is Wrong with Market-Based Forecasting of Exchange Rates?, *International Journal of Business and Economics*, 3, 107–121.

Moosa, I.A. (2008) *Quantification of Operational Risk under Basel II: The Good, Bad and Ugly*, London: Palgrave.

Moosa, I.A. (2012) The Failure of Financial Econometrics: 'Stir-Fry' Regressions as an Illustration, *Journal of Financial Transformation*, 34, 43–50.

Moosa, I.A. (2013) Why is it so Difficult to Outperform the Random Walk in Exchange Rate Forecasting?, *Applied Economics*, 23, 3340–3346.

Moosa, I.A. (2014) Direction Accuracy, Forecasting Error and the Profitability of Currency Trading: Simulation-Based Evidence, *Economia Internazionale*, 68, 413–423.

Moosa, I.A. (2015) The Random Walk versus Unbiased Efficiency: Can We Separate the Wheat from the Chaff?, *Journal of Post Keynesian Economics*, 38, 251–279.

Moosa, I.A. (2016) *Contemporary Issues in the Post-Crisis Regulatory Landscape*, Singapore: World Scientific.

Moosa, I.A. (2017a) *Econometrics as a Con Art: Exposing the Limitations and Abuses of Econometrics*, Cheltenham, UK and Northampton, MA, USA: Edward Elgar Publishing.

Moosa, I.A. (2017b) Blaming Suicide on NASA and Divorce on Margarine: The Hazard of Using Cointegration to Derive Inference on Spurious Correlation, *Applied Economics*, 49, 1483–1490.

Moosa, I.A. (2017c) Covered Interest Parity: The Untestable Hypothesis, *Journal of Post Keynesian Economics*, 40, 470–486.

Moosa, I.A. (2017d) The Econometrics of the Environmental Kuznets Curve: An Illustration Using Australian CO_2 Emissions, *Applied Economics*, 49, 4927–4945.

Moosa, I.A. (2019) The Fragility of Results and Bias in Empirical Research: An Exploratory Exposition, *Journal of Economic Methodology*, 26, 347–360.

Moosa, I.A. and Al-Deehani, T. (2009) The Myth of International Diversification, *Economia Internazionale*, 62, 1–24.

Moosa, I.A. and Baxter, J.L. (2002) Modelling the Trend and Seasonals within an Aids Model of The Demand for Alcoholic Beverages in the United Kingdom, *Journal of Applied Econometrics*, 17, 95–106.

Moosa, I.A. and Bhatti, R.H. (1999) Some Popular Misconceptions about the Theory and Empirical Testing of Purchasing Power Parity, *Journal of International Economic Studies*, 13, 147–161.

Moosa, I.A. and Burns, K. (2013) A Reappraisal of the Meese–Rogoff Puzzle, *Applied Economics*, 46, 30–40.

Moosa, I.A. and Burns, K. (2014) The Unbeatable Random Walk in Exchange Rate Forecasting: Reality or Myth?, *Journal of Macroeconomics*, 40, 69–81.

Moosa, I.A. and Burns, K. (2015) *Demystifying the Meese–Rogoff Puzzle*, London: Palgrave.

Moosa, I.A. and Korczak, M.A. (2000) The Role of Fundamentalists and Technicians in Exchange Rate Determination, *Economia Internazionale*, 53, 97–106.

Moosa, I.A. and Moosa, N. (2019) *Eliminating the IMF: An Analysis of the Debate to Keep, Reform or Abolish the Fund*, New York: Palgrave Macmillan.

Moosa, I.A. and Ramiah, V. (2014) *The Costs and Benefits of Environmental Regulation*, Cheltenham, UK and Northampton, MA, USA: Edward Elgar Publishing.

Moosa, I.A. and Vaz, J. (2015) Why is it so Difficult to Outperform the Random Walk? An Application of the Meese–Rogoff Puzzle to Stock Prices, *Applied Economics*, 47, 398–407.

Morck, R. and Yeung, B. (2011) Economics, History, and Causation, *Business History Review*, 85, 39–63.

Moshiri, S. and Abdou, A. (2010) Privatization, Regulation, and Economic Growth in Developing Countries: An Empirical Analysis, *International Journal of Interdisciplinary Social Sciences*, 5, 79–106.

Muhlenkamp, H. (2015) From State to Market Revisited: A Reassessment of the Empirical Evidence on the Efficiency of Public (and Privately Owned) Enterprises, *Annals of Public and Cooperative Economics*, 86, 535–557.

Mukherjee, C., White, H. and Wuyts, M. (1998) *Econometrics and Data Analysis for Developing Countries*, London: Routledge.

Mukherjee, D. and Pozo, S. (2011) Exchange Rate Volatility and Trade: A Semiparametric Approach, *Applied Economics*, 43, 1617–1627.

Murphy, R.G. (1984) Capital Mobility and the Relationship Between Saving and Investment Rates in OECD Countries, *Journal of International Money and Finance*, 3, 327–342.

Myers, S.C. (1977) Determinants of Corporate Borrowing, *Journal of Financial Economics*, 5, 147–175.

Myers, S.C. (1984) The Capital Structure Puzzle, *Journal of Finance*, 39, 574–592.

Naguib, R.I. (2012) The Effects of Privatization and Foreign Direct

Investment on Economic Growth in Argentina, *Journal of International Trade and Economic Development*, 21, 51–82.

Naudon, A., Tapia, M. and Zurita, F. (2004) Ignorance, Fixed Costs, and the Stock-Market Participation Puzzle, Documentos de Trabajo 262, Instituto de Economia.

Navarro, P. and Ross, W. (2016) Scoring the Trump Economic Plan: Trade, Regulatory, & Energy Policy Impacts. https://assets.donaldjtrump.com/ Trump_Economic_Plan.pdf.

Neely, C. and Sarno, L. (2002) How Well Do Monetary Fundamentals Forecast Exchange Rates?, *Federal Reserve Bank of St Louis Review*, September, 51–74.

Nelson, J.A. (2014) The Power of Stereotyping and Confirmation Bias to Overwhelm Accurate Assessment: The Case of Economics, Gender, and Risk Aversion, *Journal of Economic Methodology*, 21, 211–231.

Noulas, A. and Genimakis, G. (2011) The Determinants of Capital Structure Choice: Evidence from Greek Listed Companies, *Applied Financial Economics*, 21, 379–389.

Nunkoo, P.K. and Boateng, A. (2010) The Empirical Determinants of Target Capital Structure and Adjustment to Long-run Target: Evidence from Canadian Firms, *Applied Economics Letters*, 17, 983–990.

Obstfeld, M. (1986) Capital Mobility in the World Economy: Theory and Measurement, *Carnegie-Rochester Conference Series on Public Policy*, 24, 55–104.

Obstfeld, M. and Rogoff, K. (2000) The Six Major Puzzles in International Macroeconomics: Is There a Common Cause? *NBER Macroeconomics Annual*, 15, 339–412.

OECD (2020) Coronavirus: The World Economy at Risk, OECD Interim Economic Assessment, 2 March.

Officer, L.H. and Willett, T.D. (1979) The Covered-Arbitrage Schedule: A Critical Survey of Recent Developments, *Journal of Money, Credit and Banking*, 2, 247–257.

Oliver, S. (2017) The Perils of Forecasting and the Need for a Disciplined Investment Process, *Oliver Insight*, 31 May.

Pagan, A.R. (1984) Econometric Issues in the Analysis of Regressions with Generated Regressors, *International Economic Review*, 25, 221–247.

Pagan, A.R. (1987) Twenty Years After: Econometrics, 1966–1986, Paper presented at CORE's 20th Anniversary Conference, Louvain-la-Neuve.

Peet, J. (1992) *Myths of the Political-Economic World View from Energy and the Ecological Economics of Sustainability*, Washington DC: Island Press.

Peree, E. and Steinherr, A. (1989) Exchange Rate Uncertainty and Foreign Trade, *European Economic Review*, 33, 1241–1264.

Petersen, O., Hjelmar, U., Vrangbæk, K. and Cour, L. (2011) *Effects of Contracting out Public Sector Tasks: A Research-Based Review of Danish and International Studies from 2000–2011*, Copenhagen: AKF.

Pilkington, P. (2014) Bank of England Endorses Post-Keynesian Endogenous Money Theory, 12 March. https://fixingtheeconomists.wordpress.com/20 14/03/12/bank-of-england-endorses-post-keynesian-endogenous-money-theory/.

Plane, P. (1997) Privatization and Economic Growth: An Empirical Investigation from a Sample of Developing Market Economies, *Applied Economics*, 29, 161–178.

Popper, K. (1963) *Conjectures and Refutations: The Growth of Scientific Knowledge*, London: Routledge & Kegan Paul.

Prasad, S.J., Green, C.J. and Murinde, V. (2001) Company Financing, Capital Structure, and Ownership: A Survey and Implications for Developing Economies, SUERF Studies, No. 12, February.

Preece, D.A. (1987) Good Statistical Practice, *Statistician*, 36, 397–408.

PSIRU (2014) Public and Private Sector Efficiency, A Briefing for the EPSU Congress by PSIRU. https://www.epsu.org/article/public-and-private-sector-efficiency.

PWC (2011) The Economic Impact of the Royal Wedding, 26 April. http://www.consultant-news.com/article_display.aspx?ID=7818.

Quiggin, J. (2009) Six Refuted Doctrines, *Economic Papers*, 28, 239–248.

Rahbar, F., Sargolzaei, M., Ahmadi, R. and Ahmadi, M. (2012) Investigating the Effects of Privatization on the Economic Growth in Developing Countries: A Fixed Effect Approach, *Journal of Economics and Sustainable Development*, 3, 61–66.

Reich, R.B. (2009) How Capitalism is Killing Democracy, *Foreign Policy*, 12 October.

Rieger, M.O. and Wang, M. (2012) Can Ambiguity Aversion Solve the Equity Premium Puzzle? Survey Evidence from International Data, *Finance Research Letters*, 9, 63–72.

Rietz, T.A. (1988) The Equity Risk Premium: A Solution, *Journal of Monetary Economics*, 22, 117–131.

Riggins, N. (2014) The Financial Rewards of a Royal Family, 22 January. https://www.europeanceo.com/lifestyle/financial-rewards-royal-family/.

Ritholtz, B. (2009) The Hubris of Economics, *EconoMonitor*, 4 November. http://www.economonitor.com/blog/2009/11/the-hubris-of-economics/.

Rivera-Batiz, F.R. and Rivera-Batiz, L.A. (1994) *International Finance and Open Economy Macroeconomics*, New York: Macmillan.

Robichek, A.A. and Myers, S.C. (1966) Problems in the Theory of Optimal Capital Structure, *Journal of Financial and Quantitative Analysis*, 1, 1–35.

Rodriguez, A. (2020) Texas' Lieutenant Governor Suggests Grandparents are Willing to Die for US Economy, *USA Today*, 24 March.

Rodriguez, L.J. (2002) International Banking Regulation: Where's the Market Discipline in Basel II?, Policy Analysis, No. 455, October.

Rogoff, K. (1999) Monetary Models of Dollar/Yen/Euro Nominal Exchange Rates: Dead or Undead?, *Economic Journal*, 109, 655–659.

Romer, P. (2020) The Dismal Kingdom: Do Economists Have Too Much Power?, *Foreign Affairs*, March/April. https://www.foreignaffairs.com/articles/world/2020-06-01/defense-economists.

Rose, A. (2000) One Money, One Market: Estimating the Effect of Common Currencies on Trade, *Economic Policy*, 30, 7–45.

Rothschild, K.W. (1947) Price Theory and Oligopoly, *Economic Journal*, 57, 299–320.

Roubini, N. (2010) A Presidency Heading for a Fiscal Train Wreck, FT.Com, 28 October. http://www.ft.com/intl/cms/s/0/dd140d16-e2c2-11df-8a58-00144feabdc0.html#axzz1 MljJh357.

Rowland, P.F. (1999) Transaction Costs and International Portfolio Diversification, *Journal of International Economics*, 49, 45–170.

Russell, J.W. (1998) The International Diversification Fallacy of Exchange-Listed Securities, *Financial Services Review*, 7, 95–106.

Sachs, J. (1996) Growth in Africa: It Can be Done, *The Economist*, 29 June.

Sachs, J. (1997) The Limits of Convergence, *The Economist*, 14 June.

Sala-i-Martin, X. (1997) I Just Ran Two Million Regressions, *American Economic Review*, 87, 178–183.

Sala-i-Martin, X., Doppelhofer, G. and Miller, R.I. (2004) Determinants of Long-Term Growth: A Bayesian Averaging of Classical Estimates (BACE) Approach, *American Economic Review*, 94, 813–835.

Sampson, T., Dhingra, S., Ottaviano, G. and Van Reenen, J. (2016) Economists for Brexit: A Critique, Centre for Economic Performance, CEP Brexit Analysis Papers, No. BREXIT06.

Santa-Clara, P. and Valkanov, R. (2003) The Presidential Puzzle: Political Cycles and the Stock Market, *Journal of Finance*, 58, 1841–1872.

Santos Silva, J.M.C. and Tenreyro, S. (2006) The Log of Gravity, *Review of Economics and Statistics*, 88, 641–658.

Sarno, L. (2005) Towards a Solution to the Puzzles in Exchange Rate Economics: Where Do We Stand?, *Canadian Journal of Economics*, 38, 673–708.

Savvides, A. (1992) Unanticipated Exchange Rate Variability and the Growth of International Trade, *Review of World Economics*, 128, 446–463.

Schiff, P. (2013) Doubting The Big Lie that Inflation is not a Threat, *Forbes*, 17 January.

Schrager, A. (2019) Has the Fed Lost its Power to Influence the Economy?, 31 October. https://qz.com/1736846/can-the-federal-reserves-rate-cuts-still-boost-the-economy/.

Schumpeter, J.A. (1978) Economic Methodology, in F. Machlup (ed.) *Methodology of Economics and Other Social Sciences*, New York: Academic Press.

Schuster, K. (2017) 5 Things to Understand about Oil-Rich, Cash-Poor Venezuela, 19 April. https://www.dw.com/en/5-things-to-understand-ab out-oil-rich-cash-poor-venezuela/a-38478166.

Semion, J. (2011) Fallacies of Free Markets, 27 December. https://www. triplepundit.com/ story/2011/fallacies-free-markets/70151.

Seo, K. (2009) Ambiguity and Second-Order Belief, *Econometrica*, 77, 1575–1605.

Serrat, A. (1996) A Dynamic Model of International Risk Sharing Puzzles, MIT Working Paper.

Shefrin, H. (2002) *Beyond Greed and Fear*, Oxford: Oxford University Press.

Shefrin, H. and M. Statman (1985) The Disposition to Sell Winners too Early and Ride Losers too Long: Theory and Evidence, *Journal of Finance*, 40, 777–792.

Shiller, R.J. (2003) From Efficient Markets Theory to Behavioral Finance, *Journal of Economic Perspectives*, 17, 84–104.

Shimer, R. (2005) The Cyclical Behavior of Equilibrium Unemployment and Vacancies, *American Economic Review*, 95, 25–49.

Sigurjonsson, F. (2015) Monetary Reform: A Better Monetary System for Iceland, 10 March. http://www.forsaetisraduneyti.is/media/Skyrslur/monetary-reform.pdf.

Simms, A. (2013) The Private Sector is more Efficient than the Public Sector. https://b.3cdn.net/nefoundation/78cfe0444c38b5b9d0_3hm6iyth8.pdf.

Simms, A. and Reid, S. (2013) The Private Sector is Superior: Time to Move on from this Old Dogma, *Guardian*, 25 April.

Sinclair, T.J. (2005) *The New Masters of Capital: American Bond Rating Agencies and the Politics of Creditworthiness*, Ithaca, NY: Cornell University Press.

Skousen, M. and Taylor, K.C. (1997) *Puzzles and Paradoxes in Economics*, Cheltenham, UK and Northampton, MA, USA: Edward Elgar Publishing.

Smil, V. (2000) Perils of Long-Range Energy Forecasting: Reflections on Looking Far Ahead, *Technological Forecasting and Social Change*, 65, 251–264.

Smith, A. (1776) *An Inquiry into the Nature and Causes of the Wealth of Nations*, London: William Strahan.

Smith, D.B. and Aaronson, W. (2003) The Perils of Healthcare Workforce Forecasting: A Case Study of the Philadelphia Metropolitan Area, *Journal of Health Management*, 48, 99–110.

Smithin, J. (1994) *Controversies in Monetary Economics: Ideas, Issues and Policy*, Cheltenham, UK and Northampton, MA, USA: Edward Elgar Publishing.

Solnik, B.H. (1974) Why not Diversify Internationally?, *Financial Analyst Journal*, 30, 48–54.

Solnik, B.H. (1978) International Parity Conditions and Exchange Risk, *Journal of Banking and Finance*, 2, 281–293.

Stankiewicz, K. (2020) Cramer: 'Unless the Fed Can Create a Vaccine or Beat the Virus, Rate Cuts Won't Matter', CNBC, 2 March.

Statman, M. (1999) Behavioral Finance: Past Battles and Future Engagements, *Financial Analysts Journal*, 55, 18–27.

Stewart, H. (2012) Wealth Doesn't Trickle Down – It just Floods Offshore, *Guardian*, 22 July.

Stockman, A.C. and Tesar, L. (1995) Tastes and Technology in a Two-Country Model of the Business Cycle: Explaining International Comovements, *American Economic Review*, 85, 168–185.

Stone, C. (2013) Pursuing 'Efficiency' in the Public Sector: Why Privatisation is not Necessarily the Answer, *Conversation*, 2 April.

Stroe-Kunold, E. and Werner, J. (2009) A Drunk and Her Dog: A Spurious Relation? Cointegration Tests as Instruments to Detect Spurious Correlations between Integrated Time Series, *Quality and Quantity*, 43, 913–940.

Subrahmanyam, A. (2010) The Cross-Section of Expected Stock Returns: What Have We Learnt from the Past Twenty-Five Years of Research?, *European Financial Management*, 16, 27–42.

Sullivan, R., Timmermann, A. and White, H. (2001) Dangers of Data-Driven Inference: The Case of Calendar Effects in Stock Returns, *Journal of Econometrics*, 105, 249–286.

Swedroe, L. (2010) Is International Diversification Worth the Costs? 1 November. http://www.cbsnews.com/news/is-international-diversifica tion-worth-the-costs/.

Sy, O. and Al-Zaman, A. (2011) Resolving the Presidential Puzzle, *Financial Management*, 40, 331–355.

Szilagyi, P.G. and Batten, J.A. (2006) Arbitrage, Covered Interest Parity and Long-Term Dependence between the US Dollar, IIIS Discussion Papers, No. 128.

Tagliaferro, A. (2019) The Unintended Consequences of Ultra-Low Interest Rates. https://www.livewiremarkets.com/wires/the-unintended-consequences-of-ultra-low-interest-rates.

Taylor, M.P. (1987) Covered Interest Parity: A High-Frequency, High-Quality Data Study, *Economica*, 54, 429–453.

Taylor, M.P. and Allen, H.L. (1992) The Use of Technical Analysis in the Foreign Exchange Market, *Journal of International Money and Finance*, 11, 304–314.

Tesar, L. (1991) Savings, Investment and International Capital Flows, *Journal of International Economics*, 31, 55–78.

Tesar, L. (1993) International Risk-Sharing and Non-Traded Goods, *Journal of International Economics*, 35, 69–89.

Tesar, L. and Werner, I. (1995) Home Bias and High Turnover, *Journal of International Money and Finance*, 14, 467–492.

Thornton, D.L. (1989) Tests of Covered Interest Rate Parity, *Federal Reserve Bank of St Louis Economic Review*, July/August, 55–66.

Tinbergen, J. (1951) *Econometrics*, London: Allen & Unwin.

Titman, S. and Wessels, R. (1988) The Determinants of Capital Structure Choice, *Journal of Finance*, 43, 1–19.

Tobin, J. (1983) Domestic Saving and International Capital Movements in the Long Run and the Short Run: Comment on M. Feldstein, *European Economic Review*, 21, 153–156.

Tourism Alliance (2017) UK Tourism Statistics 2017. http://www.tourismalliance.com/ downloads/TA_395_420.pdf.

Turrini, A. and van Ypersele, T. (2002) Traders, Courts, and the Home Bias Puzzle, Centro Studi Luca d'Agliano, University of Milano, Development Working Papers, No. 159.

Utzig, S. (2010) The Financial Crisis and the Regulation of Credit Rating Agencies: A European Banking Perspective, Asian Development Bank Institute Working Papers, No. 188.

Van Rooij, M., Lusardi, A. and Alessie, R. (2011) Financial Literacy and Stock Market Participation, *Journal of Financial Economics*, 101, 449–472.

Van Wincoop, E. (2000) Borders and Trade, Federal Reserve Bank of New York, Mimeo.

Vasiliou, D. and Daskalakis, N. (2009) Behavioral Capital Structure: Is the Neoclassical Paradigm Threatened? Evidence from the Field, *Journal of Behavioral Finance*, 10, 19–32.

VisitBritain (2012) International Demand for British Tourism: Alternative Outlooks, September. https://www.visitbritain.org/sites/default/files/vb-corporate/Documents-Library/documents/VisitBritain_TE_Scenarios_v2.pdf.

Von Mises, L. (1978) The Inferiority Complex of the Social Sciences, in F. Machlup (ed.) *Methodology of Economics and Other Social Sciences*, New York: Academic Press.

Voulgaris, F., Asteriou, D. and Agiomirgianakis, G. (2002) Capital Structure, Asset Utilization, Profitability and Growth in the Greek Manufacturing Sector, *Applied Economics*, 34, 1379–1388.

Warner, J.B. (1977) Bankruptcy Costs, Absolute Priority and the Pricing of Risky Debt Claims, *Journal of Financial Economics*, 4, 239–276.

Waxman, H.A. (2008) Credit Rating Agencies and the Financial Crisis, Hearing before the House Committee on Oversight and Government Reform. http://oversight.house.gov/ images/stories/Hearings/.

Weber, T. (2011) Davos 2011: Why Do Economists Get it so Wrong?, BBC News, 27 January.

Wei, S. (1998) How Reluctant are Nations in Global Integration?, Harvard University, Mimeo.

Weiner, G. (2019) Low Inflation in 2019 – Is it Just a Big Lie?, 29 March. https://supersavingtips.com/low-inflation-big-lie/.

Welshnotbritish.com (2014) That Royal Myth about Tourism, 1 February. http://www.welshnotbritish.com/2014/02/that-royal-myth-about-tourism.html.

Werner, R.A. (2016) A Lost Century in Economics: Three Theories of Banking and the Conclusive Evidence, *International Review of Financial Analysis*, 46, 361–379.

Wheelock, D.C. (2010) The Monetary Base and Bank Lending: You Can Lead a Horse to Water . . ., Federal Reserve Bank of St Louis, Economic Synopses, No. 24.

Whitmore (2008) The Perils and Pitfalls of Oil Price Forecasting, RadioFreeEurope, 17 December. https://www.rferl.org/a/The_Perils_And_Pitfalls_Of_Oil_Price_ Forecasting/1360914.html.

Williams, G., Parikh, A. and Bailey, D. (1998) Are Exchange Rates Determined by Macroeconomic Factors?, *Applied Economics*, 30, 553–567.

Wong, P. (2011) Earnings Shocks and the Idiosyncratic Volatility Discount in the Cross-Section of Expected Returns, Working Paper, University of South Carolina.

Worstall, T. (2017) Post-Brexit UK Trade – My Apostasy, I Think the Gravity Model is Wrong, *Forbes*, 20 May.

Wright, A. and McCarthy, S. (2002) Does Purchasing Stock in Australian Multinational Corporations Create International Portfolio Diversification?, *Multinational Business Review*, 10, 79–83.

Young, C. and Holsteen, K. (2017) Model Uncertainty and Robustness: A Computational Framework for Multimodel Analysis, *Sociological Methods and Research*, 46, 3–40.

Yuan, A. (2004) International Diversification: Benefits and Costs from a Mutual Fund Perspective, Leonard N. Stern School of Business, New

York University. http://www.stern.nyu.edu/sites/default/files/assets/doc uments/con_043408.pdf.

Yule, G.U. (1926) Why Do We Sometimes Get Nonsense-Correlations between Time-Series?, *Journal of the Royal Statistical Society*, 89, 1–64.

Index